JAM CULTURES

The Tavern

Jalal ad-Dun Rumi (1207-1273)
Translated by Coleman Barks

This being human is a guest house.
Every morning a new arrival.
A joy, a depression, a meanness,
some momentary awareness comes
as an unexpected visitor.
Welcome and entertain them all!
Even if they're a crowd of sorrows,
who violently sweep your house
empty of its furniture,
still, treat each guest honorably.
He may be clearing you out
for some new delight.
The dark thought, the shame, the malice,
meet them at the door laughing,
and invite them in.
Be grateful for whoever comes,
because each has been sent
as a guide from beyond.

JAM CULTURES

Inclusion: having a seat at the table, a voice and a vote

Jitske Kramer

Translated by Mischa Hoyinck and Robert Chesal

Management Impact

Written in cooperation with Jacqueline Hoefnagels

Translation: Mischa Hoyinck & Robert Chesal

Graphic design: Douwe Hoendervanger grafisch ontwerp [lid bno] www.douwehoendervanger.nl

Editing: Piet Hugen

Cover image: Unsplash/Praewthida K

Photos of the author: Rein van der Zee (p. 230 and p. 300); Mettina Jager (cover)

© 2020 Jitske Kramer, Human Dimensions & Boom uitgevers Amsterdam

Management Impact is a division of Boom uitgevers Amsterdam

ISBN 978 94 6276 358 6

E-book ISBN 978 94 6276 399 9

FSC
MIX
FSC® C155997

www.jitskekramer.com

INTRODUCTION

About diversity, inclusion and Jam Cultures

1 DIFFERENCE

About our tendency to clone and the pros and cons of stereotyping

2 POWER

About the pecking order and who has the power

3 TRUTH

How to deal with multiple truths

4 TRUST

How discomfort releases energy

5 COURAGE

About jamming in a flow and with extremes

Appendices

About Jitske Kramer– 301

INTRODUCTION

About diversity, inclusion and Jam Cultures

p. 10

DIFFERENCE

About our tendency to clone and the pros and cons of stereotyping

p. 38

POWER

About the pecking order and who has the power

p. 88

TRUTH

How to deal with multiple truths

p. 136

TRUST

How discomfort releases energy

p. 182

COURAGE

About jamming in a flow and with extremes

p. 232

INTRODUCTION

About diversity,
inclusion and
Jam Cultures

COMMUNITY

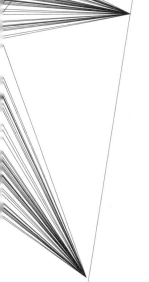

The essence

In essence, inclusion is about who is allowed to participate, who is allowed to express their opinion and who is allowed to help shape decisions. Inclusion is also about who is denied these opportunities, because some people are not permitted to participate. They're excluded—from work, politics, or education, for instance. Once they're sidelined, they can only stand by and watch. Others are allowed to participate, but have no say in the ground rules, the basic conditions; these might be about the distribution of wealth, or what conduct is permissible, or what goals a particular business should try to achieve. Being allowed to take part but not speak their mind makes these people feel ignored, so they grow demotivated and leave—though some may stay (and complain). And then you have those who are allowed to participate and speak their mind, but whose voice is consistently ignored in decision-making. True, this is inclusion, but it falls short of people's needs and spreads negativity. Obviously, we can't discuss everything with everyone all the time. There are limits, and often leadership is required. Nevertheless, we need to make the game so attractive that everyone wants to get involved and feels that they belong.

Inclusion is about people being able to be themselves and work well with others at the same time. It's about achieving unity while remaining open to all sorts of differences within the group and beyond. It's about learning to deal with differences and about clashing opinions with people we don't know, don't always understand and in some cases, don't even like. Hence, inclusion is about limits, leadership, power, privilege, conflict, emotions, curiosity, differences and similarities. It's about actively engaging people, inviting dissenting opinions and including these in decision-making. The less diverse the group, the more pressure its members feel to adapt to the dominant majority. The more diverse it is, the more challenging it becomes for everyone to get on the same page.

Everyone deals with the inclusion paradox all their lives: how to be yourself, yet adapt. Part of you searches for what makes you different, what makes you stand out, for a clear identity that gives you the agency and restrictions you need to maneuver in the world as an authentic, autonomous individual. However another part of you seeks security, looks for the common ground you share with others. You want to belong, be part of a whole, and live your life in mutual trust and loyalty.

You want both of these at the same time. Together, yet independent. *Independently connected.* The challenge is to connect with people without losing yourself. To be yourself without pushing others away. To set boundaries where you need to, and open up where you can. Every individual must find their own, unique balance. In relation to others, every individual must also deal with the question of who gets to draw the boundaries and who gets to guard them. Who gets to play and who doesn't? This process is called inclusion, and it is informed by the dynamics of power and difference. I call this 'jamming', because it's like a jam session where we're all trying to find our own voice, summoning the courage to make it heard, and tuning in to each other to create a better sound.

A celebration, or a challenge?

How many times have we heard the tired phrase 'celebrate diversity'? Greater diversity is presented as a treasure trove of opportunities, creativity, music, dance and good food. Although diversity can produce a variety of ideas that leads to creativity and innovation, in reality it doesn't always feel positive. Particularly when you just fundamentally disagree with a certain co-worker. Or if you can't mention the love of your life because being openly gay is ridiculed in the workplace. Or if you feel you have to work harder than others to get that promotion because of your ethnic background.

Inclusion means dealing with differences, strangers, emotions and conflict, scarcity and privilege, inclusion and exclusion, power and powerlessness. Nothing is harder than jointly creating

IMAGE: UNSPLASH

an environment where everybody gets to participate, regardless of their ethnic background, skin color, religion, social class, level of education, sexual orientation or gender.

Diversity has fascinated me for as long as I can remember. I thoroughly enjoy all the different types of people I meet and their wide array of stories, parties, behaviors, languages, ideas and religions. Those differences make us human. I shudder at the idea of everyone being exactly the same. And yet, sometimes I do have a problem with the fact that my neighbor disagrees with me about how to cut back the tree on our joint property line. And I can get really upset with my son for wanting to shower in his underwear at school. I get incensed when I hear that Muslim girls have a harder time finding internships than my own daughter. And as a woman, I get very angry when someone takes me less seriously than any of the men in my workplace. Diversity disrupts my flow and forces me to look in the mirror. I don't always like that.

Diversity is a topic fraught with emotion. If you bring up exclusion, discrimination, privilege or unconscious bias, you'd better prepare to take some flak, or at least eye-rolling. Most organizations prefer to talk about working together on a common goal, leadership, technology, social innovation and strategic renewal. Inclusion may be essential, but it's not an easy topic. Living and working side by side with other great people (and sometimes not so great people!) tends to be messy, and a delicate process, too.

Five Essential Themes and Eight Principles

This book puts forward five themes I consider essential for creating a more inclusive environment: difference, power, truth, trust and courage. Every chapter contains an explanation of the theme and the theory behind it, questions to help you reflect on the subject and activities to deepen your understanding. As you read these five chapters, you will find that I have interwoven them with eight principles of living and working more inclusively. I came up with these principles while working in organizations and discussed them in my earlier book *Wow! What a Difference!* All eight principles are summarized in Appendix III of the book you are now reading. They are: Do Not Clone, See the Power of Power, Challenge the Truth, Enjoy the Unknown, Not Either-Or But And/And, Hunt for Alternative Views, Vary the Rhythm, and Do It Together.

The Jam Circle in Chapter 1 shows you how to work with difference. The circle is based on these questions: how much diversity are we willing and able to take on? And how much diversity do we have to deal with, simply because we live and work side by side? I can't provide one ultimate answer to these questions. It's up to you, and the people you live and work with, to do that together. Appendix I contains a Jam Cultures Questionnaire and in Appendix II, you'll find a Jam Cultures Canvas. Both documents will help you continue the dialogue about inclusion, power and diversity and translate these discussions into concrete steps in your own social environment.

Throughout this book, you will also find personal reflections. These are passages that I read aloud during my talks. They're my attempt to express the emotions surrounding diversity and inclusion. They're my expression of the underlying and unacknowledged feelings linked to our interactions. These texts led to some heated debate between me and my associates who read and critiqued the rough drafts of this book. Some strongly encouraged me to scrap them, for a variety of reasons: they were too childish, they were stylistically jarring, they read like spontaneous talk and not the kind of language you would want to print and they read like they came straight out of a New Age magazine and would alienate managers. Others argued the opposite. They said the passages were highly relevant, personal, sensitive and a badly-needed respite from the logical and rational. The debate itself was what convinced me to include the texts. After all, that's what I think diversity is all about. It's about speaking up, letting my own voice ring true and overcoming my fear of being ridicule. It's about formulating my thoughts and feelings, taking the risk of expressing them in public, and hoping that others are willing to listen to them—rather than dismiss them because they sound strange or wrong. It feels scary; I know that those who leave the beaten path risk rejection. And you will probably read these personal texts even more critically, now that I have drawn attention to them like this, which makes me even more vulnerable. But that's how it works in diversity: anything that's different and stands out always sparks controversy. It is *matter out of space* (see Chapter 4 on Trust). Once we've found a way to pigeonhole a person or an idea, the discussion peters out. And that's exactly what happened to my personal texts, once the layout for this book was done. Suddenly, these jarring, childish words looked like lyrics and one of my critics suddenly saw the light, saying, "Oh, now I understand their place and their function in this book." Aren't humans great?

Inclusion is not a rational issue that we can resolve merely by understanding theories. It's an emotional matter requiring us to use all our senses in order to get somewhere together.

Jamming with difference
Jamming means acting from a position of uncertainty, because you don't know exactly where you're headed. But one thing is absolutely certain: everybody is genuinely interested in listening to each other.

JAM
CULTURES

I SEE YOU. YOU SEE ME. WE SMILE. CAUTIOUSLY AT FIRST, BUT
WITH GROWING CURIOSITY. WE EMBRACE EACH OTHER IN OUR
FIRST ENCOUNTER. WE DANCE OUR DANCE OF SIMILARITIES.
AND WHEN WE FEEL OUR DIFFERENCES, SUDDENLY AND
UNEXPECTED, WE SMILE OUR OTHERNESS AWAY. WE'LL DEAL
WITH THAT LATER, BUT NOT TODAY.

I WANT FAMILIAR, BUT YOU GIVE ME STRANGE. YOU CHALLENGE
MY OBVIOUS. MY HEART BEATS. I WHISPER: I WANT THE
ENERGY, BUT NOT THE TENSION. YOUR STRANGE PUTS ME OFF
BALANCE. I TRY TO FIND OUR HARMONY BUT LOSE MYSELF A
LITTLE. NOTE BY NOTE.

OUR UNCERTAINTIES VIBRATE BETWEEN US. I SPEAK MY MIND.
YOU EXPRESS YOUR THOUGHTS. OUR UNSPOKEN DESIRES FILL
IN THE SILENCE BETWEEN US. I FEEL TEARS WELLING UP IN MY
EYES. MY BODY TREMBLES AS I THINK OF LOSING THAT WHAT I
KNOW.

SLOWLY, I FEEL THE FLOW OF POSSIBILITIES. OUR WORDS
FORM THE RHYTHM OF OUR SPEECH. WE TALK ON AND ON AND
ON AND ON... WE ARE MOVE BY EACH WORD THAT WE HEAR.

EVERY WORD MAKES OUR TOGETHERNESS GROOVE. EACH
SILENCE BRINGS NEW SOUNDS TO OUR BEING. OUR IDEAS ARE
DANCING TO THE BEAT OF OUR DIFFERENCES. THEY GIVE THE
RHYTHM WE MOVE TO. ME AND MY SOUND. YOU AND YOURS.
I REDISCOVER MYSELF IN THE FLOW OF OUR TOGETHERNESS.

LET'S FIND OUR GROOVE. JOIN THE JAM.

Jitske Kramer

About me: who am I to talk?

Over the past 25 years, I've occupied myself with diversity and inclusion in all sorts of ways.

I read and wrote about it while getting my Cultural Anthropology degree. I worked on it as a trainer/consultant/facilitator in both for-profit and not-for-profit organizations in the Netherlands and abroad. Every one of my books and presentations addresses this issue, either directly or indirectly (see www.humandimensions.com). As a team, my co-workers and I have trained several thousand people in Deep Democracy, a method designed to teach inclusive decision-making (see www.deepdemocracy.nl).

Sometimes I receive critical looks that translate into: who are you to talk about diversity and inclusion? After all, I'm white, heterosexual, highly-educated, upper middle-class, with a Christian background, and my bodily functions are all in good working order. Sure, I am a woman, but don't belong to a significant minority in the Netherlands. I could argue that I have a Friesian name and that I was passionate korfball player—go ahead and Google it—until the age of 18. Talk about First World problems. So, who am I to claim any expertise on exclusion, microaggression, discrimination or everyday racism...?

I can draw on a few personal experiences, actually. Like moving from the west to the north of the country as a little girl, like being the only kid who liked comedy and protest songs when everyone else was a Madonna or Michael Jackson fan, like being the only white member of a traveling Ugandan theater group, like being a woman in the male-dominated world of public speakers and entrepreneurs. But that's all small stuff compared to the experiences of those who've had to flee their country, who've lived as expats for years, who've suffered discrimination based on their skin color, sexual orientation or religion. I can empathize with these experiences, but I haven't lived them. I'm privileged in the sense that I can blend in again after a heated debate on inclusion. I can opt to dip into the stressful issues of diversity, but afterwards I can just as easily retreat to my comfort zone. I live most of my life as part of a dominant, privileged majority.

In my work, I've been personally criticized for being a white, privileged, highly-educated, liberal, heterosexual woman. I've been told it's easy for me to talk. And I've angrily been told *"this is not your fight,"* as if I were trying to co-opt minority issues for personal or professional gain. When, in mixed company, I've mentioned my occasional insecurity about which words are appropriate for discussing diversity and skin color, I've been accused of hijacking the debate to yet again foreground white people and their emotions.

Such moments are uncomfortable. Others frame my attempts to explore my own position on these issues as examples of white arrogance or ignorance. When I express my discomfort, and say my timing must be off but my intentions are good, I am told that my intentions "make no difference." Checkmate. And when I bring up the shortage of women in talk shows and conference programs, I appear to be promoting myself. Like I said, diversity and inclusion are uncomfortable topics.

Yet, I also meet people of all colors, backgrounds, walks of life and ages who are overcome by emotion, touched, helpless or hopeful. That's because they identify with what I talk about, because my words reflect their feelings. It's because they finally know what they need to do, because anthropological studies and theories give us words that help us to identify and describe inclusion processes.

Everything I do revolves around these questions: 'What does it mean to be human?' 'How can we be human and live in connection with other humans?' 'Why do people act the way they do?' 'Why don't they act differently?' 'And why do they resort to violence when they disagree?' I lie awake at night contemplating these questions. I think these are questions everyone should care about, no matter what your origin, life experience, or political affiliation. I must consider them from my own personal background, you must do it from yours. Because we're both human. That's why.

About you, my readers

We don't know each other. You'll get to know me a little through this book, but I won't get to know you at all. I don't know who you are, what you look like or what your background is. You might be a manager or a teacher. You could be religious or devoutly atheist. Perhaps you are a refugee and know first-hand what it's like to live in different cultures. Or you might never have moved and experienced how tense it can be to be around people from a different culture. You might be a student, or a seasoned board member. Maybe you're opposed to letting more immigrants settle in your country, or maybe you're all for it. You could be mainly interested in organizational dynamics, or mainly in social dynamics. You might be male, or female, or neither ... the truth is, I will never know.

When you start writing a book, your first question is: who am I writing it for? How much does my target audience already know? What do they want to learn? What is their context, their 'habitat'? Their role, their position? I don't know. Because I don't know you. The only thing I know is that you're a fellow human being and that we inhabit this world together. And that's why I have written this book for you as human beings. It may contain stuff you already know; so you might as well skip those parts. And if it offends you because of how I phrase certain things, my apologies. Perhaps you'll deem my tone too lighthearted or too heavy-handed. Too non-committal? Too positive? Maybe you'll think my examples are too focused on ethnicity, gender, religion, age, LGBTQIAPK+, competences, leadership, lower-ranking employees, or not enough on social context. Or too much on social context ... And that's all fine.

I hope to evoke a sense of wonder, and to spark more questions, incentives and insights that will activate us to make the world a far more attractive playing field for anyone and everyone. In management speak, that's called inclusion, sustainability and agility. In plain English, that's called good for everyone, including yourself; good for the planet; and being flexible when things turn out differently. I will mostly write in plain English and leave it up to you to add the management jargon in your own mind. And I hope that we will learn to talk and collaborate in ways that honor and make use of all our differences at as many board room tables, cafeteria tables, conference tables, school tables and kitchen tables as possible. That process is what I call jamming. It would be great if this book contributed to that.

Inclusion, what's that?

Inclusion is a somewhat technical term for something essentially human and warm. It's about having a seat at the table, having a voice and having a vote. It's about exploring how we connect with others. How we enter into genuine relationships. How we co-create. It's about holding space for the pretty as well as the nasty. Giving room and taking up room. Autonomy and togetherness. It's about a way of collaborating, living and being that allows everyone to be themselves. To shine, but also to cry. To feel hope and fear, power and helplessness.

Inclusion is about how to be humans together. Genuine and meaningful relationship blossom when we see the good in each other, but also when we share our less pleasant sides. If we are to put people at the center of our actions, we need to have the courage to show each other every side of ourselves. That is, without immediately excluding or disqualifying others because they look different, have a different nationality, talk funny or have different ideas. Inclusion means making room for sadness and looking for love in the small stuff. Not passing each other like ships in the night and shaking hands only with each other's job profile, but approaching each other with sincerity, open-mindedness, curiosity and wonder. Leaving room for real talk, doubts and desires, while connecting with mutual similarities and differences. Inclusion means stopping the tyranny of both the majority and the minority. Inclusion means opening up to each other, but also setting limits for yourself.

This might strike you as soft, idealistic and way out there on Planet Kramer. I can say the same thing in management speak: Inclusion is adapting your processes in order to keep talent on board, eradicate a culture of fear, increase active participation, grow employee support, root out bullying, hold leaders accountable for the organizational climate, reduce the talent drain, place responsibility as far down the corporate hierarchy as possible, initiate participation processes, optimize vertical collaboration in the supply chain, adjust KPIs to more customer-centered targets, create coherence from incoherence, be agile, put the focus on soft controls such as integrity and trust, boost corporate values, encourage personal entrepreneurship, break down silos, increase individual professionalism and prevent internal division between departments ... In other words, inclusion.

Conventional organizational science dictates every indicator to be measurable, transparent and verifiable. Obviously, that's not always possible. Some things can't be understood, measured or quantified. Perhaps it's precisely those intangibles that cannot be pinned down that are the most important things. Sometimes, the invisible undercurrent is more influential than its visible manifestation. Even in the workplace. After all, we cannot and need not understand everything. People generally just mess around with the best of intentions. Things that we can only feel—say love, loyalty and trust—are no less real.

Exclusion is the result of too much inclusion
Too much inclusion and connection with likeminded people leads to exclusion of others. Pigeonholing, wall-building and discrimination are not caused by exclusion. Paradoxically, they are caused by over-inclusion, by an excessive love for the people that look and think like us. People close the doors of their homes to protect their loved ones, not because they hate strangers.

Inclusion Defined as Do's and Don'ts

Inclusion is about what happens in the attraction and repulsion process. It's about understanding each other and the will to understand each other. About who gets a seat at the table, who can join the action, who is allowed to voice their opinion and who, ultimately, has the power to decide. If we organize this interaction and decision-making process well, there's connection and flow. If we fail to do this, we're faced with alienation and conflict.

While inclusion means that everyone's welcome, it doesn't mean that any type of behavior is welcome. This a line we need to agree on and draw. And therefore, inclusion is about power. After all, who is allowed to draw the line, and where? Who sets the standards, who defines what's normal and who determines the distribution of money, jobs, promotions, food and other privileges?

Do	Don't	Do	Don't
Listen to all stakeholders and opinions for the sake of making progress.	Negotiate endlessly or debate tirelessly in order to reach weak compromises.	Make use of each other's differences.	Teach each other a lesson.
Engage the right people, with the necessary knowledge and experience, involved.	Involve everyone in everything.	Support people so they can shine.	Outdo the other, or protect those who underperform.
Look at an issue from all sides with an eye to the organization's mission, strategy and goals.	Listen to everyone's opinion on every problem under the motto: anything goes.	Solve problems on the basis of equality, without avoiding the pain.	Beat around the bush and waste your time on political games.

ILLUSTRATION: SUGGESTION & ILLUSION. FROM: KRAMER, WOW! WHAT A DIFFERENCE!

Boundaries

It's enough to make you crazy when you think about it, but there can be no inclusion without exclusion. As Dutch sociologist Paul Scheffer explained so clearly in his essay *The Freedom of the Border*, an open society can thrive only within limits. Within those boundaries we can feel free and safe. As human beings, we identify with a group and the uniqueness of that group is always defined in relation to the other. We've never been able to define who we are without reference to others.

To put it differently, because others are other, we can be ourselves. The boundary between us and them makes us who we are. Tribes, communities and organizations exist by virtue of that line between us and them, between who belongs and who doesn't. We form our own cultural identity by setting ourselves apart from the other, by seeing the difference between ourselves and the other. And sometimes we lose ourselves because of the other.

In order to promote inclusion, equity and human rights, we need to set limits on behavior and values that are at odds with these positive values. How do you protect yourself while maintaining an open and inquisitive attitude toward people who are not open-minded and curious about you, but instead want to teach you a lesson? Similar questions arise in companies, teams and families.

Societies are made up of subcultures, a multitude of all sorts of smaller communities. Not all these subcultures have the same values. Likewise, organizations have divisions, departments, teams and project groups. A single, global tribe for all of humanity seems a long way off. If subgroups, conflicting interests and competition are givens, the key question is how to foster trust and harmonious coexistence despite all the differences between these groups. An inclusive society or organization does not get rid of differences, but handles them well.

Liminal zones as a meeting ground

At some point, people from various groups or subgroups encounter one another. Traditionally, this has happened in marketplaces and along trade routes, where people exchanged stories, goods and gods, argued and fell in love. These days, the meeting grounds are in many places: from office parties where the various ranks gather around the same buffet, to the schoolyard where parents, teachers and kids meet. In *The Invention of Humanity*, Dutch historian Siep Stuurman describes how the quality of our liminal—or border—experiences determines the meaning we assign to the other and otherness. A bad experience can lead us to conclude that the other's lifestyle is not worth further exploration. In essence, you see the other as someone of slightly less value than yourself, and if you're really honest, maybe even a little bit less human. This feeds aggression against people who are different. On the other hand, a positive experience fosters our sense of community, prompting us to stand together and fight social injustice rather than each other.

People depend on each other. It's crucial that we find ways of working together well in those liminal regions.

Setting limits

We can't exist without boundaries. We live in groups, large and small. The question of who draws the boundaries and who guards them is a tense and often painful part of our joint humanity. I am particularly fond of Vernã Myers' words: "Diversity is being invited to the party. Inclusion is being asked to join in and dance." However, the problem with this definition is that there's someone who extends the invitation. Someone who decides whether or not to invite you. That's fine if your community is a business or some other organization with clear borders, a border patrol and a selection committee.

The problem arises when you look at the world as one big venue where everyone automatically attends the party. Then no one is in a position to extend an invitation. And yet, an essential part of your sense of community is the freedom to choose who does and doesn't fit in with the group, who gets to join and who doesn't, who you want on your team. I enjoy the personal freedom of deciding whether or not I want to welcome someone into my home or to include them in my

No cake for you

I was sitting at an outdoor café, alone. As I do from time to time. I enjoy it. The guy at the next table was there to celebrate his birthday, it turned out. More and more friends and relatives of his showed up and pulled up a chair. Some knew each other, others did not. The group kept getting bigger until the circle enveloped me and my table, too. Another woman walked up, greeted everyone, and cheerfully struck up a conversation with me. After about five minutes, she asked how I knew the guy whose birthday it was. I laughed and said I didn't. She fell silent, looked at me with an inquisitive expression, and turned her back on me to continue her conversation with other guests. I sat there in silence, a bit lost. The cake arrived. Everyone sang Happy Birthday, except me.

Strangers were included, but only if they knew the guest of honor. If not, you were left out.

work environment. Which begs the question: which criteria do I apply to this choice? How much diversity, and which type of diversity, can I, should I, and will I engage in? I'll talk more about borders and liminal zones in Chapter 1 on Difference.

People-centrism is an arrogant idea

Putting top priority on people and human relationships is considered an innovative thought. Especially in the workplace and in organizational change management, with its love of objectivation, rationalization and simplification. But there are also people who feel this people-oriented approach short-changes Mother Nature and the true diversity of life forms on this planet.

The Ecuadorian *buen vivir* concept celebrates the relationships between people, animals and plants, as I learned from a lecture on world philosophy by Dorine van Norren, a Dutch diplomat with a doctorate in International Law and Development Studies. The idea that people can be absolutely free in thought and behavior is absurd if you assume that people, animals and plants form one intricate ecosystem. If this is your frame of reference, concepts like 'development' and 'progress' no longer make sense either. In the *buen vivir* concept, there is a continuous flow of realities connecting everything with everything else. In this world view, the idea that we humans should take care of and conserve nature loses its currency, too, because that idea presumes we are superior to animals. Inclusion, in *buen vivir*, means diversity of not only people but animals and plants, as well. Even a river has a voice that needs to be heard. In this way of thinking, sustainability *is* human nature rather than a means to an end or one option among many. If we really acted on the idea that our humanity equals our exchange with animals and nature, board meetings would take on a whole new look and sound. To my mind, this is next-level inclusion—giving equal weight not only to every human's opinions, desires and interests, but also to those of every animal, plant, tree, mountain and body of water.

Inclusion and You

Questions to reflect on and discuss with others

- How easily do you include others in the groups you feel at home in? For example, your family and friends, but also in your workplace: your team, department or organization.
- When did you last make new friends?
- To what extent are you willing, able and forced to adopt other people's norms in order to belong?
- Were you, in your childhood, ever excluded? How did that feel?
- What is a good reason for excluding someone?
- To what extent do you take other people's interests into account in your thought and behavior? Do you consider future generations? Animals? Nature?
- How do you feel when you want to participate, but you're not allowed? Or when you have ideas relevant to the discussion, but you're not allowed to contribute to it? When a decision has an impact on you, but you're not allowed to be part of the decision-making process?

Diversity: visible and invisible differences

In and of itself, diversity is not such a difficult concept. It's about differences. It's about the differences we can see and those we can't. Living and working side by side is all about dealing with those differences. Diversity does become more problematic when you realize not every difference is welcome in every group. You can find yourself excluded because of visible differences. You may one day find, for example, that you're not appointed to the board because of your age. Boys who take ballet may be ridiculed by their classmates. Black politicians are still an exception in Dutch politics.

When it comes to invisible differences, the question is which ones you're allowed to mention and which you're not. I find it interesting that people often introduce themselves at work by naming certain invisible differences, while leaving others out. For instance, "I'm 45, married and have two kids," but not "My favorite color is blue, I believe in Allah and my motto is …" We can choose whether or not to reveal our invisible differences to others. We tend to reveal what fits in with the mainstream of the group and avoid what sticks out. When introducing ourselves, we're more likely to say "I just got married" than "I just got divorced". Likewise, women over 45 are more likely to state "I have kids" than "I have no kids". And if they do mention it, they tend to downplay their nonconformist answers to avoid awkwardness, by saying things like, "It was a conscious choice, don't feel sorry."

Sometimes the group is fine with you having your different beliefs or characteristics as long as it isn't confronted with them. "It's fine for you to believe in your god," they tend to say. "But why do you have to show it by wearing a yarmulke, headscarf or crucifix?" Or, "it's fine if you're attracted to men, but you don't need to flaunt it." The problem is that people feel tension, stress, sadness and anger when they have to hide what's important to them. Moreover, it also begs the question that's key to all the issues surrounding inclusion: who sets the standard? Who decides what's normal? And when are you excluded? I will discuss the role of power in greater detail in Chapter 2 on Power.

Diversity is about a mix of visible and invisible differences. Inclusion is about how we deal with this mix.

▶ *The Iceberg of Visible and Invisible Differences.*

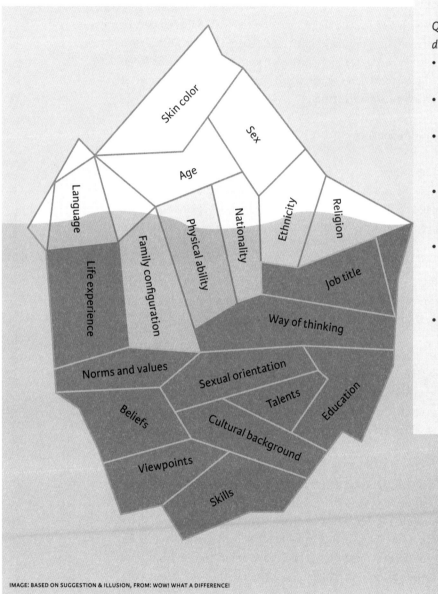

Skin color
Sex
Age
Language
Nationality
Physical ability
Ethnicity
Religion
Family configuration
Life experience
Job title
Way of thinking
Norms and values
Sexual orientation
Talents
Education
Beliefs
Cultural background
Viewpoints
Skills

IMAGE: BASED ON SUGGESTION & ILLUSION, FROM: WOW! WHAT A DIFFERENCE!

Diversity and You

Questions to reflect on and discuss with others

- What role has diversity played in your life?
- What role does it play now?
- Which invisible differences do you sometimes keep to yourself? Why?
- Which invisible differences do you not want to discuss with coworkers? Why not?
- How many generations back can you trace your own family's history of diversity and inclusion?
- How much diversity is there in your workplace? What type of diversity? Are you part of the majority or a minority?

INTRODUCTION

Diversity: a pain, or cause for optimism?

Diversity is sometimes embraced with a smile, and sometimes greeted with sighs, anxiety or anger. It's an emotional topic. Once you start talking about it, the discussion can quickly turn into an exchange of accusations. If you argue for more diversity, you're bound to be labelled a 'goody two-shoes'. If you make a case for stricter limits, you'll probably be called a 'racist'. It seems like there are only two narratives to choose from.

Two stories, each based on a very different idea:

Story 1: Living with diversity is impossible
People seek out others who are like them. That's always been the case and that's not going to change. That's the stuff we're made of. We protect our own people first, set clear boundaries and build walls to protect ourselves. Diversity is complicated. It's a hassle, and not a good idea.

Story 2: Living with diversity is possible
No two people are the same. That's always been the case and that's not going to change. That's the stuff we're made of. People have always sought out others, for trading purposes and to exchange knowledge and beliefs. Diversity is fun, productive and something to be enjoyed.

I think both viewpoints are true. There's a tension between the two that we can't avoid. It's true that the residents of Amsterdam have 188 different nationalities that usually get along peacefully. And it's true that we can have great fun barbecuing with other European nationalities when we're on vacation. However, it's just as true that the Dutch people at a campground gossip about the French and that there are ethnic subcultures in Amsterdam that don't get along with each other.

The flames of this tension are fanned by real and perceived disadvantages and the unequitable division of wealth, labor, education and privileges. Conflicts arise mainly when we experience a shortage of food, work, education, space, when we all want the same and have to share the available resources. Conflicts arise when we feel we're being short-changed. When we believe there's an elite that only looks out for itself and doesn't take others into account. And when we feel that this is based on our cultural or religious background, the color of our skin, our age, gender or sexual orientation ... that's when things get ugly. It makes us furious. And that's exactly the problem.

In many places, people live and work together in harmony: in neighborhoods, boardrooms and schoolrooms. But at the same time, there are many places where tensions arise because of perceived or real differences and inequalities between groups of people. Inequalities that seem to be steadily getting worse, too. People love the familiar, at the same time that they follow their drive to experience the unknown. That's why we travel halfway across the world to experience new things. It's why we gape at exotic dances and rituals, enjoy strange foods and flock to buy foreign technologies. All the while knowing that we'll soon be able to return home, to get back to our routine.

No two of us the same

I reason from the assumption that no two people are the same. Everyone's unique. Sometimes we like this and sometimes we don't. Take your spouse: it can be great fun when he or she thinks of doing something else than you had in mind, but it can also be incredibly irritating. If we're painfully honest, we like diversity most when it's a slight variation of ourselves. But truly different ideas, opinions and beliefs are generally experienced as a nuisance. Particularly when they question our world view, our behavior, our beliefs and lifestyle. Diversity can rock the boat, and differences can be painful. That prompts us to fight and build walls. Sometimes that is necessary. But most of the time, it isn't.

'The only people we can think of as normal are those we don't know very well.'
– Alain de Botton

Diversity creates excitement, opportunities, challenges and problems. A lack of diversity encourages routine, convenience and coasting, but not innovation or change. Dynamism and creativity are usually the result of contact and clashes between groups of people and cultures. Without them, we'd be stagnant. Cultures adopt each other's skills, concepts, frames of reference, foods, music, language and religion. New ideas are both tempting and threatening. 'Imported' innovation often calls up resistance and anxiety about the group's existing identity. Fresh ideas can reinforce a group's cohesion, but can also disrupt it and cause conflict.

Diversity and inclusion. Why? Just because!

Many organizations keep returning to the question whether diversity is demonstrably 'better'.

Business case upon business case is written to determine whether the organization needs to explicitly address diversity and inclusion. These debates are often dominated by an incumbent, homogenous group that shares many characteristics with the typical majority.

In Western Europe, this means: speaker of the national language with no detectable accent, white, well-educated, male, not openly religious, member of the upper-middle or upper class. This group typically doesn't see the problem. To them, everything is going just fine. It's all about quality, right? Anyone who's really motivated can elbow their way into the group and in the long run, we will automatically become more diverse anyway. This book is full of reasons why that group is wrong. We need to stop questioning whether diversity and inclusion are necessary and profitable. That's procrastination and an (unconscious) smokescreen intended to avoid discomfort and to justify inaction.

I will enumerate four reasons for changing this mindset, in the hope that this makes it easier to do so. I've come across these reasons in all kinds of discussions I've been part of, and in memos, mission statements and vision statements I've read. Which of these ring a bell? Which ones would people in your workplace recognize?

1 Diversity and inclusion: because of the times we live in

The world keeps changing faster and faster. The pace is picking up because of globalization. Because of the internet we can reach the farthest corners of the earth. We take numerous flights every year and human migration is increasingly common. We retire later, change jobs more often and work with people of all different generations. We need to process more information of increasing complexity. All of us need to acquire a growing diversity of skills to meet the demands of our jobs and society. Everywhere you look, we need thinkers and doers, innovators and conservators, superspecialists and generalists. We're better equipped to do business in China if one or more of our employees is Chinese. A post-merger transition will only succeed if it includes people from all the countries and disciplines involved. In short, diversity is coming at us from all sides. Those of us who insist on staying in our own, little cocoon are quickly losing relevance.

And let's not forget that we're facing huge, complicated problems that affect the entire planet. The issues are no longer familiar-sounding variations on a theme. They're not square 2D puzzles. Our problems are dynamic 3D puzzles with missing pieces. Cause and effect are fuzzy. These issues are wicked, indeterminate, indefinite and tangled. Finding solutions to them will require us to cooperate with as many different people as possible. Climate change problems can't be solved by single countries, or even by the European Union. Same goes for the division between rich and poor, refugee crises and plastic pollution. We need to collaborate across cultural, financial, religious, political and geographical borders. The future requires us to be sustainable, diverse and agile. So, an inclusive mindset and inclusive skills are indispensable.

2 Diversity and inclusion: because it's social and fair

The fact that Ahmed is less likely to be hired than John is simply not fair. The fact that men are paid more than women for the same work isn't either. It's abhorrent that good-looking people have better chances of landing a job. It's shocking that someone in a wheelchair often can't get past the front door, literally speaking. And I could go on and on.

This unfairness is something people only begin to appreciate when confronted with it directly. The successful white male who thinks it's nonsense that Muslims face discrimination on the job market, suddenly sees the light when his own daughter marries a Moroccan man and he personally witnesses the prejudice. The same man realizes age discrimination is real when he's passed over for a promotion because he's too old and he notices others no longer take him seriously.

The topic of diversity tends to release a lot of energy, especially since it is linked to feelings of fairness. In some, it awakens their activist side, in others it evokes fatigue and an unwillingness to discuss the issue. After all, quality is the only thing that counts. Absolutely, quality is important and yes, you do want to feel that you click with someone. But the diversity debate has a direct bearing on this. Because who is the judge of what constitutes quality? Particularly when it comes to unquantifiable qualities like leadership and authority. Newcomers might not have a big local network, but they could well have other networks.

3 Diversity and inclusion: because it makes the pond bigger

In the *war for talent,* fishing outside your own pond is a great advantage, simply because it's a numbers game. Fishing in a larger pond increases your chances of finding what you're looking for. It enables you to adjust to an expected labor shortage. The risk of managing by numbers is that HR might be the only department that puts its best foot forward, while the rest of the organization never takes ownership of the pursuit of greater diversity. Newly hired 'minorities' will soon leave the company again. No one likes being hired as the token woman or person of color. Diversity should not become an HR hobby, while senior management complains about the quotas used and laments that hiring is no longer based on quality and talent. In short, everyone needs to agree that promoting diversity goes hand in hand with seeking quality and upholding inclusion.

4 Diversity and inclusion: because it improves quality

The fourth reason why diversity and inclusion are indispensable is that research has proven over and over again that multiple insights, angles and networks improve quality. Let me cite a few of the many available studies: more women in senior positions is the key to economic growth (EU report, 2010); investment teams whose members are from diverse backgrounds perform dramatically better than homogenous teams (*Harvard Business Review,* August 2018); in complex disciplines like law, medicine, science and management, there is a positive correlation between the quality of the products and services delivered and the diversity of the professionals involved (NBER 2018 analysis in USA). Based on task-oriented thinking, diversity may not be the best solution for strict routine tasks, but how many jobs require just routine work these days? An organizational policy based on the idea that more diversity improves quality produces more synergy than a policy aimed at helping an organization to accurately reflect society's diversity in numbers. Under the former policy, diversity is no longer an HR hobby or a political correctness box to tick because teams and their leaders truly feel the need for more diversity in their group.

'Real equality will be achieved only when lazy, birdbrain women are also appointed in high-level positions.'
– Beatrice de Graaf

"Equal rights for others doesn't mean fewer rights for you. It's not a pie."
— source unknown

Many scholars and entrepreneurs say this century's biggest challenge is to create synergy between different types of people, talents and skills. That's why today's management books are all about co-creation, scrum, agile, town halls, participation, and so on. It's not just about gathering different types of people at the table; the trick is to keep them there.

Jam Cultures

This book is called *Jam Cultures* because dealing with diversity and striving for more inclusion always reminds me of what happens in jam sessions; musicians improvise while creating a melodious tune. To me, jamming means being open, hopeful and vulnerable and daring to take a shot in the dark. It requires you to be sure you've mastered your own instrument and that you can make it sound the way you want. It's about continually practicing self-reflection and having the courage to take the first step, to stay open and show curiosity. Trusting the other and yourself. Dealing with the fear that the other won't like what you're doing. Improvising together with what you bring to the music, with what you have. In jam cultures, people know how to jam with differences.

Jamming can be scary and lonely when searching for flow and connection. It can be sheer heaven when it works. And sometimes, it doesn't work. Then, you need to face the situation, accept it, and bide your time. Or take immediate action. Join in and at the same time, play your own tune. Truth *and* dare. That's when the magic happens and you lift each other up.

Just wing it - Kyteman

In 2014, trumpetist, composer and producer Kyteman and his band took the jam session and ran with it. He booked several venues and theaters without having decided on any fixed sets or even a particular musical style. He and his band didn't practice songs, melodies, rhythms or chord progressions, but a musical sign language that involved dynamics, breaks, rhythm changes, types of chords and musical rebellion. This language allowed them to improvise and adapt to any musical situation they found themselves in. Every song was created on the spot, right there on stage. As I'm writing this, I'm listening to the CD taped during those live sessions. You can feel the emotion and the creative tension. When everything jells, it's like magic. Everything flows together: the musicians, melody, rhythms and audience. Kyteman describes his theory about having a good jam session on his website. He describes how everything flows from disorder. There's no plan, clear direction, definite idea or structure. But you play anyway. Musicians don't concentrate on pre-determined notes and melodies, but open themselves up to each other, the audience and the whole context. There's just one simple rule: make magic out of thin air. Whenever an idea pops into a band member's head, the rule is to just wing it. See what happens and keep listening. And then, Kyteman says, everything suddenly fits together and you keep going. That's jamming.

Music unites

Thousands of years ago, Homo Sapiens out-evolved the Neanderthals. Some scientists believe this is because our ancestors were able to make music and sing. Music creates a sense of community and offers a way to share experiences and stories with large groups spread across long distances. So, music promoted cooperation and hence survival.

Even today, it's obvious that music unites people. In stadiums, at concerts, during weddings and funerals. Singing together makes us happier. It's no coincidence that so many people sing in choirs. When we watch the Eurovision Song Contest, we feel connected as Europeans.

Music is also conducive to our individual sense of well-being. Music boosts our oxytocin levels. When we're alone, it makes us feel less lonely. And there's another great thing about music. When we make music together, we each sound unique but our other differences recede to the background.

Jam Cultures Animated Videos

I have commissioned four animated videos to illustrate the concept of inclusion. You can find them on YouTube. They're there for you to use. Your team can watch them, or you can show them at events and training sessions.

Video: Inclusion: Beyond Us and Them

What happens when someone who is different than the rest joins your team. For one, it creates discomfort, whether you like it or not. After all, we like people who are similar to us. But these 'natural' preferences can cause fragmentation.

https://www.youtube.com/watch?v=3Y5egnYoCRk

Video: Sabotage and the Wisdom of the Minority

We tend to gloss over our differences based on magical thinking; if we pretend there are no differences, we'll avoid trouble. But in reality, people who can't be who they are and say what they think will feel unsafe.

https://www.youtube.com/watch?v=IP4KbyRnUDc

Video: Groupthink "This is how we do it"

Groupthink has its perils, and it's hard to break out of. It's good to know what the group expects of you, to know the rules of the game. Voicing a dissenting opinion can be risky because the group can assume a trench mentality.

https://www.youtube.com/watch?v=jwHfmlbJX5Q

Video: Diversity and Inclusion as a jam session

Magnifying the differences is the best way to make them manageable. Focus on the contradictions. Inclusion is a joint effort. Openly support the person in the group who dares to stick their neck out. Say what you do want. It doesn't have to be either-or; it can be both. Change up the rhythm. Treat it like a jam session and improvise!

https://www.youtube.com/watch?v=mxWyh4u9nxQ

References

- Kramer, Jitske (2014). *Wow! What a Difference! Utrecht: Human Dimensions Publications.*
- Scheffer, Paul (2016). *De vrijheid van de grens. [The Freedom of Limitation]* Amsterdam: De Bezige Bij.
- Stuurman, Siep (2017). *The Invention of Humanity: Equality and Cultural Difference in World History.* Harvard University Press.

About buen vivir

My description of *buen vivir* is based on notes I took during Dorine vanNorren's lecture at a philosophy festival in Utrecht, the Netherlands in April 2018. Dutch diplomat Dorine vanNorren has a doctorate in International Law and Development Studies. She wrote her dissertation on the relationship between sustainable development goals and a comparative study of African Ubuntu philosophy (South Africa), the native buen vivir concept (Ecuador) and the Buddhist idea of gross national happiness (Bhutan). VanNorren has worked for various Dutch government ministries, advisory councils and UNESCO.

About Kyteman

- In 2014, Guido van de Wiel (www.mijnmoment.com) wrote an interesting blog post about his experiences during a Kyteman gig.
- Website: www.colinbenders.com

About diversity and quality

- Montesquieu Institute (2010): More women in senior positions – key to economic stability and growth. https://op.europa.eu/en/publication-detail/-/publication/fa515107-36e5-4870-8a17-afc442635d0c/language-en
- Gompers, Paul and Kovvali, Silpa (2018). 'The Other Diversity Dividend'. *Harvard Business Review.* https://hbr.org/2018/07/the-other-diversitydividend

- The National Bureau of Economic Research study 2018: The Allocation of Talent and US Economic Growth. http://klenow.com/HHJK.pdf

DIFFERENCE

About our tendency
to clone and the
pros and cons of
stereotyping

Don't Clone

JAM CULTURES

Safety knows no time
I wrap my thoughts softly around your thinking.
I hear only what I want to hear.
When I doubt you and what you say, you reply: 'all is fine,
since we're so safe and secure together.
I rock my worries away, with you.
Our together is really ours.

I am slowly suffocating in our togetherness. I sense
how ideas are chasing their own tail. How the same
people keep doing the same things. How thoughts are slowly
fossilizing. How opinions cluster until they become sacred cows.
I claw around, looking for different views. I crack.
I open the windows of comfort and stretch my thoughts.
I breathe.

I don't want to melt together into one same thought.
I want loose and tight at the same time. I want
ideas to clash and rub each other the wrong way.
To challenge and oppose and provoke and push me
to broaden my horizon. I want risks. I want more.
Don't clone.

Jitske Kramer

Our encounters are nothing new ...

... we like to travel. We humans have been roaming the planet for ages, trading, fighting and falling in love. Despite our countless encounters with the unknown, we still prefer to work with people like ourselves. Just look around you in your workplace. Why do we seek out the familiar? And do we really want to be that way?

We like to surround ourselves with people who are pleasant to be with and good at what they do. We do that at school, among friends and at clubs, and definitely at work. And we tend to take ourselves as the benchmark for what is pleasant or good. Nearly everyone has had the experience of meeting a new coworker and instantly knowing whether you'll hit it off or not. Here's my take on this: if you immediately think you will, you have cloned. You must have felt a sense of recognition, prompted by your conscious or unconscious antenna for people who resemble you in their behavior, appearance, lifestyle or opinions. In this chapter, I'll explain why we love and surround ourselves with people who are like us, and why we only seem able to either worship or revile people who are not like us. I'll discuss the pros and cons of cloning; how to become (more) aware of your own cloning behavior and how you can stretch your own preferences a bit to include people who are different. You'll find out what's so appealing and dangerous about stereotypes, how to deal with contradictions, and what role leadership plays in diversity.

The fuss about difference: nature or nurture?

People feel safe and easy to work with when they share our basic appearance, lifestyle, norms and values, our way of thinking and solving problems. Birds of a feather flock together. It's easy to understand each other, because we can predict each other's behavior based on what we already know and recognize. We share the same ideas about how the game is played. This prevents embarrassment and misjudgment. You have to wonder whether this is simply what we're made of, whether we're incapable of peaceful cohabitation with strangers and foolish to try to change that. Then again, maybe this is all learned behavior, which implies we could change it if we wanted to.

▶ *The pond in the 'Senegalese village' at the 1905 Liège world's fair, postcard (heliotype), 1905.*

Human Zoo

Just a century ago, it was entirely normal to take your family to the human zoo to gape at so-called savages. Ethnological exhibitions were highly popular. People from all over the world were put on display for the supposedly civilized world to see what they looked like and how they lived. This black and white photograph from 1905 shows a mock Senegalese village on display at the Liège World's Fair. It shows mothers and children bathing in a specially dug pond. It's almost unimaginable, but these 'freak shows' featuring live human exhibits like Saartjie Baartman—the Hottentot Venus—or real Sami, or Inuits, actually existed!

And in some ways, they still do. It's just that these days, we travel to where these 'exotic' people live, to see them in their natural habitat. We fly to Namibia to catch a glimpse of the traditional Himba lifestyle, or to Thailand to see the Padaung (better known as Longnecks) and capture them in selfies. Some of us travel to 'save' or 'help' the other, while others want contact, not so much with a particular person, but with an ideal: the romantic image of the noble savage, the natural people that still have a connection to Mother Earth and are happy, even if they have no earthly possessions. I'll be the first to admit that I've been guilty of both of these motives in the past. At the same time however, I've always looked for a way to break out of those contexts and truly make contact with strangers as equals. This is hard work for both sides and all involved. It's demanding, yet essential to our cohabitation as human beings.

The history of the human zoo shows how Western Europeans saw 'the other' less than a century ago. White people considered those of a different skin color to be barbaric. They felt superior and smugly condescended to 'civilize' the 'poor darkies'. You can sense the vast inequality in these encounters, an inequality that we like to think of as long gone. However, it still lurks behind our thoughts and deeds in many ways. If not individually, then certainly on a wider, socio-economic level. Anthropology professor Gloria Wekker calls this our 'cultural archive', an unacknowledged reservoir of knowledge and emotions, based on 400 years of colonial domination, which continually informs our feelings, thoughts and actions without us even realizing it. From there, this reservoir spills over into our regulations, procedures, policies, teaching and institutions. This is why schools in the Netherlands often teach only half-truths about the Dutch involvement in the slave trade,. And I bet similar issues play in schools all around the world, showing mainly the positive story of the national history.

White innocence
Waking people up to the full story often provokes anger, disbelief, hostility and aggression. This is what Gloria Wekker, calls shattering 'white innocence'. In her eponymous book, she argues that whiteness is "so ordinary, so lacking in characteristics, so normal, so devoid of meaning" that it has become colorless. As if being white is such a natural, invisible category that it doesn't matter. Ethnicity is always about people of color, never about white people. In this 'colorblind' approach, it seems as if Dutch society is free of racism. But, as Wekker says:

At my lectures on working in an international environment, I'm often told that the Dutch are known for their openness and tolerance for other cultures. Then I'm asked what's stopping other nations from taking the same attitude. That's the myth the Dutch have internalized and desperately cling to.

"There is a fundamental unwillingness to critically consider the applicability of a racialized grammar of difference to the Netherlands. However, in the main terms that are still circulating to indicate whites and others, the binary pair autochtoon-allochtoon/autochthones-allochthones, race is firmly present .... Both concepts, allochtoon and autochtoon, are constructed realities, which make it appear as if they are transparent, clearly distinguishable categories, while the cultural mixing and matching that has been going on cannot be acknowledged. Within the category of autochtoon there are many, as we have seen, whose ancestors came from elsewhere, but who manage, through a white appearance, to make a successful claim to Dutchness. Allochtonen are the ones who do not manage this, through their skin color or their deviant religion or culture. The binary thus sets racializing processes in motion; everyone knows that they reference whites and people of color respectively."

In 2016, the Dutch state decided that in its own communications, it would replace the terms *allochtoon* (immigrant) and *autochtoon* (native) with the descriptors "residents with a migrant background" and "residents with a Dutch background." The change did not alter the ideas that inform our thoughts and actions. Few of us would be willing to acknowledge that we base what we say and do on underlying assumptions of inequality. We sincerely believe we don't discriminate. "We have foreign friends," we think. "We eat world cuisine, and had such a great time with the locals on our vacation. We're curious, we read books..." —at least that part we know is true!— "...and we don't judge people on their looks or gender. We're only interested in finding the right person for the job and we don't care about their skin color, sex or sexual orientation, how they spend their spare time, or how old they are."

We even sincerely believe in our own sincerity. But chances are, all your friends feel the same way and when it comes down to it, like attracts like—so liberals are most comfortable associating with other liberals. More disconcertingly, it's likely that your liberal thoughts about yourself aren't even accurate.

White fragility

When you delve deeper into this topic, you'll come across the term 'white fragility'. It was coined by Robin DiAngelo in 2011, during her tenure as professor of Multicultural Education at Westfield State University. She used white fragility to describe the defensiveness white people display when challenged on their ideas about race and racism and particularly when they feel called out for white domination and privilege. Or, as Gloria Wekker puts it, when they are jolted out of their white innocence.

DiAngelo, who has twenty years of experience teaching diversity training courses, argues that white people are bad at talking about racism. As soon as this word is mentioned, they feel personally attacked, claim that they treat everyone the same, that they're colorblind and don't care whether someone's red, black, white, yellow, or purple. They point out that they have black friends and demonstrated for equal rights. They raise their voices, get angry or start crying about the injustice. Those tears are known as 'white tears', or white people's emotions about racism.

Why is this? In *Hallo witte mensen [Hello, White People]*, Anousha Nzume argues that white people have the luxury of never having to deal with the color of their skin and are therefore not trained to deal with bad experiences linked to their skin color or culture. That could well be. As a white person, I experience a great sense of shame for things I knew nothing about, discomfort with my position in a larger story of perpetrators and victims in which I, my peer group and our ancestry suddenly find ourselves on the wrong side of history. And I am reluctant to share my emotions about this, because I don't want to cry white tears. I often feel as if I have to walk on eggshells in this discussion in order not to say the wrong things. I'm afraid I'll be misunderstood or even scolded by all sides. It's uncomfortable. And before you know it, I stop talking about it altogether, thus reinforcing the existing inequality and accompanying racism. Mumbling a token apology to the tune of 'color shouldn't matter' is nothing but a conversation stopper, masking some very real problems. It stops me, and us, from taking real action. If we stop talking out of embarrassment and the fear of saying the wrong thing, we stymie ourselves. That's something I want to avoid.

According to DiAngelo, the strong negative emotions surrounding terms like racism and discrimination could be an unconscious defense mechanism intended to keep these problems at bay, in order not to face them, let alone solve them structurally. I hope I don't display this mechanism myself, but I do frequently see it stifle debate in the workplace and in public. And when debate does get off the ground, it often gets clouded by a moral battle about who's woke and who isn't, who identified the injustice first, who is best able to handle stress, who bears the heaviest burden, who suffers most, or who is the most compassionate. And to the majority of people, those who are trying to open their eyes to an issue—to racism, climate change or the injustice of a given policy—are just a bunch of annoying do-gooders. This is a difficult dynamic that we need to break out of if we are to achieve more inclusion.

It is entirely human for defense mechanisms to kick in when someone opens your eyes to something you never knew existed, to discrimination and exclusion that you have unwittingly participated in. Of course, you need space to deal with these feelings. Yet, it can be highly irritating for the people who finally speak out about what has often troubled them for years, and sometimes for generations, that the dominant group hijacks the conversation. This group will talk, cry and offer explanations instead of listening and asking questions. The most common response is: "Yes, but I had a hard time too." Before you know it, you are trapped in a toxic cycle of feelings and accusations involving victims, perpetrators, onlookers and prosecutors. The trick is to recognize and validate everyone's emotions at such moments of openness; to try not to sweep aside the minority's pain but to let it manifest itself in full. Do so while also making room for the majority's sadness, without allowing it to overshadow the minority. We need to acknowledge each other's inability and collaboratively look for new approaches, no matter how messy that process might be. The Jam Circle that I describe later in this chapter can help us to deal with this.

Sometimes, in our discussion of inclusion and exclusion, I think we should be talking about human *fragility* instead of white fragility. After all, we're all hampered by our human vulnerability, our discomfort with injustice and privilege. Then again, I'm ashamed of this thought, because I wonder if my rephrasing veils the real problem. As if my own white innocence and white fragility make me unable to really see and feel what's going on. I don't know where the truth lies.

I do know that finding ways to openly discuss these topics is crucial, because inequality exists and gets in the way of inclusion. This goes not only for skin color, but for every characteristic that is not mainstream. By acknowledging what's going on, we can learn to deal with it differently. Note that I use the word learn. It's not going to happen overnight. We need empathy and willpower, we also need our brain, which doesn't always cooperate.

In the brain
We're pretty good at reading the facial expressions of people we know. We can tell whether they're angry, sad or pleased. We can judge them pretty accurately. We're less adept at doing

this when it comes to strangers, particularly when they're physically different from the people we know. This creates discomfort. When I first arrived in Uganda, I had trouble telling people apart. Just as in that horrible cliché: everyone looked alike. Reading people's facial expressions was a real challenge. After a while, I got used to it and learned to distinguish between different faces. When I look at photographs from that time now, I can't imagine that I ever had trouble seeing the differences.

In another example of this phenomenon, one of my coworkers and I attended a conference in Indonesia. She's at least a foot taller than me and has curly ginger hair. Yet people there were unable to tell us apart. We were dumbstruck.

Once upon a time, when people still lived in caves and turf huts, we needed to be able to make snap decisions about potentially dangerous situations. Obviously, the biggest dangers didn't come from within your own tribe. It was other tribes we had to be wary of. They competed with our tribe for scarce resources. Of course, some tribes also forged friendships; they intermarried, traded and celebrated common religious holidays. But it was always smart to play 'wait and see' first. Besides, people spent most of their time with their own family, relatives and tribe. Some tribes didn't interact with strangers for months on end. So it was especially important to maintain close ties with the members of your own tribe.

Perhaps you think this is ancient history, but until recently, many people still married someone who lived down the street, or in the same neighborhood or village. Even today, that is often the case. Most people still don't forge close friendships with those of a different faith. Just think of your own circle of friends. To take the Netherlands as an example, although secularization has progressed steadily here since the 1960s, the Dutch still have a stubborn habit of focusing on the familiar. The desire to keep it in the tribe is partly in our DNA, but it's also learned behavior. After all, everyone else does it too. You're weird if you bring home a foreign bride or groom. "Marrying outside your faith is an invitation to the devil," my grandmother used to say. Just imagine how awkward it would be if your boyfriend didn't speak a word of English and you brought him along to your uncle's birthday party in rural Ohio. Recognizing that we all have a tendency to clone is the first step in discarding that behavior. After all, acknowledging it to yourself means you can also learn to overcome it.

Recent neurological research shows how relations with the familiar are reflected in the brain. In *Deep Diversity*, Shakil Choudhury describes in detail and step-by-step how our brain creates neurological pathways that have a profound effect on our emotions and stereotypes. For example, four-month old infants still respond in exactly the same way to any face they see. However, by the time these babies are nine months old, their brains reveal clear differences. When these babies see someone who looks like their primary caregiver, the areas of the brain that regulate trust, empathy and interaction light up significantly more. When they see someone with a different skin color, their brains react in the same way they do with any random object. Particularly the areas that involve empathy light up less. You might recognize this in yourself when you look at images of a disaster. Any disaster involving multiple casualties and injured people is bound to affect you, but when the victims physically look like your own children or your parents, the emotional impact is deeper. It's painful to admit this, but deep down you know it to be true.

Our brain is wired to assess in an instant whether we are safe, or in danger. In order to make such flash assessments, the brain makes no distinction between observing and interpreting. We see something, and boom: good or bad. Safe or dangerous. Unfortunately, the brain is hopelessly ill-equipped for our multifaceted, multicultural world. To connect with people who look different than our primary caregivers, we need to make an extra effort: wait, they look very different from me and I've never seen them before, but why should that be alarming? In this case, we can't simply trust our reflexes and intuitions. That's hard to accept, the more so because the database we draw these knee-jerk reactions from is being fed non-stop by rumors and media output about certain groups of people. It's no surprise, then, that many of us still end up seeking and finding a mate from within our own 'tribe'. Your challenge is to beat your own legacy system, because it doesn't serve its purpose any more. It's outdated!

Being more aware
We live in a constant swirl of subjective, personal experiences. We're carried along by a torrent of emotions like pain, pleasure, sadness, anger, love, disappointment, fear, joy. We bob along on a stream of experiences: our connections with each other, relationships that were broken off or never get off the ground, loneliness, spiritual connection, and so on. It's a never-ending stream of thoughts, judgments, prejudices and assumptions. We're swept up in sensations that come and go, whether we realize it or not.

Being more aware means more actively regulating our emotions, thoughts and physical sensations, and interacting with those of others. It means being aware of the effect we have on others, and others on us. Understanding how this continually, mutually affects us in the intersubjective reality all of us together create, consciously and unconsciously. Against the backdrop of the ever-changing contexts in which we live. While that swirl of experiences and emotions goes on and on. This we call life.

Dangerous nonsense

Our contradictory tendencies to stick to our own tribe and to forge close ties with strangers are both ingrained in us. We are a genetic mix through and through. The idea that there ever was a pure, original ethnicity or culture is a big, dangerous lie. It's a lie because people have always traded with others and borrowed each other's beliefs, gods and art. We've made love and had children together. And the idea of an original group is a dangerous one because it's so attractive to so many people. It feeds into people's need to belong and have clear boundaries. It fuels the idea of superiority. And these feelings in turn reinforce our brain's old knee-jerk preference for the familiar.

If we want to strengthen our innate tendency to seek out the unknown and connect with strangers, we need an equally attractive story about inclusion and diversity. We are perfectly capable of bonding with each other for reasons other than skin color, ethnicity and faith. In fact, it happens all the time. All it takes is a little more effort from everyone involved, because it means breaking with routines and letting ourselves be surprised by new ideas. We can only live together in an inclusive, open, democratic way if we do our absolute best. Otherwise, it won't happen.

The anthropological turn: the invention of humanity and equality

Through history, people all over the world have often cast strangers as less than human, as animals or barbarians. In the 20th century, people started getting used to the idea that we're all part of the same biological species, but that didn't mean we embraced equality. Some were considered more human than others. The point is this: humanity and equality are not natural truths, but concepts invented by people. In *The Invention of Humanity*, Siep Stuurman calls this shift in thinking about equality and humanity the anthropological turn.

The invention of humanity

The invention of humanity means that we assume that the other, the stranger, has the same human characteristics as we do. In other words, we

A friend for a reason, a season or for life
You can build all sorts of relationships with all sorts of people. You can connect because you share something: a language, a religion, a place where you live, a job, a dream, a taste in music, a lifestyle, age … Connections with others can run to different depths and change according to their context. And that's fine. Every person is unique. You don't have to love everybody equally. Not hating each other is a good place to start when you want to co-exist. So is assuming that the other means well.

assume the other is just as curious about life as we are. We assume the other feels envy and love like we do. The other, like us, has certain ideas about leadership, planning, child-rearing problems, ambitions, nightmares and dreams. Even if a stranger's behavior seems odd, you assume it's human and prompted by needs and doubts similar to your own. Others are not dumb or uneducated beings that still have to learn to curb their barbaric emotions. What's more, thanks to the invention of humanity, you realize that the other looks at you through the same strange lens. If you think the other is weird, they must think the same of you. The fact that we can surprise each other is exactly what makes us human: different but not inferior. This thought may sound very logical, but you only need to read a few news articles to realize that not everyone has taken the invention of humanity on board yet. Just think of denigrating remarks like "that backward culture" and "they're all criminals and rapists".

Being aware of our shared humanity enables you to look at your own culture through a stranger's eyes. This way of thinking opens the door to the idea that we're all members of an overarching, meta-community that unites all the tribes, cities, villages and peoples on this planet. A community that's not devoid of conflict, obviously, but one that nonetheless shares human characteristics and in which different cultures can coexist.

Differences are then no longer fixed and rift-like, but rather accidental outcomes of a shared background of possibilities that can only be understood in a group's particular time and context. The stranger's culture is no longer an unpredictable, muddled bunch of objectionable, absurd ideas and customs, but a coherent whole, with its own internal logic – just like your own culture. What's more, by looking at your own culture through the eyes of a stranger, you can question your own assumptions and customs.

The invention of equality
We often say all people are equal. It seems self-evident. Although one look at our history shows you that equality is a controversial idea. Stuurman argues that inequality has always been our point of departure. Our history is full of references to subjects, inferiors, minions, servants, subordinates, underlings, vassals, barbarians, heathens, savages and slaves. Many of our written sources emphasize how irrational, hostile, inferior, unintelligible, inscrutable, uncivilized and uncouth strangers are. They could be converted or saved, perhaps. However, don't let the positive choice of words delude you: they were beneath us. That is, if they were considered human at all. The human zoo is a painful reminder of this attitude. Stuurman

describes the European Enlightenment as an era in which the Europeans discovered ever more savages... In that light, it's almost unimaginable that we're making light of equity and equality.

Equality is also a human invention and a logical extension of humanity. It didn't always exist. It is not a fact or a given. The notion of equality has reared its head at various points in the past, usually prompted by a dissatisfaction with unequal human relationships. For example, the eighteenth-century Christian abolitionists appealed to their contemporaries to admit that all people were created in God's image. The prevailing thought was that Africans lived like animals, were hardly rational and could therefore be used as machinery. In the new story of equality, enslaved people regained their humanity, with a human soul. Never could they, or should they, be used and traded like goods. The concept of equality has found its way into all sorts of mythical and religious stories, novels, poems, arguments and parables. It changed the discourse about human relationships and hence our behaviors, procedures and institutions. Words speak just as loudly as actions, because the way you talk, and therefore think, influences your actions.

If equality is the ideal, then we have to admit we're not there yet. Institutionalized racism is still a daily reality. Even within the limits of equality, many people are still implicitly or explicitly excluded: illiterate people, non-Europeans, refugees, people with the "wrong" religion. Meanwhile, the gap between the rich and the poor keeps widening day by day, and that too is exclusion. There are still people who talk about strangers as if they're stupid and somehow of lesser value. On the other hand, if equality and equity are not your ideals, you may find all this talk about inclusion and diversity a bit over the top.

There will always be cultural differences, but there will always be cultural similarities, too. That's because we're all human. We could reword that as: culture is the unique set of answers a group formulates to universal, human questions. Keeping this sense of proportion enables us to meet and connect with others, coexist with other cultures and learn from each other. It means we no longer gape at each other like savages, but respectfully view one another as people, with similarities and differences. In every respect. So, a religion is not backward, but

A white South African woman told me she was raised by her black nanny. She lived with her parents, but they both worked long hours and traveled frequently. So, she got her daily care and cuddles from her nanny. At the same time, though, she heard her parents talk negatively about black people, saying they couldn't be trusted, for example. As a child, she didn't know what to believe. How confusing to grow up with such mixed signals.

1 DIFFERENCE

different. This means I don't have to embrace it, but I also don't look down on it. Someone in a wheelchair is not a failed human, but a normal person who gets around differently. Equality and humanity are valuable principles for inclusion.

More inclusion, with an open mind, but without the rose-colored glasses

If peaceful coexistence with diversity is possible in any one place, it should be possible everywhere. And it is possible, as we can see in Amsterdam, New York, Berlin and elsewhere. It is also proven possible in many, many families. It's not a genetically determined given that living and working together with a highly diverse population is doomed to fail. I believe in the fun, the necessity, the energy and the opportunity generated by working and living alongside people of various backgrounds. At the same time, we must be realistic and dare to discuss the limitations of diversity. Inequality exists. Sometimes, you just want to withdraw and be in your cocoon with like-minded people. Sometimes, you simply don't like a person or you disapprove of a certain cultural or religious practice. Denying this leads to dangerous blind spots. It's important to realize that our brain is apparently wired to endorse xenophobia rather than reject it, because we can use this awareness and self-reflection to combat our own fear of the other. So let's strive for more inclusion by being open-minded, but without looking at it through rose-colored glasses.

You don't have to love someone to live and work alongside them. Tolerance is a minimum requirement; acceptance reinforces that foundation. It's important to leave each other some room. I give you some space and you give me some space. That's what I keep repeating to my teenage children too: live and let live! We don't need to be on each other's case the whole time. Let's respect the law and, in the liminal space where we meet, the public space, let's be polite to each other. And yes, let's by all means discuss what counts as "polite" and who decides as much. That's exactly what this book is about.

'The purpose of anthropology is to make the world safe for human differences.'
– Ruth Benedict

*'All people are
the same; only
their habits differ.'
– Confucius*

How much diversity are we willing and able to accept? What do we have to accept?

Most people are willing to live and work alongside people who are different. As long as they are not *too* different. We want to surround yourself with people we can connect with. That makes sense. We don't want to spend all day sitting across from someone whose guts we hate. The question is whether we can stretch our preferences just enough to become familiar with more different people. In the same way that you can learn to read people's faces in a foreign country, you can learn to accept the fact that other people do certain things differently. To an extent, it's just a matter of getting used to it. We need to let go of the idea that we should shun all contact with the unknown.

▶ *Mural (2014) in the British resort Clacton-on-Sea. The local authorities were quick to remove
it after receiving complaints about it being racist and offensive. At that point, no one knew it was
the work of the world-famous Banksy.*

IMAGE: © BANKSY.CO.UK

We all have multiple identities

Everyone is part of several groups at the same time. And every group constitutes a small part of someone's identity. Take me, for instance. I'm a woman, mother, entrepreneur, traveler, speaker, daughter, and a resident of the city of Utrecht. It helps to see other people in all their facets and to realize that we share some of them, but not all. We can connect in what we share. We can amaze and complement each other in the areas where we differ. If we look at each other as multifaceted beings, diversity becomes a lot less abstract.

Ways to deal with diversity in a group: fragmentation and inclusion

So, we meet. We start to work together in a team, or live side-by-side in a neighborhood. At this point, all sorts of processes are set in motion, such as integration, making space, demarcation and inclusion and exclusion. This acculturation process comes in roughly four forms—exclusion, segregation, integration and assimilation—all of which are based on the us-them divide, with a dominant group that hardly needs to change and a minority that is allowed to, or expected to, integrate in some way. I call these fragmentation strategies, because all four keep the divisions between the majority and the minority intact. The fifth form of acculturation is inclusion, which is the opposite of fragmentation and the subject of this book.

Let's first have a brief look at the four fragmentation strategies.

1 Exclusion

Excluding people, that is, preventing them from participating, makes dealing with diversity relatively simple, because you just don't. At best, you occupy yourself with controlling access and guarding the walls. You can't learn anything from each other, but because you are safely ensconced in your fortress, you're not bothered by the other either. The ideas underlying this strategy often run along the lines of: "our own people first", and "we've got it made, but we earned it, and we don't want to lose it."

In business hiring practices, I see the strategy described above put to use in the search for a 100% perfect match, guaranteed by difficult assessments and all sorts of personality tests. This is also known as a culture fit. There's nothing wrong with it, but it does sharply increase the risk of stifling innovation and creating a large pool of clones. This happens at start-ups that only hire young cowboys. But it happened at the Dutch state tax authority, too, where for decades they only hired people with a strong penchant for routine, certainty and structure.

And that proved to be the organization's Achilles heel when it fell badly out of step with the times and needed to be restructured. The workforce was far too homogenous and couldn't make the necessary adjustments. Boundary-setting and exclusion can also follow a divestiture, or be aimed at the competition, and is sometimes combined with head-hunting efforts.

When exclusion politics are linked to the idea that there is such a thing as an indigenous population, things can get tense very quickly. This situation is particularly volatile when such ideas are combined with an ideology advocating genetic purity. That's when walls get built or reinforced and defended with violence. When this is going on, inclusion is a long way off.

2 Segregation
In this form of acculturation, others are allowed in, but kept in their own neighborhood, a ghetto, often in the margins of society. This keeps their disruptive influence to a minimum. That's how we end up with trailer parks, art colonies, student ghettos and red light districts on the wrong side of the tracks.

In business, you'll find groups who've been given a project and a budget to do something in the margin, as long as they don't cause too much trouble for the rest of the company. Ironically, the diversity and inclusion project group often finds itself in this marginalized, sidelined position. The powers that be will show up once in a while to stress how important this topic is, but they're unavailable to project members at any other time and they don't provide enough budget to bring the project's stated goals within reach.

3 Integration
Integration is an interesting strategy. People are often asked to integrate while maintaining their own cultural identity. This is the same as telling people to adapt to the dominant cultural discourse, to adopt its rules of conduct and its appearance codes, yet to remain who they are. This is a mission impossible. It's only chance of success is if the dominant majority is prepared to meet the newcomers part of the way. If the majority makes a move, too, we're talking inclusion. In practice, integration often means assimilation.

4 Assimilation
To assimilate means to adapt. In this strategy, the integrating minority is expected to adopt all the do's and don'ts of the dominant group. In the workplace, this is done through on-boarding

programs. New hires are then thoroughly inducted in the mores of the organizations—painted 'blue' or another color, whatever the organization's color happens to be. The better the newcomer is at adapting, the more successful they're thought to be. The dominant culture finds this a comfortable method, because the hassle of experiencing differences is nipped in the bud right from the start. Another process aimed at assimilation are consciousness-limiting teambuilding events, where everyone is re-indoctrinated and efforts are made to "get everyone on the same page again" in order to spread and roll out this strategy ever further.

In society, we demand that newcomers assimilate by making them take an integration test and by complementing them with remarks like "I don't notice at all anymore that you're black." In *White Innocence*, Gloria Wekker put it as follows: *"Belonging to the Dutch nation demands that those features that the collective imaginary considers non-Dutch—such as language, an exotic appearance, "having a tinge of color" (the demeaning way some Dutch people describe being a person of color), outlandish dress and convictions, non-Christian religions, the memory of oppression—are shed as fast as possible and that one tries to assimilate. ... In the public sphere the assimilation model of mono-ethnicism and monoculturalism is so thorough that all signs of being from elsewhere should be erased. Of course, those who can phenotypically pass for Dutch, that is, those who are white, are in an advantageous position."*

Inclusion

Inclusion is based on "us" only, instead of "us and them." Everyone involved considers each other equal and contributes to trying to find the best way to coexist. In this strategy, minorities have an equal say and the dominant group meets the newcomers halfway in order to find solutions that everyone can live with. In inclusion, we decide together on the rules of the game. Minorities not only have a voice; they also have a vote. As Dutch historian Johan Huizinga described in his book *Homo Ludens: people who play the game can obey the rules, but they can also debate what the rules ought to be. In inclusion, you continue to play the game, even when new people join. You take the time to re-evaluate the rules and to make new ones if the situation calls for it.*

How to ensure everyone can join in

If people have little or no say, let alone are allowed to participate, there's a real risk of disintegration, fault lines and fragmentation. More inclusion requires a willingness on all sides to shift in order to reach the highest joint potential. Inclusion is not about elbowing your way in, but about being allowed to join.

Fragmentation	Inclusion
Trying to reduce differences	Seeing differences as a given
Us-Them thinking	Everyone is connected
Conflict between groups	Everyone is equal
People don't say what they think	Being allowed to say what you think
Productivity of the unit goes down	Being allowed to be who you are
Strife, competition	Connection, belonging, co-creation

Exclusion

Integration

Segregation

Assimilation

Inclusion

ILLUSTRATION: SUGGESTION & ILLUSION, FROM: WOW! WHAT A DIFFERENCE!

The Inclusion Paradox

In the introduction, I already mentioned the Inclusion Paradox: be yourself yet adapt. That's a tall order, and it's required of us all from early childhood. You're told to be yourself, to use your talents, to let your uniqueness flourish, to become who you are meant to be and to be authentic in your approach to life. At the same time, you're expected to restrain yourself, not get conceited, integrate, adapt to the group, fit in, and be considerate. Depending on your upbringing either be yourself or adapt got more focus. We scorn people who do not integrate sufficiently. But when you assimilate too much, you betray yourself. This paradox is at work everywhere, for everyone and every group. There are many ways of dealing with it. Organizations that uphold individuality will favor the "be yourself" adage: every man for himself. Organizations that stress the collective will be more likely to adhere to the adapt adage: if everyone loved their neighbor, this would be a better world for all of us.

▸ *The Inclusion Paradox.*

BE YOURSELF, YET ADAPT

IMAGE: SHUTTERSTOCK

The good thing is that this paradox is not truly a contradiction. You don't really have to choose. Being yourself and adapting are both valuable endeavors and both visions hold truth. You might be interested to discover for yourself which side you favor, which side your organization favors and what you teach your children. If you tend towards the 'be yourself' side, this means you'll need a set of basic agreements to unite all those unique individuals around you into a workable whole. If you find you are more likely to tackle things from the 'adapt' side, you'll need to look for ways to accommodate diversity in the group's clear-cut frame of norms.

The paradox shows us that inclusion has its limits, too; everyone is welcome, but not every behavior is acceptable. A co-worker may be quiet and a bit rough around the edges, but it's not too much to expect him to say 'good morning' at the water cooler. This does not force him to be someone he's not. He does not have to be all jolly, reveal details of his private life or joke around with you, but he can be expected to show politeness and proper conduct in an organization, on a team, or in the family, classroom or club. Inclusion does not mean anything goes. Everyone is accepted and anyone can join in, but there are boundaries for behavior. Clearly, this paradox will cause less personal stress about adaptation and authenticity if your own visible and invisible identity markers closely resemble those of the dominant group. That's where power and decision-making power come into the picture. I'll get to that soon.

Unconscious fear

We were here first; are they going to take over? Are they here to take our privileges and wealth away from us? Will my kids be able to find a job or a home when they grow up? If that team becomes part of our department, will I need to give up my desk? Are we going to have to change our meeting style? Will I still be able to leave work early on Fridays? What's going to happen to me? All people fall prey to this us-versus-them thinking. We're curious about the other, but wary of them, too. Can we stay ourselves? Will they adapt? This is the inclusion paradox rearing its head and causing tension. At the same time, there will be people who shake their heads at all this fear and fuss. New perspectives and new people are fun. They open the door to innovation! It all depends on which story you believe in...

Can I trust you to look beyond my non-conventional appearance? To defer your judgment? Can we be ourselves entirely when we encounter each other? Can I trust that you will respect my limits and show me goodwill?

1 DIFFERENCE

It's often said that once people meet each other, things aren't as hard as everyone had assumed. Ignorance breeds intolerance, so contact alone will help us understand each other better. All true, but the contact has to be genuine. Merely eyeballing the other may just fan negative emotions. Latent prejudice and fear can be reinforced. Look, now there are even more of them! What if they...? Contact and getting to know each other means talking with each other, laughing and crying together. It does not mean sending management down to talk about things without making real contact. That's likely to backfire.

Stereotypes have pros and cons

Our minds are full of assumptions, stereotypes and prejudice. Clearly, these hinder us from straightforwardly accepting people who appear not to be like us. But we need to make assumptions to create the semblance of order. Otherwise the world would appear chaotic to us, with nothing for us to hold on to. We make sense of it all by agreeing on rules and by pigeonholing people, things and behavior. For example, when I go to work, I wear clothes. Check. When I'm attracted to someone sexually, I don't just jump them, but I introduce myself first. Check. When I write a project proposal, I make sure to include the available budget. Check. If a coworker does something I don't like, I don't hit them, but I give them feedback using appropriate language. Check.

Rules and norms provide direction in life. They relieve us from an endless series of choices. It's comfortable to know how to behave, how not to embarrass myself. And I feel a connection with people who observe the same rules and norms. It makes life so much more livable. That's why we apply this ordering principle to categories of people as well. It's convenient to know how I should act toward women or children. And toward managers, too, because they behave differently than construction workers, hairdressers or lawyers.

Just act normal
"Just act normal.
That's not normal.
You be normal."
These are phrases
Dutch people use a lot.
Even Dutch politicians
talk this way without
stopping to think about
the fact that they're
including and excluding
people. Who decides
what's normal, anyway?
And so what if someone
doesn't conform to what
is generally considered as
normal behavior? Do you get
a red card? Are you sent away?
And just imagine everyone
acted 'normal,' whatever that is.
If they did, there would never be
any change or progress.

A meeting room with ten men in suits and one woman. Can't she get us some coffee?
A young woman is quickly deemed
to be too young and inexperienced
for a particular role, while a young
man tends to be called 'promising'. Women have to work harder
to overcome prejudice and get the
same promotion. Just like people from
minority groups.

Likewise, the French, English and Japanese all come with their own 'instruction manual'. And while we're at it: the same goes for Muslims, black people, white people, senior citizens and people in wheelchairs. Just like norms, stereotypes about groups of people help to create order in the chaos of life. Quite handy really.

Pros of stereotyping	Cons of stereotyping
makes things simpler	appraisal turns into judgment
structures a chaotic world	judgment turns into prejudice
provides guidelines	prejudice turns into stereotype
enhances group identity (us-them)	stereotype becomes 'the truth'
offers comfort	'truth' leads to cloning, discrimination, racism

The flip side of this ordering is that we often forget to check whether the person we're appraising actually fits into the pigeonhole we've created for them. Besides, we're not so good at checking and adjusting those pigeonholes, or keeping them pliable. Before you know it, all sorts of conscious and unconscious prejudice creeps in, which we then start to see as the truth, opening the door to discrimination. Particularly because our us-them thinking has kicked in and we've lost the ability to connect with each other. That's the danger of pigeonholing.

What's more, people who don't fit into a pigeonhole create cognitive dissonance. Our brain can't handle it. We raise our eyebrows if a woman is not caring and considerate. What's wrong with her? Consider this: my nana was really fond of her Surinamese nurse, but never dropped her prejudice towards other Surinamese. The nurse simply didn't fit the mold. But that was no reason to adjust the mold. People who don't conform to what is expected of them arc labeled anomalies. We make it clear that they're not like the rest of their group. Most people don't want to stick out like a sore thumb. As a consequence, they adjust their behavior to fit the mold.

People will always continue to pigeonhole others. Under strain, we judge and condemn others even more severely. That's what our brains are wired to do. There's nothing wrong with this, as long as we remain aware that these pigeonholes are just socially agreed upon, made-up structures that can never do justice to a whole person and that need regular updating.

Such social constructs are also known as classifications. In creating cultures, we're constantly cranking out classifications. That's our way of jointly deciding on what is right and wrong, pretty and ugly, true and false. These decisions provide a cultural framework that delineates the space in which we can be who we are. But they can also create a lot of friction between different cultures: how could you think *that* is beautiful, right or true?

Classifications we use when we look at people are not fixed realities. But they're not as innocent as they might seem. Remember the 1994 genocide in Rwanda? The distinction between the Hutus and the Tutsis, the two ethnic groups in the country, was a myth thought up and implemented by the colonial rulers, the Germans and later the Belgians. The Hutus and Tutsis had coexisted peacefully for hundreds of years as shepherds and farmers. They spoke the same language and drew no ethnic distinction between themselves. The only difference was that the term Hutu was used for those who farmed and Tutsi for those who herded cows. In essence, these terms were used to denote how many cows someone owned. This could change, so people could change from Hutu to Tutsi and vice versa. However, the Belgians wanted to strengthen their grip on power in Rwanda and decided to reserve the term Tutsi for the taller, slightly lighter-skinned people with a slightly narrower nose. Suddenly, less than 15% of the population were Tutsis, and the rest of the population, who had not been designated as such by the Belgians, were branded Hutu by default. The Tutsis were appointed tribal leaders by the colonial administration and started to consider themselves the new elite. This didn't sit well with the Hutus, who began to claim positions in the new ruling class. This in turn did not suit the Belgians' plans. They had no interest whatsoever in an ongoing democratization process where everyone clamored for power and equal rights. Years of anger, rebellion and protests followed, leading the Belgians in 1955 to provide extra political support to the Tutsis, effectively handing them all political and economic power. This just fueled fury among the population. Because it was difficult to tell the Hutus and Tutsis apart, which caused confusion, the Belgians started to issue identity cards. In the 1960s, the Belgians finally decided to support the Hutus in their call for more active participation

Someone talks to you in broken English. Unconsciously, you start speaking louder and louder, using ever shorter sentences.

A man in a wheelchair enters. Without thinking, you ask his companion what the man would like to drink.

and power. But the unrest continued to grow and eventually exploded in 1994. In the genocide, those identity cards issued by the Belgians decades earlier sealed people's fate.

The moral of this story is this: cultural identities and pigeonholes are not natural or unchangeable truths. They're made up by us humans. Always. The good news is that, in theory, we could create a joint, worldwide human identity if we really wanted to.

Mindbugs, or cultural earworms

All those pigeonholes we've created and all those ideas we've formed about each other are judgments. And like I said, judgments can come in handy when you're trying to order the jumble of life. But if I judge you before I've even met you, I'm prejudiced. Mahzarin Banaij, professor of Social Ethics at Harvard University, has coined the great term *"mindbugs" for such prejudice.* Mindbugs are the neural pathways that we don't want, but that our brains have created for us anyway. Something similar happens in music. Think about the earworms you can't get out of your mind, those phrases of a song that keep bugging you.

A stereotypical image can be a step in the right direction

We have no clear idea of who strangers are. For that reason, we can sometimes see them as dangerous, chaotic or confused. Sometimes a stereotypical image can help to replace this directionless perception with a clearer pattern of thought and action. Strangers are still different then, but at least they can be understood to some extent. I once worked in a large, international group in which the people from Albania and Lithuania expressed disappointment that we Western Europeans did not know any stereotypical jokes about them. That made them feel like they did not count, like they had no place in our work and interpersonal contact.

1 DIFFERENCE

Frequently used, loaded terms	
Race	Race is a human construct. It's not a biological reality
Racism	In the most general sense, racism means people believe that there are different human races, and that one race is superior to another. The term has negative connotations and is often used in conjunction with violence, discrimination and suppression. *Merriam-Webster's Dictionary* defines racism as "a belief that race is the primary determinant of human traits and capacities and that racial differences produce an inherent superiority of a particular race".
Ethnocentrism	Ethnocentrism means you put your own people or group first and center-stage and judge others from that position. Since we like to see ourselves as good, or even, the best, the other tends to get the short end of the stick. Every positive characteristic is attributed to your own group, while the negative characteristics are assigned to, and magnified in, another group.
Xenophobia	If people's fear of the foreign is great, it's called xenophobia ("xenos" is Greek for strange or foreign).
Racist (as a label for a person)	People tend to think of racists as bad people who purposefully exclude others and say mean things about people with a different (non-white) skin color. As if only bad people are racist and good people are by default non-racist. If racist equals bad, then being called a racist or being accused of discrimination feels incredibly offensive.
Racial discrimination	According to the UN Convention on the Elimination of All Forms of Racial Discrimination issued in 1965, racial discrimination is "any distinction, exclusion, restriction or preference based on race, color, descent, or national or ethnic origin which has the purpose or effect of nullifying or impairing the recognition, enjoyment or exercise, on an equal footing, of human rights and fundamental freedoms in the political, economic, social, cultural or any other field of public life."
Institutional racism	An institution is a human-made system of rules that influences our economic, social and political actions. Institutions can be formal, as in the case of laws and regulations, or informal, as in unspoken codes, conventions and common habits. Anthropologists also refer to this as a set of explicit and implicit behavioral norms. Institutional racism refers to the system of written and unwritten rules which systematically disadvantage anyone who is not in the dominant ethnic group, usually by government, business, religion, education and other large organizations with the power to influence many people's lives. These are systems that continue to reproduce racism because they are collectively unsuccessful at delivering appropriate professional services to any person without regard for their skin color, culture or ethnicity. In practice, these grand words translate into situations such as these: if John is disruptive in class, he's labeled "that annoying kid," but if Ahmed is disruptive, he's called "that no-good Moroccan." It's easier for John to find an apprenticeship than it is for Ahmed. You could see these as isolated incidents. But taken together, they form a pattern we call institutional racism. People of the dominant group often fail to see these patterns and find them unimaginable because they seldom experience them directly. In the West, we call this phenomenon white privilege.
Reverse racism	White people often claim that remarks about them as a group constitute reverse racism. But racism is inextricably linked to a subordinate group vis-a-vis a dominant group. White people are not in a subordinate position and can therefore never be the object of racism. Sure, they can be subjected to all sorts of mean-spirited remarks and prejudice, but to call that reverse racism defies the definition of racism itself.

'WHY DOESN'T YOUR MAMMA WASH YOU WITH FAIRY SOAP?
Made only by THE N. K. FAIRBANK COMPANY.
CHICAGO, ST LOUIS, NEW YORK, BOSTON, PHILADELPHIA, PITTSBURGH, BALTIMORE

ILLUSTRATION: FAIRBANK COMPANY

Coders are highly intelligent, slightly overweight guys with ponytails, who only wear black T-shirts and whose life outside of work consists of playing video games. Accountants are boring, conservative men with no sense of humor. Lawyers would sell their own mother if that made them any money. Gay men have a great fashion sense and are always up on the latest trends. HR managers are young, empathic women with a picture of their young children on their desk, who lack any real ambition and don't know a thing about innovation or new business models.

If we were conscious of these mindbugs, we could adjust them. Unfortunately, our brain often outsmarts us with its lightning-fast associations and connections between tiny bits of information. If we start seeing these as the truth and base our actions on them, things go wrong. Then we hire staunchly boring men as accountants and don't take HR seriously. If there's a vacancy for a manager, we automatically see a man in our mind's eye. And if we need a smart, innovation-oriented type of person, we just know that's not someone with a rural accent. After all, city dwellers are far better at dealing with complex issues than country folk. At least, that's what our brain tries to tell us.

We're often surprised when people don't fit the molds we've thought up for them. If a woman is caring and considerate, it's considered normal. If a man thinks of bringing cake to the meeting, we're surprised and complimentary: "wow, how thoughtful, John!" If a woman is hired as a CEO, it's such a rarity that the national news runs a story on it — at least that's what it's like in the Netherlands, where women rarely win the top job. When a man is appointed chairman, it's hardly newsworthy. Women are not supposed to bang their fists on the table, while men are not supposed to get emotional and cry. And it's women's bad luck that "male" behavior tends to be rewarded in positions of power and prestige, except when women display it. Instead of being rewarded, women are often put down as arrogant or bitchy. In other words, not considerate and caring enough... That's not a mindbug, that's a mindf*ck.

Earworms: why you can't get some tunes out of your head

Mothers connect with their 3-month-old babies by other means than words. More so than language, it is the melody of their speech that creates the contact. Researcher Martine van Puyvelde, working with a team of 12 professional musicians, discovered this by analyzing the tonal frequencies in 854 mother-baby 'conversations'. It turned out that 85 percent of the time, the mothers and their babies tried to find harmonizing tones. They composed their own little musical phrases, in a sense. The moments when they were not harmonizing, they were not in close contact with each other, either. The melodies they 'composed' were similar to popular ditties like the Beatles' 'Ob-La-Di, Ob-La-Da'. Possibly, the researchers concluded, melodies like these get so firmly etched into our brain because they resemble our earliest social experiences of emotional safety.

65

Most people think they personally don't have that many mindbugs. That's unfortunate, because it's not true. Everyone has these persistent cultural earworms. They're dug in deep in our brain, feeding off our experiences and the stories we hear. It's an uncomfortable thought, but they also influence our intuition. Which means you can no longer trust your gut feelings in assessing situations and people. The key to improvement is awareness: knowing and checking what you think and feel. That doesn't always work out. You won't always manage. Mindbugs don't just take over in stressful situations, but during our daily routines, too. And when we let our guard down, like when we've had a few drinks. Mindbugs control our automatic pilot. Which doesn't mean you necessarily resort to negative treatment of others. But it does mean you tend to give preferential treatment to people you most closely identify with. It's all quite subtle, instantaneous and unconscious and that's exactly why mindbugs are so hard to overcome.

We have loads of ready-made thoughts and ideas on the shelf. Each of these may possess a kernel of truth. But they are neither true of entire groups, nor of that one specific person. This has surprising effects. In one of her lectures, Esther Mollema, a Dutch expert in inclusion and diversity, asks this question: "Why are hurricanes with female names significantly deadlier (in terms of numbers of casualties) than hurricanes with male names?" Her answer is: "Because we underestimate the threat that Bonny, Emily and Fiona pose and take fewer precautions than when we prepare for Alex or Karl to hit." If only this were a joke....

I've got a riddle for you
A man and his son get into a road accident. The father dies on the spot, while the son is raced to the hospital in an ambulance. Minutes later, in the OR, the surgeon walks in, sees the boy and exclaims, "I can't do this surgery. That's my son." Can you solve this riddle?

Boston University conducted research based on the riddle in 2014. Only 14% of the 197 students who were presented with it were able to provide the solution. Even female students who considered themselves feminists were often wrong. The same happened when the riddle was inverted, so that the mother had been killed and a nurse came in and saw the boy. The results are even more surprising considering the fact that many of these students had a mother with a good job, including medical doctors who worked in hospitals!

As part of the study, 103 children were also presented with the riddle. They scored just as poorly, but at least they thought of creative solutions like "the surgeon is a ghost" or "the whole thing was just a dream," which were apparently more self-evident than a female surgeon.

Watch out: mindbugs are contagious

You can catch out mindbugs by becoming aware of them, by reading about them, talking about them and taking training courses about them. As far as I'm concerned, that comes with a danger sign. First of all, mindbugs can become hyperactive because you've woken them up, so you see them in everyone's behavior. There we go again, sexism. We need to check whether this is actually the case, before this thought in turn becomes a mindbug along the lines of: it's always the women that are discriminated against. But there's another danger too, and it's even more threatening. We can be infected by mindbugs we didn't have yet. Here's an example:

In June 2017, a web article was published on broadlyvice.com about a Georgetown study with the following headline and lead: *"People Don't View Black Girls as Children, Even When They're as Young as Five. According to a new study, adults view black girls as less innocent and less needing of protection than their white peers."*

Participants in the study (unconsciously) thought that black girls were more adult than white girls, to be more knowledgeable about adult topics like sex and therefore needed less protection and support than their white peers. These are shock-

Some examples of frequently occurring mindbugs. If at any point while reading this, you catch yourself thinking for a nanosecond: "but that's true, right?", you've got a mindbug.

- Men are better leaders.
- Women are more caring than men.
- People with autism are gifted.
- People with a recognizably non-Western name are not well-educated.
- Young people are flexible, older people are not.
- Women who wear a headscarf are traditional and conservative.
- People who don't speak the dominant language perfectly have fewer skills.
- Beautiful, thin people are smarter.

Want to know more about your mindbugs? Take a test: https://implicit.harvard.edu/implicit/

ing mindbugs that might explain why the authorities see black girls as more culpable and therefore punish them more harshly for wrongdoing. Which would in turn explain why black girls are five times more likely to be expelled from school and three times more likely to end up in juvenile detention than their white peers.

Let me be absolutely clear: this is awful and obviously must be addressed. However, the point I would like to make is that we have to view these mindbugs and their consequences in their cultural context. I doubt that people in the north of the Netherlands have the same unconscious prejudice as people in Washington, D.C. They have a different collective memory, a different history, a different social structure, different sentiments and sensitivities. Because we read about such mindbugs from elsewhere, they suddenly take hold in our brains, too, and before you know it, they start catching on and making undesirable connections that weren't there before. If before we saw black kindergarten-age girls in the same light as white kindergarten-age girls, now there's suddenly an option to see them as mini-adults! Mindbugs are not just quick and elusive, they're also contagious. By making them tangible, we're making them more contagious. If someone hums that melody, it suddenly gets stuck in your mind too. And yet, making them tangible, becoming aware of them and explicitly naming them, is an effective way to tackle them. In fact, it's the only way we know of to combat them. We'll have to develop the tools to track these bugs down in our own minds, so you can tell them to shut up. For me, the solution is to use an anthropological perspective that allows you to look at the meaning of a phenomenon in your own frame of reference, time and location. Taking this perspective also teaches you to look critically at your own cultural assumptions by asking you to look at yourself through someone else's eyes. Nothing has meaning in and of itself. So let's keep looking and being amazed. Let's not unquestioningly copy/paste arguments and findings from one context to another.

IMAGE: CORNWALLPRIDE.ORG

About gender

Because it comes up so often in this context

Your sex is determined at birth. This is the moment when it is decided how people will address you (he/she), how you're supposed to act, what professions are suitable for you and what clothes are considered appropriate. One body part directs everyone's thoughts about you and the world around you. It opens a whole gamut of cultural norms, assumptions and expectations. Taken together, these are what's known as gender: the cultural expression of the difference in biological sex. Gender is about behavior, dress codes and other expressions of identity that are expected of men and women in a particular cultural context. Every society on earth has certain images and expectations of men and women, of masculinity and femininity. Children are taught these things from very early on, making them seem like biological givens (nature), while in fact they are thought-up concepts (nurture). Lipstick? Woman. Tie? Man. Modest handshake? Woman. Firm handshake and eye contact? Man. In essence, gender roles are stereotypical images of how men and women should behave. If you adhere to the customs of the group, you fit right in.

Gender diversity

But what if your sense of identity is different than the flavors your surroundings offer? Unfortunately, people who don't feel at home in any of the pigeonholes we've defined are considered strange and often treated with hostility. People, especially as a collective, are notoriously bad at dealing with behavior that deviates from the norm and defies their comprehension. It confuses them. It calls up questions, uncertainty and even aggression. Being yourself is all very well, but within certain bounds, please.

Gender is usually divided into two flavors: male and female. Even though there are many other forms of gender. Many people identify neither as men nor women and call themselves gender queer. Some are intersexual; they have both male and female sexual characteristics. Others may feel uncomfortable with the gender identity that goes with their sex. These are transgenders. And when you're born as a boy or a girl and your sense of identity fits your sexual characteristics, you're cisgender. Transsexuals identify completely with the opposite sex, want to permanently live like the opposite sex and therefore opt to have their sexual characteristics changed. And there are many other types of sexual identity and gender diversity. Some of the best known are lesbians (women who are attracted to women), gays (men who are attracted to men), straight (people who are attracted to the opposite sex) and bisexuals (people who are attracted to both men and women).

All these different flavors are often summed up in the term LGBTIQAPC or LGBT+. This acronym stands for Lesbian, Gay, Bisexual, Transgender, Intersexual, Queer, Asexual, Pansexual, Cisgender. Queers are people who do not want to be identified as either gay or heterosexual, and don't want to be pigeonholed. Asexuals are people who feel no sexual attraction to others, but can fall in love. Pansexuals are people who are attracted to people, regardless of their sex or sexual preference.

Gender neutral
Gender neutral doesn't mean there are no more distinctions between men and women. What it does mean is that people have more individual freedom to experience gender in different ways. Let's stop calling boy toys boy toys and just call them technical toys. So that our gender molds become less prescriptive in what boys and girls are supposed to enjoy.

The Jam Circle: Jamming with Difference

In my definition, jamming is the process that unfolds when we spontaneously co-create something. The result of this process is called Jam Cultures. I have summarized this process in the Jam Circle. Inclusion is both the point of departure and the outcome of jamming. You play with everyone, you listen to everyone and it works only if everyone is allowed to create their own sound, and actually dares to do it.

To get into the flow of the jam circle, we use connection and difference, we seek out the power differentials, we include people's different truths, we trust each other and we have the guts to do all this together. These are also the chapters of this book: difference, power, truth, trust and courage.

The great thing about this process that we do it all the time, in rapid bursts, even in the two minutes we spend together at the water cooler. While we're also living side by side and interacting in longer, slower waves.

Obviously, your group will eventually settle on a rhythm, a flow, a way of doing things that fits the group. This becomes a culture full of unwritten rules. That's wonderful and necessary. In Jam Cultures, one of those rules is that you are allowed to challenge the existing mores at any time. That you don't have to bite your tongue, but can say what you want, as long as you also listen to what others have to say.

The flow of the jam circle

Live your life
Enjoy everything that comes your way. Be your non-neutral, pleasant and unpleasant self. Sing, fight, cry, pray, laugh, work and admire. Enjoy others. Work and dance. Open yourself up to others and think whatever you think.
And then, wow. You will experience a difference. In the other. Big or small. You have disrupted your routine.

Open up
Difference evokes emotions. Beautiful and ugly emotions. Anxiety about power and rank. Fear about who will have the upper hand, fear about needing to change. Acknowledge these feelings. Whether you feel lost or attacked, or even if you don't know what you feel, stay open and alert, but don't forget to take good care of yourself. You don't have to react to everything. It's more important to feel where you are, where you stand, than to know where you are. And forget about knowing where you need to go and how to get there. Knowing comes later. For now, hold space.

If you feel fear or anger, if you break into a sweat, you might look for ways to let your emotions cool down a little so you can see and think clearly. Take long, slow breaths. Relax your body even while your muscles want to tense up. Have an internal dialogue and listen to all the emotions and judgments that well up in you. Which of your needs is being frustrated? Which assumptions triggered? Which desires do you feel? What do you need help with? If you feel anger, acknowledge that and listen to the beliefs and values that are being challenged. Assume that you probably misunderstood the other's intentions. This means transcending your own baggage of emotions and judgments. Watching the movie of you as if you were in the audience. Only when you turn down the volume of your own inner screaming and swearing, can you gradually make room for the other's experience and intentions.

And then you will find that you can listen to the other with an open mind, curiosity and amaze-
ment. Simply because you don't have to resolve anything yet. Surprise yourself.

Explore
Explore the differences, similarities and every possible angle with an open heart and eyes
wide open. Even if what you see breaks your heart. Even if you feel aggression welling up.
There are so many ways to see and experience the world. Explore every option from a place
of wonder. Be curious out of empathy and the recognition that there's a kernel of truth in
everything and that everyone carries a piece of the truth in them. So don't listen from a place
of judgment, assumptions and interpretations. That is not to say that you have to unquestioningly accept or agree with everything the other says. You keep observing and thinking
clearly and critically so you can get to know, sense and understand every possible perspective. You challenge your own beliefs. You ask whether anyone has other ideas. Whether anything needs further exploration. Question your own thoughts, observations and conclusions.
There's no need to be certain (yet).
And then you'll find that you can experience, sense and understand the situation from multi-
ple perspectives.

Create
Then it's time to decide on how we're going to live, work and exist alongside each other. Can
we create a joint story? Are our different ideas, needs, interests and desires compatible? What
do we agree on? Some of these decisions are practical, like what we are going to spend our
money on. Others are moral or ethical choices or positions. Power and ranking always play
an important role in this creation, decision-making and negotiation process. Are we trying to
achieve the best possible solution?

We're not looking to make a lifelong deal, by the way. Transience is part and parcel of jamming. Inclusion is an accumulation of temporary, workable solutions that work for everyone
but can change over time. If we find a joint solution that no one has apparently ever thought
of, we're jammin' bigtime, we're in a groove, in a zone, creating real synergy where one plus
one is three. But if we can't get the session going, if we can't get into the groove, we need to
look for elegant solutions so we can each go our own way.
And then we start acting in accordance with our decisions. We enjoy ourselves, each other and
our lives.

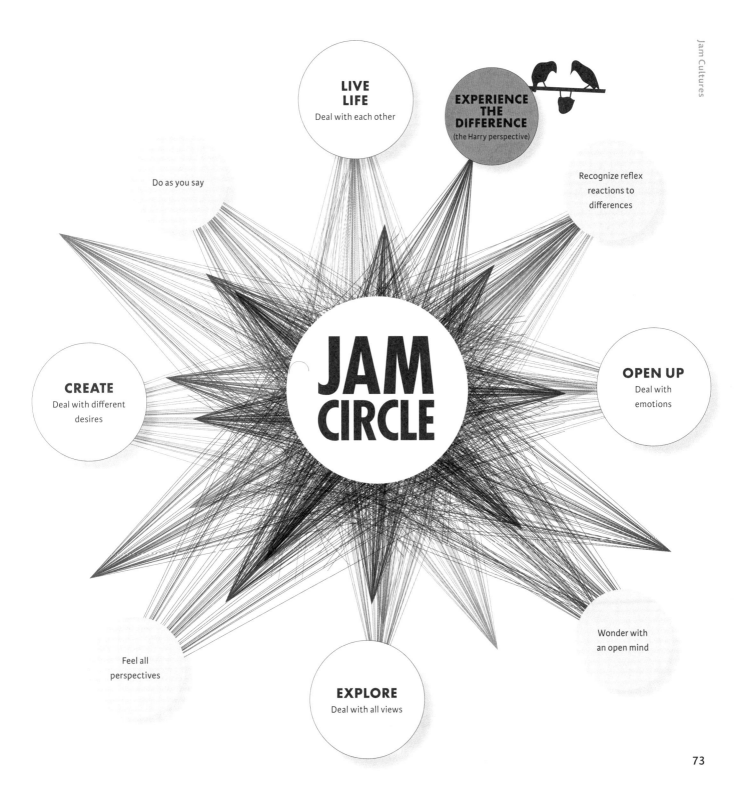

Join the jam!

Top Ten Tips for a Hot Jam Session

Just like improvisational theater and jam sessions, discussions benefit from a few ground rules. These secure the process, even if the content is fluid. If we know where we stand, and feel where the other stands, we can get started and keep going. Even if we don't understand each other so well (yet).

1

Join at the right chord (a group of three or more notes sounded together, as a basis of harmony) and in the right key. What emotions are at play? How are people talking? What is the tone of the conversation? Join.

2

Then add your rhythm to make the whole more interesting. Make your voice heard, talk at your own tempo, in your own style. This gives the debate more color.

3

Add your melody, your musical thoughts, your unique combination of pitch and sustain, your personal sound. Give your opinion, your unique mixture of thoughts, beliefs and associations. Make yourself heard.

4

Play all out, with everything you've got. That creates resonance and magic. Don't turn the debate into a game, but put your heart and soul in it, open up to yourself and others.

5

Jamming also has a competitive edge. Try to measure up to your fellow musicians and make sure you grab your first solo. Know your place, understand the group hierarchy, recognize that people are not the same. If you want to be heard, don't hesitate but step into the spotlight. If you're the first to speak up, your story and your idea will set the tone for the rest of the debate.

YouTube offers many tutorials on how to jam best with others. I've selected the Top Ten Tips and translated them into communication tips. Cooperation and inclusion as a jam session ... *join in and jam!*

9 Don't panic when things don't go exactly as planned. Go with the flow. If you temporarily get lost, you can find your way back by listening to the rest of the band. Genuine talks can never be planned. Working together is unpredictable. That's okay. If you end up in a tangle, don't let the stress get to you, but listen to where everyone is so you can pick up the thread and continue to talk.

6 Another thing jamming requires you to know is when and how to make room for others and their sounds, that you understand call and response. Don't turn the debate into your personal monologue. Make way for others, allow yourself to be surprised and integrate this new sound into your own melody. This tip is particularly important if you're high in the pecking order. Soloing is great, but not if you drown out everyone else.

8 Make sure you practice a lot and understand the structure of jam sessions, so that you're ready to jump in and play when there's an audience and you don't know the other players. Practice your communication skills, and techniques in dealing with differences.

10 Have fun! Make sure the food is good, invite friends over and make new ones. Find the groove, the magic of jamming. Create a pleasant atmosphere and good working conditions. Leave room to be surprised by yourself and others. And have fun together!

7 Jamming can be incredibly frightening, but it's where you really learn to improvise. Real talks can be scary as hell, but that's where real life happens - in confronting and meeting the other.

1 DIFFERENCE

Inclusion: dealing with opposing forces

Inclusion means putting people and the interaction between people center stage. This also means you have to focus on all sorts of elusive feelings, irrational behaviors, ambiguities, contradictions, laziness, passive aggressiveness and avoidance. We're not robots, you know. If you focus on people, you have no choice but to also look at people's less pleasant conduct. No one is all fun. Everyone has downsides, and that goes for you and me, too. People never completely agree with each other; we all have contradictory thoughts and needs. That's where it gets interesting, because we all want to be heard. Of course we think others should be heard, but we'd rather not hear what we don't like, even though that's exactly what's needed. Inclusion is impossible if everything disagreeable is ignored or swept under the rug. That would mean that people can never be their whole selves and that we're letting opportunities slip away.

Ways of dealing with opposing forces

An additional challenge is accepting that we, too, need to adapt. It's easy to point out what the majority agrees on, but sometimes the dominant group needs to take it down a notch, or even shut up for a minute. We all want harmony, but you can't make music together if you don't listen to each other. When you're jamming, you can't all solo at the same time. That just makes noise. But if you let one musician do all the soloing, then you're defeating the purpose of jamming, too. We all want to play our own solo, albeit accompanied by the routine and safety of a basic beat.

In order to achieve this, we need to order the multitude of options. There are roughly four universal ordering principles that help us deal with difference and distinction, as anthropology professor Arie de Ruiter explains to his students every year. These four principles are continually and simultaneously at play, but different ones take precedence over the others at different times. No doubt you

Someone has to lead the way
Despite the hatred every day
Have the guts to take a stand
Draw a merciless line in the sand
Someone has to stop the pain
with much more heart and much less
brain; and try the thing that no one
dares ....maybe you can be the one that
cares? – Jitske Kramer (loosely based on
a poem by Marnix Pauwels)

will recognize them in yourself and the world around you. People who are aware of them can play with them and use the various processes to improve the way they work together. One way is not necessarily better than another. The challenge is to find the right mix.

The four ordering principles are:

1. *Complementary.* This principle is based on the idea that our mutual differences complement each other and that we're better off united. We complement each other in a harmony of differences. We look for synergy. We turn parties into partners. This process has led to many a good marriage and successful joint venture.
2. *Corresponding.* We know we're different, but we prefer to ignore it. We look to recognize ourselves in the other. We primarily focus on our similarities and tend to reduce something new to something we already know. We wonder what our joint passions are, what we both like and want. This may also lead to good marriages and successful joint ventures, as long as those differences are recognized at some point.
3. *Contrasting.* This principle is based on the thought that difference is competitive. Difference leads to conflict, hassle and a tug of war. In this arena, you have to be very sure of yourself to prove your point. You seek a position of power. You realize you need other people's help to attain your goals, but at the same time, those others and their differences get in the way of your ambitions. You prefer to solve this tension by making others defer to your rules. Creating a common interest and a shared vision are key, as a basis for organizing common practices. We try to tackle the obstacle of difference by doing (almost) everything together. But because different interests and subcultures strive for differentiation, this type of integration carries a bigger risk of fragmenting the system and the group. After all, it creates and maintains tension.
4. *Hierarchical.* We're different and that's just fine, as long as it's clear who's in charge here. We need someone to tell us whether something's true or not true. That does require all of us to believe this person.

Leadership and inclusion

Leadership roles have changed a lot. People speak up, they're better educated and have access to many sources of information. That's why a lot of energy is focused on the issue of a shared vision and mission. This is often an attempt to create clear rules and an unambiguous story to get rid of the "obstacle of difference" (see the Contrasting Principle above). Leaders are no longer able to sit in their penthouse boardrooms and surmise the surroundings and know everything better. The issues have become too complex and the world is changing too fast. Leaders cannot impose their truth on others without violence. Particularly because more and more people look at leaders as almighty beings imbued with divine wisdom anymore. That's still a hard pill to swallow for most board members, senior managers, teachers and team managers. Culture building is no longer about recreating uniformity, but about organizing diversity. And one of leadership's key roles is to organize and facilitate meaningful meetings in the liminal zones.

Everyone has access to multiple realities, everyone thinks and forms opinions. That's why we all need to realize—and especially our leaders need to see—that we need more than one way of dealing with our diversity. Obviously, we need to reach some basic agreements which allow us to work and live together. These basic structures provide a framework that provides room to act in, or jam. That requires leadership, but not the type of leadership that knows everything in detail and manages by content. Instead it requires inclusive, courageous leaders. Ones who dare to manage by similarities and differences; ones who dare to step in when tensions rise and don't stand by and watch as people get bogged down in conflict. It requires leaders who know they don't have to solve everything, but who do have the moral courage to involve everyone in the conversation.

We can't do without leadership

To paraphrase Simon Sinek in *Leaders Eat Last*: leaders create a safe space in which people can flourish. In exchange, they receive privileges, extra money and culinary food. Under threat, they're expected to face the danger first and head-on. When leaders faced with danger attack their own subordinates by firing people and shutting down whole departments, that's when things go wrong in organizations. Such moves transgress a deeply human contract. They are anything but inclusive, and they're deeply damaging to any group.

People can't do without leadership. Even in self-managing teams, we need good support with a clear framework and leaders who create an environment where people can develop. If you fail to set boundaries as a leader, if you lack the courage to engage in difficult talks, set targets and standards for conduct, you're wasting your group's potential. We need leaders who are flexible, leaders who challenge us, who have a vision for the future, dare to take a stand and are unafraid to make moral decisions. We need leaders who help us settle arguments, engage in ethical debates and distribute wealth fairly. We need leaders who cherish us without smothering us. Harnessing and making good use of diversity requires a mix of strong and connective leadership. Our ideas on what this leadership should look like are quite divergent: how directive, how formal, how distant, how laissez-faire, how controlling, how caring....

In times of unrest people call for strong leadership

The more diversity, the more subgroups, liminal zones, contradictions and potential conflicts. This creates unrest and uncertainty about ourselves, the other, and how to handle this. If you look around, you'll notice that it's precisely in these circumstances that people in the workplace and in society start to call for strong, charismatic leaders. People who say they know what's going on, set boundaries, start helping their own groups, have a clear story. People who are prepared to put an end to the reigning chaos and bring order, albeit reasoning from a principle of inequality. Calling out for such a leader is much easier than continuing to muddle through ourselves, because that would require us to examine our own emotions. How can we, particularly in these confusing times with so many alarming differences, continue to base ourselves on equality and still show strong, inclusive leadership?

Inclusive leadership

It doesn't help for leaders to start acting all distant and neutral and above the fray. Diversity and inclusion require engagement and independence. That's not the same thing as neutrality, as I learned from Bart Brandsma, a Dutch expert in polarization. Neutrality, not saying what you think, makes you elusive and therefore vulnerable to attacks from all sides. Independence is stronger and more supportive. In order to be independent, you do have to speak up and say where you stand, what you consider important. While also showing that you're open to other people's opinions.

We love to separate things into pretty and ugly, good and bad, true and false. Certain types of leadership can be good or bad, but also beautiful or ugly. This means leaders' behavior can be both beautiful and bad at the same time. That's a very dangerous mix.

Inclusive leadership requires independence, decisiveness and a willingness to follow when necessary. To show yourself and efface yourself. Below I will list Ten Key Points for Inclusive Leadership. It is not an exhaustive list. You can probably think of more. I will develop each of these points further in the course of this book.

1

Power. Challenge. Convey vision. Inclusive leaders are able to convey a mission and do so decisively, setting it as a challenge. They are inspiring, passionate, and a good match. Once in a while, they nudge people out of their comfort zone.

2

Love. Open up. Listen to others, regardless of their station in life or background. Inviting towards all involved.

3

Be the public face. The leader is the spokesperson for the organization and tells the story to the outside world. The story makes clear how the organization's differences are combined into a unified whole.

4

Make content-based decisions. Inclusive leadership means arranging consultation and decision-making in such a way that not just the right people have a seat at the table, but the right perspectives are represented, too. This ensures that decisions can be best suited to the current situation. These decisions don't necessarily coincide with the leader's opinion. Leaders are not expected to have a solution to every problem. In fact, they might lack the expertise needed for more complicated issues, but others may be able to provide it. On the other hand, there are times when leaders need to cut through the crap and make hard choices. Because people ask for it. How the decision-making process is structured is key to ensuring inclusion.

5

Challenge the system to accept new routines. Not by threatening, or pushing and shoving, but by changing the rules and procedures that block inclusion.

6

Creating space – a daily safe space to jam in. Creating the context in which tension can get dissolved. Creating room for difference, dialogue and debate. Contradictions and conflicts are a normal part of life. You don't need to solve those as a leader; you can't have all the answers. However, you do need to ensure there's a safe space by creating procedures, time, frameworks and codes of conduct that leave space for important discussions to take place and genuine connections to be made. I'll have more on this in Chapter 4 on Trust. You need to create room for differences and similarities; beauty and ugliness. For minorities and minority standpoints you need to consciously create extra room, because this is usually overlooked. If anyone is excluded, humiliated or discriminated against, the leader must address this. Dare to safeguard the group's standards and to make clear what is and isn't acceptable.

7

Holding space – extra attention at special moments. This is the safe space squared. When conflicts are blown wide open, arguments erupt and people lose it, the leader is there to help ease the tension. Holding space is about giving room to problems, particularly when this is complicated. It means examining what's going on, no matter how painful or sad, so there's room for the next step and the solution to emerge. In other words, it's not about focusing on a solution, but about making visible where we are. Opening up and exploring every angle. Bringing every emotion and power issue to the table, so that we can examine them together, operating from a place of trust. Inclusive leaders know how to stay afloat in this open-ended tension.

8

Show engagement and independence. Inclusive leadership is neither sleight-of-hand, nor a method. On the contrary, it invites people to join in with all they've got and bring all they are. To work together with heart and soul on the organization's or society's objectives. With everyone's pleasant and less pleasant sides in full view. This requires leadership to do the same. This is known as showing vulnerability, but as far as I'm concerned that's a throwback to when leaders were supposed to be big, strong know-it-alls. I prefer to say that leaders only need to show their humanity, including their doubts. Bring their own voice and take a step back to hear others, too. Inclusive leaders take a stand, but can be independent at the same time because they listen to everyone and anything. They ask questions and are prepared to change their opinion. They speak freely. They jam.

9

Provide leadership in the liminal zones. We're used to thinking in relatively clearly delineated units such as teams, organizations or nations. However, these boundaries are never absolute. They're actually just human constructs, devised to make our lives seem more manageable. When there is more diversity, we're more frequently invited and challenged to connect with others at or near those boundaries. In zones where different interests converge, different lifestyles mingle and co-creation is an option. Inclusive leaders have the ability to stretch the boundaries between networks and bridge the gaps between them; to counteract groupthink; to unite people with different areas of expertise; to encourage and facilitate exchange on the edge of the differences. It no longer works to apply the same rules to everyone in any situation. As an inclusive leader, you need to step up and get involved in this force field of differences. Don't stand on the sidelines to see how others are handling social and cultural clashes. This means you need to curb the impulse to step aside and look on from a neutral, distant or even indifferent perspective at the wrongs and tensions in your tribe. As the leader of a jam session, you join the jam, while keeping an overview. Engaged yet independent. That takes courage.

10

Regulating your own emotions and insecurity. Inclusive leaders act from a position of not having all the answers. They prepare the group for what's to come. They regularly confront themselves and others with new insights and shake up routines. This message is not always welcomed. Straddling the boundaries between differences can be lonely, emotionally speaking. It means putting yourself in a spot where you show your feelings and let them inform, but not dictate, your actions. It means being able to step in and out and resonate with every perspective. It requires an intense mix of neutrality and compassion with every possible perspective.

Five important boundaries between groups of people
Inclusive leadership requires that you show leadership in the
liminal zones, the areas close to the boundaries where differences are expressed. *Source: Boundary Spanning Leadership,
published by the Centre of Creative Leadership.*

1

Vertical
Across hierarchical levels

2

Horizontal
Across roles, areas of expertise,
departments

3

Stakeholders
Beyond the organization's boundaries (business partners, customers, job market, shareholders)

4

Demographic
Across various subgroups (gender,
ethnicity, age, nationality, religion,
sexual orientation)

5

Geographical
Across distance and time zones

How to show more love for diversity and difference

Can we allow more people who are different from us into our heads and hearts? Absolutely. And then we'll see that it's complicated, but necessary. That it enriches our lives. That if there's a will there's a way, and that obstacles can vanish into thin air.

So, challenge yourself. And allow the people you work with to challenge you. Learn to understand how your preferences can influence your decisions and how prejudice can unconsciously steer your thoughts and feelings. This requires alertness and attention. It requires you to open up to difference and at the same time set limits where necessary.

Stop cloning. One way to do this is to stop using job descriptions that are so restrictively worded that they exclude whole categories of people. Judge ideas, not people. Widen your preferences when working with others. Recognize yourself in what is different and what you share with the other. Stop saying you're color blind. Skin color matters. Don't become a clone of everyone else. Show yourself, dare to be different. This can be difficult, because you may feel required to 'be yourself yet adapt'.

Realize that differences are part of life. Diversity is not an obstacle to overcome, but a human given we need to learn to live with. Jamming is the way to go. Which requires leadership aimed at maximizing contradictions and acting from a position of uncertainty. Just wing it.

'Everyone else is a living example of how things can be different.'
— Professor André Wierdsma

Questions to reflect on and discuss with others

There's enough food for thought. Below you will find a list of questions you can explore, either by yourself or with others. Share your insights on social media, so we can all benefit: #jamcultures.

- When was the last time you cloned?
- What mindbugs are buzzing around in your brain?
- What pigeonhole have you holed up in?
- What pigeonholes have you put others into?
- When, why, how often and to whom have you said: "Come on, don't overreact?"

- How aware are you of the fact that your perceptions are strongly influenced by your age, sex, skin color, etc.?
- How can you widen the circle of those you trust and your set of preferred behaviors?
- Looking at your social environment, what fragmentation strategies do you see?
- Are you more on the "be yourself" or the "adapt" side? What do you tell your children? Your coworkers? Customers?
- Are you an inclusive leader? Why or why not?
- Where do you draw the line in behavior? How do you deal with this in an inclusive manner?

A few questions I borrowed from Anousha Nzume's *Hello, White People*, specifically for white people:
- When was the first time you realized you were white?
- How did being white affect your adolescence?
- How many times a day are you confronted with your whiteness?
- How often do you see people who look like you in terms of skin color being portrayed in a positive light in the media?
- How often do you stop to think that your answers do not speak for people of color?
- And how would you answer all these questions if you were speaking for the organization you work for? And from your professional role?

And here's a question for men, specifically:
- How often have you adapted your clothes or behavior to avoid sexual advances? Pose the same question to at least ten women in your life.

Do something

Reflecting and talking are important, but so is taking action. Below I've provided a few ready-made ideas to put into action. Clearly, this list is not intended to be exhaustive. Add your own ideas and make the list longer. Share your insights on social media, so we can all benefit: #jamcultures.

- Go out to dinner at a restaurant whose cuisine is totally new to you.
- Look for people in your surroundings that don't look like you at all and invite them for a cup of coffee, lunch or a drink. Who knows, you might end up making new friends, while tackling a few of those persistent mindbugs.

- For the white people among us: refuse yourself the luxury of denying your skin color for one day. Look, listen, talk, ask questions, walk around the supermarket, watch the news, read the newspaper and imagine that everyone white was black and the other way around. You could do the same with men and women.

- Read your kids' history books. If you conclude that what they learn is too rosy or too one-sided, at least talk about it with them. Approach the school. Send an e-mail or, better yet, make an appointment to discuss this.

- Make sure minorities are promoted and find their way up, in order to grow the pool of talent. If management come up with a list of high potentials who are almost all members of the majority in your workplace, you need to open the discussion. Don't just talk to your management; talk to those who have a minority background, too. Are their motivations and talents visible enough?

- It happens all the time: negative responses or doubts when a woman in her thirties is recommended for a senior role. Yes, people, breaking news: a lot of women get pregnant and have kids. That's how it works and it's part of life. As coworkers, managers and employers you need to be as flexible as possible. That's not just human, it's also your best bet, because you'll be repaid in loyalty and innovation.

- It's true that the pool of female and bicultural "management potentials" is smaller than the pool of white men. That's the way the cookie has crumbled and it will take a while before this is rebalanced. All the more reason to start your search for new candidates for a role early, because it might take a little longer. And make sure that you give your in-house talent enough chances to grow and develop so you can eliminate prejudice and other obstacles as soon as possible.

- Take steps to include more people in the media who speak a dialect. And stop subtitling them. Just put a little effort in. I say we should start with the weather and have that presented in every possible dialect.

Inclusion Principle: Don't Clone
- Understand how your preferences influence your decisions.
- Widen your preferences.
- Consciously work with people who are different from you.
- Judge ideas, not people.

1 DIFFERENCE

References

Brandsma, Bart (2016). *Polarisatie. Inzicht in de dynamiek van wij-zij denken.* [Polarization: Understanding the Dynamics of Us vs. Them Thinking]. Schoonrewoerd: BB in Media.

Choudhury, Shakil (2016). *Deep Diversity: Overcoming Us and Them.* Toronto: Between the Lines.

DiAngelo, Robin (2018). *White Fragility: Why It's So Hard for White People to Talk About Racism.* Boston: Beacon Press.

Huizinga, Johan (1950). *Homo Ludens. Proeve eener bepaling van het spel-element der cultuur.* [Homo Ludens: A Study of the Play-Element in Culture]. Edited by L. Brummel et al. https://www.dbnl.org/tekst/huiz003hom001_01/

Kramer, Jitske & Braun, Danielle (2018). *Building tribes. Reisgids voor organisaties.* [Building Tribes: Travel Guide for Organizations] Deventer: Management Impact.

Nzume, Anousha (2017). *Hallo witte mensen.* [Hello White People] Amsterdam: Amsterdam University Press.

Said, Edward (1993). *Culture and Imperialism.* London: Vintage.

Sinek, Simon (2017). *Leaders Eat Last: Why Some Teams Pull Together And Others Don't.* New York: Penguin Books Ltd.

Stuurman, Siep (2017). *The Invention of Humanity: Equality and Cultural Difference in World History.* Harvard University Press.

Wekker, Gloria (2017). *White Innocence: Paradoxes of Colonialism and Race.* Durham, NC: Duke University Press.

Study of the role of music in the mother-infant relationship. Musical earworms

Van Puyvelde, M., Vanfletteren, O, van Loots, G, De schuyffeleer, S., Vinck, B., Jacquet, W. & Verhelst, W. (2010). "Tonal synchrony in mother-infant interaction based on harmonic and pentatonic series." *Infant Behavior & Development, 33* (4), 387-400. Summary: http://www.vub.ac.be/pers/persberichten/2013/02/13/zit-muziek-moeder-baby-relatie

Study of the surgeon and injured son riddle

Study by Boston University in 2014 about the riddle of the injured son and the surgeon: http://www.bu.edu/today/2014/bu-research-riddle-reveals-the-depth-of-gender-bias/

People don't view black girls as children

"People Don't View Black Girls as Children, Even When They're as Young as Five", June 28, 2017; https://www.vice.com/en_us/article/pade5n/people-dont-view-black-girls-as-children-even-when-theyre-as-young-as-five

Arie de Ruiter PhD

Arie de Ruiter is professor emeritus of Anthropology. I was fortunate enough to attend several of his lecture series. Every time, he sparked off new ideas in me. Seldom have I met such an encyclopedic mind.

Boundary-Spanning Leadership

This great term was coined by the Centre for Creative Leadership in their eponymous book. For an accessible article on this topic: https://www.ccl.org/wpcontent/up-loads/2015/04/BoundarySpanningLeadership.pdf

Ernst, Chris & Chrobot-Mason, Donna (2010). *Boundary-Spanning Leadership: Six Practices for Solving Problems, Driving Innovation and Transforming Organizations.* Maidenhead: McGraw-Hill Education-Europe.

2

POWER

About the pecking
order and who has
the power

See the power of power

JAM CULTURES

I am so sorry. So sorry that we are the greater number.
That we were here first. And that we have just that little more than you.
You can't hold that against us. We worked very hard for it.
And you can do the same. Fight your way in! Show who you are
and what you can bring us! You are more than welcome to join.

Why are you crying? I can see you're doing your best.
That you struggle and smile and swear your way in.
I cheer you on. Silently. My head, my heart, filled
with my self-invented helplessness.
Sometimes I am shocked to see how we point
our freedom at you, like a weapon.
I am so sorry.

Why are you shouting? I am listening.
I am asking questions. I am giving you
support.
I don't know how, but I am doing it.
I go to battle for you. I want to give
back to you
what wasn't mine in the first place.
But give me time.
I am so sorry. Let's scream together.
Cry together.
Laugh together. Let's do together all
what we can do. Together.
You're welcome.

Jitske Kramer

If you felt a bit uncomfortable after reading the previous chapter ...

... this chapter is going to be even less pleasant. It's about the dark side of diversity and inclusion. Forget about options and opportunities, innovation and creation, optimism and positivism for a minute. Forget about the mindless consumption of exotic foods and world music. This is about finding ways to jam on an equal footing. It's about who is allowed to fully take part, and who isn't. And hence it's about who ultimately sets the standards, who has the power to decide who gets a piece of the pie, whose voice gets heard, and who really has a vote. We're going to take a look at why it often goes wrong and how power can get in the way of inclusion. Let's examine what makes people think: "Sure, of course everybody can join in, but we were here first." That thought doesn't exactly help foster jam cultures, but unfortunately it's quite common. Let's look at what factors obstruct a cultural jam session. In short, this chapter focuses on power as a jam-stopper, an obstacle that's not easily avoided. We can only restore the flow if we're prepared to delve into this problem and fully explore it, no matter how painful that is.

Variations are fun

We don't mind if others are a variation of ourselves, but the differences shouldn't be too pronounced or involve matters of principle. Say we were all taking a hike and one of us said: "We don't need to walk the whole way; we could also skip." We'd probably find it funny and creative. We'd see it as quirky, a bit of extra fun. But imagine we're hiking North and one of us suddenly wants all of us to turn around and hike South. We probably wouldn't take kindly to the suggestion. It wouldn't feel like a lark. More likely, it would strike us as annoying. We'd say "C'mon, just go with the flow." What's even more annoying is that it's always the same people who want to go against the grain. And going against the grain is one thing, but trying to make all of us go the other way is quite another. They shouldn't slow us down, distract us, hold up a mirror to us, contradict us, or consider themselves better than us. Because then we'll get pissed off, or at least deeply annoyed.

Wealth is
not distributed
equally.

One simple example is clothing: are you free to choose what you wear? Sure, we are. Or so we think. But imagine if you wore a Spiderman costume to work. Or, what would people think if you wore something that was fashionable in the 1950s, but not anymore? Our individual sense of fashion is subject to specific, but implicit rules. You might not ever want to wear a white leotard, or blue culottes. Maybe you wouldn't ever want to work in a place where you're expected to wear a suit; those are individual choices. But there are also sociocultural frameworks that apply to clothing, some of which have even been put down in laws. In the Netherlands, you're supposed to wear clothes. You can't walk around naked, at least not in the street. You're also not allowed to cover your face, so burqas, balaclavas and full-face helmets are banned in public buildings and public transport. Those who ignore the rules and walk around naked or completely covered in the public domain, risk a fine. We've decided that neither nakedness nor full-face coverings belong in Dutch culture. You may disagree, but if you flout the rules, you risk a fine.

Embracing diversity is easier said than done, because it's no small feat to take on the uneven distribution of power, sexism or institutional racism. If you don't watch out, your diversity policy will prove half-baked, or worse, mere window-dressing. In reality, things will still be business as usual, but covered with a nice rainbow, some exotic snacks and interesting tribal drums from the African continent. That's what embracing diversity looks like when it's done to stymie debate rather than start a real conversation about changing pernicious habits, norms and values.

Culture as a weapon

Ultimately, inclusion is about who gets to make what decisions and who gets to enjoy what privileges. Some members of the group have the power to impose cultural rules and laws on others and to provide or withhold access to the group. Those who have mastered the rules of the group gain power, become leaders and influence the rules. Culture creates power brokers and power brokers create culture. Those in power get to decide how early we have to start at work, when we can leave, who gets a promotion, which IT system the company is going to buy and whether interns will be paid. They also decide what medical care is covered by our health insurance, who qualifies for social security, how many years we have to go to school, whether a new airport will be built, whether or not to reintroduce the military draft, and so on. Culture and power are intertwined. It's good to be aware of that and to know your own place in it.

Definition of power
Because rulers can impose their ways and ideas on others through education and the media, culture is sometimes seen as a weapon the elite can wield. The elite can define what is right and wrong, can frame and direct. In the workplace, this becomes apparent during off-site team-building activities. No effort is spared to make everyone embrace management's ideas and to wipe out dissident thought: let's get everyone on the same page and rearing to go. If you look at it from this perspective, such activities are the most mind-numbing, conscious-ness-reducing experiences you can imagine.

Poorly distributed power keeps people dumb
When the ruling class doesn't listen to the different ideas in a group and when this group uncritically accepts whatever the ruling class says, the rulers' decisions and actions will not be as good as they could be. Unevenly distributed power makes everyone dumber. One important element of inclusion is that you make decisions *with* people rather than *for* people, so that everyone not only *feels* heard, but actually *is* heard. We often shy away from this because we're afraid of plurality, of seeing everyone's cards on the table, of the upheaval this would cause. The paradox is that ignoring all these different voices actually causes a lot of problems and undercurrents and decreases the quality of decisions. I explored this subject in depth in my book *Deep Democracy*.

The uneven distribution of power is a touchy subject, especially when we feel the unevenness is based on gender, ethnic or religious differences. It angers us. We avoid the subject, lie about it and feel ashamed of it. We refuse to believe it's true, we rebel, we say it's of no concern to us. But it keeps us awake at night. It makes us leave organizations, end marriages and start wars. The imbalance in power is real, and just as with our tendency to clone, becoming aware of it is a major step forward. If we want to jam, we have to learn to deal with that power differential and use it to our advantage.

Away with the leaders? No

Perhaps because power relations are a sensitive subject, the debate on the need for leadership can get rather heated. Some people question whether we need leaders at all, while others insist that we all need a leader. Many management books and papers focus on distributed leadership or self-managing organizations. There even is a movement that propagates doing away with hierarchies in organizations. Based on my book *Deep Democracy* and my penchant for inclusion, I often get lumped together with the latter school of thought. Yet in *The Corporate Tribe* and *Building Tribes,* I wrote about the importance of good leadership, because we're hierarchical animals and like functioning in a pecking order. So, where do I stand on this issue?

I believe we have no need for a 'kingpin' with absolute power, but at the same time, organizations do need leadership. Leaders ensure decisions can be made and everyone who wants or needs to is included in the discussion. Self-management sounds great, but isn't always necessary and doesn't always work either. One organization I know of that had haphazardly introduced self-organizing teams saw its absenteeism rate skyrocket to 20 percent. As soon as leadership is removed, people lose their bearings and don't know who's responsible for things anymore. Doing away with leaders means doing away with the chain of command and with knowing who to turn to when things go awry. If the old chain of command is not replaced with a new one, people will be left in the lurch and will have to call out their less conscientious coworkers themselves. This is usually a less inclusive and democratic process than you'd hope. It tends to quickly descend into survival of the fittest with the biggest mouths taking on informal leadership or cutting corners because they feel confident no one will dare call them out on it. Others, the people who care about customer value, start to work twice as hard to make up for the coworkers who are slacking off. The values underlying the whole self-organizing endeavor—full equality, openness and transparency—are completely lost in the fray. Lack of clarity about leadership causes a lot of strife and stress, because everyone in the workplace feels insecure about whether their actions are right or wrong and who they should turn to when there's a problem.

There will always be differences between people. A clear chain of command makes it easier to deal with conflicts and tension. We are equal, but we occupy different positions of power. Obviously, we do need to make sure this chain of command is based on fairness, and even more importantly, that we treat the people below us fairly. In jam cultures, leaders don't take care of everything, but they create the conditions in which people feel called upon to resolve tensions themselves. Inclusion means recognizing that everyone is equal, but not the same. It also means structuring the chain of command in a way that allows everyone to be heard. Good leaders find ways to make everyone feel equal. Not on the same footing, but worth as much as anyone else. Just as Kyteman was clearly the leader and front man of his band's jam sessions, yet still expected all his band members to find their own sound and add it to the mix. Leaders establish the frameworks, creating a climate and conditions in which everyone dares to take risks and everyone can shine. Personally, I've done lot of improvisational theater in restaurants, acting in collaboration with waiters and a maître d'. Our best nights were when we all understood our mutual power relations and we had a tough maître d'. That enabled us to go all out. If the maître d' didn't take control, we all held back a little and the improvisations just wouldn't flow. People need clear leadership and rules in order to fly. We need leaders who know when to hold on and when to let go. This doesn't mean leadership can't rotate. It can, as long as everyone is aware of it.

Even the kingpin needs someone to look up to
We all need something or someone to look up to. Everyone needs guidance and affirmation from higher up. That is to say, even the kingpin (the CEO, the headmaster, the patriarch or matriarch) needs someone to look up to. That could be their mother, a god, a vision or a world view. It's interesting to know who or what the kingpin considers more important than themselves.

'Let me explain to you one more time …': mansplaining and whitesplaining

Mansplaining was coined by Rebecca Solnit in her 2008 essay *Men Explain Things to Me*. The term refers to men explaining things to a woman and positioning themselves as an authority in the field, even though she is actually the expert. For example, men explaining Newton's laws to a female physicist; men telling female medical doctors how to treat a disease, or men explaining how to hit the ball to a female top-50 tennis player. The all-time low is the man who apparently felt the need to explain to his wife how to put in a tampon.

The term *whitesplaining* is used for a similar process in which white people feel the need to explain the world to black people, for example, what it's like to be discriminated against, or what does and doesn't constitute racism.

Obviously, men are allowed to explain things to women and white people can talk about how they experience racism. As long as we see each other as equals. Clearly, that's what both terms are about: the sense that the other person does not consider your experience or knowledge as equally valid, and feels the need to correct you. And that's a subtle way of pushing you down a notch in the pecking order. It's disrespectful and annoying as hell. The trick is to open up the discussion about this in such a way that the discussion deepens rather than hardens. It's important to avoid a battle about who is morally right in this. It's key to keep checking each other's intentions and to stay open about them.

The invisible chains of culture

In December 2018, the Netherlands Institute for Social Research (SCP) published the umpteenth study that's appeared on the position of Dutch women in the labor market. The SCP concluded that just 60% of Dutch women in a relationship were economically in-

Switch It Up - mind game
In August 2018, shortly after former parliamentarian Femke Halsema was appointed mayor of Amsterdam, daily paper *Trouw* ran a story under the headline: "Van Uhm helps Halsema audit firefighters". Twitter exploded with questions about the framing of this news. Why didn't the headline read "Halsema asks Van Uhm to audit firefighters"?

I enjoy this game of switching the male/female or black/white perspective in newspapers, on TV, on the street, in conference halls. In my head, I replace the men with women (and the other way around) and all people of color with white people (and vice versa). That makes it painfully clear where the bias is. Can you imagine a leading newspaper printing this headline: "New CEO of X is a man"?

dependent. In most relationships, men are the main breadwinners and both sexes expect merely a token contribution from the woman. The report confirmed what was already known: Dutch women are more likely than women in other countries to opt for a part time job, even before they have kids. During a debate I moderated, several people suggested there was nothing wrong with this, particularly if women chose part time work out of their own free will. But the question is how free they really are. After all, the norm is that women take on the lion's share of care-related tasks in a relationship. This makes the one-and-a-half breadwinner model more like a default setting than a conscious choice. Going against the grain means having to explain yourself and exert yourself more than when you just go with the flow. I can still recall how disapprovingly other mothers looked at me when I dropped my kids off at school and hurried to my full-time job. They even openly questioned my choices. "But you did want those kids, right?" It's commonplace for Dutch employers to nudge women into part time jobs, even young women fresh out of college. This occurs particularly in industries with many women employees, where part time jobs are the norm and most jobs openings are for part time workers. So your freedom of choice is not absolute; cultural expectations create a pre-existing script of behaviors, procedures and facilities that you have to contend with.

Hiding behind 'my culture'

And finally, one last way to use culture as a weapon. It's common wisdom that we've been culturally pre-programmed and can't resist the automatic decisions our brain makes. Another widely held idea is that we should always strive to be authentic and true to ourselves. Put these two ideas together, and you get a strong tendency for people to say: "Yup, that's me. That's who I am, that's my culture and there's nothing I can do about it." Well, I have just one thing to say about that: No. You always have a choice!

PHOTO: SAMUEL CORUM/ANADOLU AGENCY/GETTY IMAGES

Pecking Orders: eat, kill or have sex

▶ *It looks like a scene from a movie, but it isn't. It was the summer of 2017. There was a far-right rally in Charlottesville, Virginia. Protesters were marching against the removal of a statue of Robert E. Lee, Confederate general during the American Civil War (1861–1865), champion of Southern independence and staunch defender of slavery. The protesters carried torches and flags, gave Nazi salutes, and chanted 'white lives matter' and 'Jews will not replace us'. During the rally, a neo-Nazi rammed his car into a group of counter protesters, killing a young woman and injuring nineteen people.*

If we come across another entity, we want to know how to categorize it. All people do it, myself included. We use three categories to classify what we encounter: What is it?

Is it good or bad? Is it ugly or beautiful? First of all, we decide *what* something is. Is it human, animal or inanimate? Can I eat it, or not? Can I sit on it, or not? Next, we classify the entity as either good or bad. Do I want it, or not? Should I kill it, or let it live? And lastly, we decide whether that entity is beautiful or ugly. Is it good for me, or not? Can I have sex with it, and to what end: for procreation, love or lust?

We do this all the time, and it takes but a split second. Our answers are always related to our own cultural context. For example, features that are considered beautiful in one culture, may be considered ugly in another one. Based on my answers, I categorize the people around me and rank them in a basic pecking order. And so do you.

Homo hierarchicus

There's a hierarchy in every group, from kindergartens to executive boards. We are homo hierarchicus, as Louis Dumont said. In every group, everywhere, one person has more influence than another. Who decides what's for dinner at your house? Who chooses where you go on vacation? Clearly, not everyone is consulted about everything. Those of us who aren't invited to the table usually aren't heard and even if we're invited to chime in, we often don't have a vote. That's ranking and we simply can't do without it. A pecking order provides clarity. Every culture has lots of implicit judgments about what that order is supposed to be. Who wears the pants in your house? The pater familias, obviously. And if it's the mater familias, in many cultures that makes us chuckle. But we also respect it. After all, the home is women's domain. Remember the mindbugs?

Determining the pecking order by ranking

The pecking order in a group is based on a mix of characteristics. Some of these are givens that you can't—or can't easily—change, like sex, skin color, age, height and origin. Other characteristics are social and/or behavioral, and can engender either admiration or fear and thus affect your ranking: a big mouth, talent, verbal creativity, sparkling eyes, large muscles. While you can't do much about the first set of characteristics, the latter are something you can work on. Meanwhile, we're not aware of it, but we're continually giving people points for all these characteristics. The sum total of your rankings determines how much influence you have on others, as Arnold Mindell, founder of *Deep Democracy*, described in detail.

Mindell's Ranking Test

Compare yourself to other people in a specific group: your team at work, your family, your sports club. Or pick a group you would be an outsider to: the Hell's Angels, an evangelical church community, a voodoo festival in Benin. What status points would you accord yourself for different characteristics? For example, would your age give you a higher or lower ranking?

The points are distributed as follows: 1 means you assess your ranking to be low in comparison to the others in the group; 2 means you think your ranking scores neutral in this group; and 3 means you believe this characteristic would give you authority and respect in the group.

1. *Origin* (ethnicity, nationality, skin color)
2. *Sex* (f/m)
3. *Sexual orientation*
4. *Age* (old, young)
5. *Authenticity* (in touch with your personal drives and goals, in touch with a god, the universe, the divine, the ancestors)
6. *Health* (mental, physical)
7. *Economic class* (poor/rich, possessions)
8. *Education* (level, subject)
9. *Social status in a particular group* (upper, middle, lower class, nobility, elite)
10. *Psychological well-being* (self-confidence)
11. *Language proficiency* (speak the group's language fluently, know and use the group's jargon)
12. *Magical power* (knowledge or skills the others don't have)
13. *Seniority* (been with the organization or in the field for a short/long time)

Mindell predicts that the further below the average of 26 you score, the bigger the chance that you don't speak up much in the group. Even if you're an expert in your field, if you give yourself a low ranking, you will not contribute much to the debate. So, when you notice you find it difficult to speak up in a group, this may have to do with how you rate your own status in this specific group.

All of us are continually ranking. Power and hierarchy bring out our animal qualities. It's no wonder we call it a pecking order. Lack of clarity in the hierarchy leads to conflicts and trouble. So, there's no point trying to get rid of ranking, but it does make sense to try and use it wisely. That's not something you can do in a vacuum; it's the ultimate unspoken party game. As Mindell says, you don't see ranking in the mirror, you only notice it in your interaction with others. Which is why your ranking changes depending on the circumstances. You might be like a boss at work because of your MBA degree, but back home your brothers might still tease you for being chicken shit. Perhaps you score lots of points at a bar thanks to your sexy dress, but the same outfit won't do you any good in the workplace.

Every cultural group has its own set of status priorities. In some circles, the amount of money you have gets you a much higher ranking than in others. Another subculture puts more weight on whether or not you're a homeowner. In one group, skin color might be high on the list, while in another, young people score higher than old. And so on.

As we saw above, ranking points are not always the result of visible characteristics. They can also come from invisible traits like your sexual orientation or political affiliation. You can choose whether you want to make those known and hence whether you want to be ranked accordingly. This is where it becomes relevant how the group ranks these characteristics. It can be painful to realize that something that matters deeply to you, like your sexuality, would lower your status if it became known to a particular group. You might choose to keep it to yourself, even if that hurts too.

Fons Trompenaars, an expert in the field of intercultural collaboration, distinguishes between acquired and assigned status. In a culture that values *acquired* skills, ranking depends on performance. In that culture, a young person will rank highly for excelling at a task. In a culture that values *assigned* status, ranking depends on a person's station in life. So in that culture, the same young person who excels at a task will be outranked by an older person, even if the older one is less skilled. There, seniority is what counts most.

The value of certain items on a ranking list can be fluid. Whether it's considered acceptable in your group to vote for a certain party depends on the news about that party. Through time, different groups have changed their views on many issues, like whether it's positive or negative to own a car, smoke cigarettes or eat meat. This means the ranking value changes, too.

Just a few years ago, you thought you were boss if you flew to other cities for a weekend break five times a year. Try bragging about that now, and you'll be asked why you don't feel guilty for taking a plane.

Ranking and inclusion

Looking at it so consciously, ranking may seem an extraordinarily complicated process, but people are very good at it. Some less than others, though. As social beings, we notice from a young age what the norm is, who's powerful and who we should try to please. Those more skilled at the ranking game can climb the ladder more quickly. The good news is, by acknowledging that we take part in this ranking game, we can do it better and more fairly. Assuming we want to do so.

If your point total is low, you tend to keep a low profile in the workplace. You're wary about speaking up because you know your rank in the pecking order. You know your influence is relatively low and your vulnerability high. If you do speak up, your cheeks will probably flush. People higher on the ladder will see this as insecurity. Or they might read your silence as proof that you have nothing to contribute and look down on you for what they regard as a non-committal attitude or even stupidity. From a high-ranking position, it's difficult to understand why others are reticent. Those at the top of the ladder often insist that it's safe to say anything. They believe that not talking is a sign of personal insecurity, a lack of assertiveness or a lack of personal leadership. Some higher-ups—the most dominant people— then add: silence implies consent.

People higher up the ladder are responsible for ensuring that everyone is heard. They can do this by showing an interest—a real interest, not just a token gesture—in what everyone has to say. What else can they do? They can ask if anyone has more ideas, and explicitly invite everyone to contribute. They can insist that even the bigmouths ask for other people's opinions. They can engage and stay independent. And they can do the hardest thing of all: just listen. Not pretend to listen,

Pecking orders and corporate ladders

Ranking is a timeless phenomenon. People create pecking orders and corporate ladders. Your position in the pecking order depends on your various traits. Some are intrinsically yours, such as skin color, sex and age. Others can be acquired, such as communication style, education and drive. The value of each varies according to cultural context. You can't see your ranking by looking in the mirror, but only in your interaction with others.

but really listen and think about what's said. Allow themselves to be moved. Allow themselves to be persuaded, to change their minds, to see things differently... even because of something said by someone of low rank.

Inclusion, ranking and competition

In the introduction, I mentioned that jam sessions are also competitive. You look at the musicians in the band, check who you can compete with, determine where in the music you can shine. If you feel strong, you grab the first solo. But be aware that the session will only flow if you also know when to step aside and smile when someone else outdoes you. It's about both sides: fully seizing the opportunity when you see room for it, and letting the other excel when they do the same. This creates a groove that yet another person can tune into. Imagine how it could be if your team at work functioned in the same way. What if production chain contracts were geared to make this possible? Just think of an education system organized according to this principle!

Acceptance of hierarchy differs from place to place

Power and ranking are universal human givens. We create pecking orders. But not all cultures look at the power balance in the same way. Social psychologists Geert Hofstede and Mauk Mulder, who have widely published on the matter, show that it can be much easier to climb the social ladder in one country than in another. In some countries, it's much easier to become richer than the average person, or to gain far more influence than others. Class differences are more readily accepted in Asian countries than in the Netherlands or the even more egalitarian countries of Scandinavia. Similarly, the respect accorded the head of state—and the expectations of decorum from this public figure— can differ sharply from one place to another. A mild joke about the Thai King Vajiralongkorn can get you imprisoned for up to fifteen years, while Dutch people can

Bob's sales are bigger than Sanjay's
According to the Dutch daily newspaper *de Volkskrant* (April 14, 2018), some call center managers advise employees with a foreign-sounding name to adopt a typically Dutch name instead. They claim it's good for sales. Apparently, you won't buy from a caller named Fatima, but a Linda can sell you your own shirt. You might need help from a helpdesk employee, but he better be named Bill, not Abdul. It's all about customer satisfaction, they say.

- If you were a call center manager, would you tell or advise your people to change their names?
- If you were a call center employee, would you change your name?
- If you were a customer, who would you be more likely to buy something or accept assistance from: Bill or Abdul?

People are not equal

Who do you unconsciously rank higher on the social ladder. Don't think too much about it, follow your first instinct.

- white or black
- man or woman
- city or country dweller
- young or old
- Christian or Muslim
- PhD or plumber
- lacrosse player or kickboxer
- operagoer or Liberace fan
- beer belly or slim and trim

The outcome is always connected to your cultural context. In Western Europe, you will rank higher as a Christian. In the Middle East a Muslim will rank higher. The ranking of these characteristics can fluctuate over time, but ranking itself is a fact. It's what people do. The important question is, how do we deal with it?

call their monarch, Willem-Alexander, 'King Pilsner' and know they'll get laughs, not a visit from the police.

Not only different countries read power differently; different organizations do, too. In one business, the management team might be extremely accessible, with their desks in the same open plan space as their employees, while in another the power gap might be unbridgeable because the senior figures are far away, in their luxurious penthouse offices.

Limited space at the top of the ladder

But it works both ways. If you're low in the pecking order don't act like you're high in the pecking order. It might be a hard pill to swallow, but if you are a fairly recent immigrant with less than perfect language proficiency or relevant cultural baggage, don't assume you deserve the same privileges of someone firmly rooted in their country, whose background and cultural credentials are unquestionable. Being that presumptuous is just as annoying as being an arrogant manager in a penthouse office. But why do I say this is a hard pill to swallow? Because no matter what skills, abilities or background you have, you can still end up lower in the pecking order than you think you deserve. Sometimes just because of someone else's mindbug. And that feels unfair, and maybe it simply is unfair. As if you're a lesser person. It can hurt, mentally and even physically. It can give you headaches and heartaches. But in the end, you have to deal with reality. This is where you are. You have to acknowledge where you are in the pecking order and take action from there. For people low in the pecking order, this can be a cruel and emotional process. And obviously, it would be great if others helped and looked at you as an equal. Unfortunately, that is often not yet the case.

Inclusion: seeing the multifacetedness in ranking

Recognizing that we all take part in ranking is a major part of the solution. It's essential to understand that a person can never have the highest ranking in every respect. Ranking is multifaceted, so you rank higher in some contexts and lower in others. Realizing this can give us all some room to breathe, without needing to upend the entire pecking order. Leaders can remain leaders even as they admit that they're novices in the field of sales. They can give their younger sales reps all the room they need without losing authority.

Upsetting the pecking order

What it boils down to: some of us are higher in the pecking order than others, and most of us are fine with that. Some people might try to climb the ladder, while others don't mind staying where they are, staying out of the heat. One key question in terms of inclusion is: how does the top of the pecking order handle its power? Those who know they are dominant and use their power fairly can allow different voices to be heard and even elicit and facilitate dissenting opinions. Courageous leaders realize that more inclusion will, in the long run, improve things for everyone. They have the courage to put their personal interests on the back burner in favor of the greater whole and the resilience to absorb the tension that inclusion causes in the short run.

If you invite people who are different to take part in the decision-making process, you know the group dynamics are bound to change. It can lead to shifts in the existing order of power and privilege. This realization makes many people very nervous. It upsets the pecking order and if you do it, you run the risk of ending up a few rungs lower on the ladder. The main danger is that people see this as a reason to

Leveling up, leveling down

There are no CEOs, board members or politicians in my family. No one in my family is in government, so I had never traveled in those circles. Hence, I was pretty nervous for my first appointment with a company CEO and board of directors. I didn't really know what to say. I was afraid they might misunderstand me, and I them. I didn't know what the etiquette was. As it turned out, there was no reason for me to worry.

The first time I went to work on a care farm, I was nervous too. There's no one in my family with special needs, so I've never traveled in those circles either. I didn't know what to say and worried I would misunderstand people, and they me. I had no idea what the rules were. My worries turned out to be totally unnecessary.

Not getting nervous about meeting someone from a different background, or a different ranking, whether higher or lower, is something you learn. And maybe you will never get past your nerves entirely.

label any change as negative and the new rules as ridiculous, because they're afraid of losing status.

Dropping in ranking hurts

It can be physically painful to descend in rank. A high ranking gets your hormones going: your dopamine and testosterone levels go up. If you lose a dominant position, you're deprived of your dopamine drip. I've seen with my own eyes that it can hurt. My father started his career in human resources and rose to a position where he had his own corner office with big windows and a secretary who brought him coffee in a porcelain cup. Then he decided to switch careers and become a teacher at a university of applied sciences. Soon after, the university introduced the New Way of Working and he spent the rest of his career working at a hot desk and buying coffee from an automatic dispenser. Luckily, my dad could laugh about it, but he also said: "to be honest, it sometimes feels like I took a wrong turn somehow." This may be a mild case. Some people go through much harder adjustments. One businessman who had to relinquish his private plane and adjust to 'normal life' said he suffered from physical withdrawal symptoms for a month. His hands were shaking and he had trouble sleeping. Just goes to show you that it takes a while to get ranking hormones out of your system. It's like going cold turkey.

Ranking as a turbocharger

Ranking can turbocharge the processes of exclusion. If the powers that be have decided what's normal and who is and isn't allowed to take part, it takes a pretty determined person to change that. It leads to explosive emotions in people who feel they're discriminated against due to negative mindbugs. Fortunately, the opposite is true too: ranking can accelerate inclusion and connection. If leaders, those with the most privileges and the highest ranking, strongly advocate inclusion, it can go fast. It's essential that these leaders put their money where their mouth is. Differently put, they have to be sincere and actually take measures that increase diversity and inclusion. If the powerful

Spotted on Twitter (comedian unknown)

Comedian: 'You hear a lot about crazy ex-girlfriend stories, mostly funny ones, but hardly ever any crazy ex-boyfriend ones. Ever wonder why?' People laughed and he paused.
Comedian: 'Because women don't make it out alive.'
One response to this post: 'We men should be glad women want gender equality and not revenge.'

are really on board, change can happen in no time. In other words: if the heart of power really wants it, it'll be done in 24 hours, so to speak.

Dominance Blindness and Minority Stress

In every group, there are various images and stories, some of which will end up in the dominant story and others won't. High-ranking individuals have a lot of influence on this process. And there is a special phenomenon that can make us impervious to each other's stories.

Dominance Blindness

When viewing things from the dominant perspective, it's difficult to see and feel what a minority group experiences. I call this dominance blindness, which is a slight adaptation of the concept of privilege blindness. Sometimes, you don't hear what others have to say, because they don't say it out loud. Sometimes, people do speak up, but you're unable to put yourself in their shoes so you can't read their signals. And in some cases, you simply don't believe what they're saying is true and you ignore it. This is what's behind the white innocence I talked about in Chapter 1. If you combine this with our tendency to clone, you'll understand why it is so hard and takes so long to diversify high-level corporate management.

Minority Stress

On the opposite side of the spectrum from dominance blindness is what I call minority stress. People who are in a non-dominant position generally have to work harder to be seen and heard. Is that unfair? Yes. And it often goes hand in hand with a particular feeling: stress. That's what you feel when the things you consider important are dismissed, not listened to, or ignored altogether. The trick is to give higher-ranking people the respect they feel they have com-

Seven check marks
The dominant group in the Netherlands has specific characteristics: white, not openly religious, from an upper-middle to upper class family, speaks standard Dutch, college educated, male and currently in upper-middle to upper class circles themselves. Or, as anthropologist and journalist Joris Luyendijk called it in one of his lectures, the seven check marks. Just three percent of the 17 million inhabitants of the Netherlands have all seven check marks. Most political leaders and senior managers have seven check marks. Statistically, this is absurdly improbable. So we have to conclude: either these people are brilliant, or there are subtle exclusion mechanisms at work.

ing to them and perhaps even deserve, while also making room for your own viewpoints, ideas, opinions and experiences. To put it differently: you need to learn to play the ranking game very, very well. Of course, the ideal situation is that those in power want you to speak and want to listen to you. That would make jamming a lot easier. But when confronted with dominance blindness, you will need to open these people's eyes and ears to your voice. Sometimes, you may need to make a lot of noise and wave protest banners, and at other times, you may get your point across better by being subtle and cooperative.

Okay, I'll go along with that

Sometimes you have thoughts or feelings that deviate from the majority stand-point, but that raises so much discomfort that you decide to 'go along' with the majority. You endorse the group's opinion even though you don't agree with it. That can feel a lot less stressful than speaking up. At the same time, the majority doesn't understand why someone with a different opinion wouldn't dare to speak up. Being in a minority position might also prompt you to rebel and sabotage, by the way. I'll talk about that later in this chapter.

Improper and illegal questions
In an interview for a job as a project manager at the local government, the candidate who wore a head scarf and would be expected to work in a mainly white neighbor-hood, was asked, "Will you be able to leave your background behind when you enter the office / when you come in in the morning?" The next question was even more troubling: "Are you prepared to join us for our traditional Friday afternoon drinks?"

Don't kid yourself: the pressure of fitting into the existing pigeonholes is so great, that we're even prepared to go along with prejudice that clearly puts us at a disadvantage. This is demonstrated by the 1940s *"Doll Test"* conducted in the USA, which was repeated in 2010. Although almost 70 years had passed, the outcomes were more or less the same. Kids were given two identical dolls, one with light skin, the other with dark skin. Then they were asked to choose between the dolls in response to questions like: Who is the pretty doll? Who is the bad doll? Which doll would you want to play with? All the kids, regard-less of their skin color, assigned more negative characteristics to the dark doll and positive characteristics to the white doll. The last question the kids were asked, was who they most resembled. In response, the black kids hesitant-ly pointed to the black doll. What a heartbreaking result. It creates so much internal stress to go along with everyone's prejudices even though you know you're not stupid, ugly or bad. Such internalized mindbugs are damaging to your sense of self-worth and to the group as a whole. If you're not part of a minority group, it's almost impossible to imagine what that's like. That's dominance blindness.

And the other way around: dominance stress and minority blindness

It also works the other way around: the dominant group can experience stress, too. It happens, for instance, in the debate about the controversial Black Pete figure who appears in the streets of the Netherlands at the beginning of December every year. The dominant group is getting more and more annoyed with all the criticism of this aspect of the Saint Nicholas celebration. "They" are ruining "our" party, they say. These are the white tears I discussed earlier. People from the dominant group get the feeling that the minority is provoking them and will keep doing so until the majority gets fed up and gives in. The same mechanism is at work in the sniggering and sexist jokes made by men in a group of 50 construction company managers when the first female manager is appointed. In both cases, the issues at stake are about power. Surely those newcomers don't think they call the shots now? They can join the party, but only if they go along with the existing norms and rituals. The underlying question in inclusion is always: who gets to decide? Or, to put it differently: Whose country is this? Whose workplace is this? Whose team? Whose city? Whose home? The sense of losing or having to share power causes stress and increases aggression towards the other, the foreigner, the newcomer, the intruder. Diversity is fine as long as just a few 'multicultural' or female participants join the show, but it's a whole different matter when

Elephants and mice
Laura Liswood's *The Loudest Duck: Moving Beyond Diversity* contains a great metaphor for majorities and minorities. Elephants stride around quite unassailable and strong. They go wherever they want to go. Yet, when they see a mouse, they jump. Then they stamp on it, to get rid of that weird creature. That's why mice learn to study elephants very, very well. They make sure they don't get in the elephants' way, but listen to how they move, adjust and facilitate. These are all behaviors we've come to call feminine. But actually, it's minority behavior. Meanwhile, the elephants keep stomping around comfortably and self-assured. They don't need to take those mice into account. They won't pay them any mind until the mice start to swarm.

Are you a mouse or an elephant? Do you personally know both positions?

they start changing the rules of the game, the prizes and costumes. Let alone taking over the stage.

Jokes, banter and microaggression

It's quite easy to make hurtful jokes out of dominance blindness. You didn't mean any harm, you had no idea you were stepping on anyone's toes. But your blindness can cut the other person like a knife. That's because it's *you* making the joke, or because so many other people have made similar jokes. That's when jokes have an excluding us-against-them effect. And there's nothing funny about that. Those of us with a lower rank are the butt-end of jokes on a regular basis. There are jokes about gay people, women, Moroccans, Hispanics, Belgians, people with special needs, and so on. Well, grow a thick skin, you might say. They're just jokes and the people who tell them don't really mean it. That's why we don't pay these jokes much mind, not even at work. Still, such mockery wears people down. One joke is okay, but constantly having to field similar jokes from every direction is more than a little annoying. In fact, it cuts so deep that there's a name for it: microaggression.

Queer bitches and bitches on the rag

Some people really shouldn't tell certain jokes. People in wheelchairs can make very cynical comments about 'cripples,' I've noticed. But I would never feel right using that word myself. It depends whether you're part of the group. The same goes for homosexuals. One of them told me it was fine for him to jokingly call his friends 'queer bitches,' but that no one outside of the gay scene would get away with that. Likewise, men who jokingly ask their female coworker in a meeting whether they're 'on the rag' again will not make any friends. But women are allowed to joke about this among themselves. Jokes and banter

Ethnic profiling

For police officers who patrol the streets, assessing a situation and profiling are an essential part of the job. Deviations from typical or average behavior are clues that something might be wrong, that they might have to intervene to prevent or solve crimes. Having read everything I've discussed so far, you can surely sense how hard it is to do this neutrally and objectively.

"Hey, I see a young black guy driving an expensive SUV. I notice, because that's out of the ordinary. Most young black guys can't afford an expensive car. So, let's pull him over to check his license and registration, to see if that car is his."

It's understandable that the police want to do their job. At the same time, however, it is so incredibly painful and humiliating for the person who is stopped and searched unnecessarily not just once, but regularly. The other day, a white coworker of mine noticed how the train conductors only checked the tickets of the colored people on the train. She asked the conductor why, to which he replied laughingly that he'd be happy to check her ticket too, if she felt so strongly about it. That's the Netherlands for you. In 2019, mind you.

can really cement group identity, but coming from the wrong people, those outside the group, they can cause the gap to widen. The important issue here is not freedom of expression, but sensitivity and empathy.

Innocent jokes: co-ed showers

In my youth, I excelled at a sport called korfball, which is similar to netball. In case you've never heard of it, I should tell you that korfball doesn't rank highly on the ladder in terms of respect. Korfball players are constantly the brunt of lame jokes. One of the remarks I had to contend with innumerable times when telling someone I played korfball, which is a co-ed sport, is: "Oh dear, co-ed showers, huh?" As a teenager, this used to really bother me. Korfball was an important part of my life and others were always poking fun at it. The jokes didn't stop until one of the more popular kids in my class said: "Stop being so childish. Korfball is a sport like any other."

Clearly, this is a relatively innocent example. It's much more painful if people ridicule your skin color, religion, or appearance. It can even be painful when people ask an honest question about where you're from, when you were born and raised in the same country they were born in, but you don't look 'indigenous'. The problem is that it isn't just one person who asks that question. You get it all the time. Even a compliment can hit you like a brick in this context: "Wow, your English is really good!" This feels like a rebuke dressed up as a compliment, because the suggestion is you don't really belong here. Even if the person saying it doesn't mean any harm.

Less innocent jokes: the Mohammed cartoons

Do you remember the commotion and deadly violence during the worldwide protests against a series of twelve cartoons about the prophet Mohammed? The cartoons were published on September 30, 2005 by the Danish newspaper *Jyllands-Posten*. The particular cartoon that sparked the most indignation and anger in Muslims the world over was drawn by Kurt Westergaard. He depicted the prophet Mohammed wearing a turban in the shape of a bomb. Muslim anger in turn sparked an uproar in the West over narrow-mindedness about a simple drawing and the threat to freedom of expression. The unrest was widespread and long-lasting, and more than two hundred people died in protests in Nigeria and elsewhere, according to *The New York Times* and other sources.

In 2006, *Charlie Hebdo, a* controversial French magazine, was one of the magazines that reprinted the Danish Mohammed cartoons. In 2011, the magazine published a special issue called *Charia Hebdo*, ostensibly guest-edited by Mohammed. The magazine's offices became the target of two terrorist attacks, one in 2011 and the other in 2015. During the 2015 attack, twelve people were killed.

IMAGE: RENALD "LUZ" LUZIER, CHARLIE HEBDO

▶ *Cover of the first edition of Charlie Hebdo after the attack in 2015. More than 7 million copies of the magazine were printed and sold. The average edition at that time sold 70,000 copies.*

So, why all the anger in the Muslim community, a non-Muslim might ask. It has to do with the taboo on depicting the prophet Mohammed. In Islam, Mohammed is the epitome of infallibility and perfection. Any representation will necessarily demean his true, divine perfection and is therefore an insult in and of itself. And for many Muslims, an insult to Mohammed equals an insult to all of Islam and its followers. On top of that, the cartoons associated Mohammed, a holy man of peace, with terrorism. This outraged many Muslims. Add to this the fact that some Muslims perceive the Western war on terror as a war on Islam, and hence on them personally. On the other side of the debate we find the Europeans who argue that Muslims will just have to get used to the fact that in today's world, people sometimes poke fun at each other. Those are the rules of the game, and if you don't like it, you can leave.

Aren't jokes always okay?

You might conclude from this that some jokes are better left untold, because they're too painful or insulting. Or you might conclude that we should be allowed to joke about anything anytime, because no one gets to impose their ideas of what is and isn't proper. And even more so when it concerns art, because if we can't write poems about it, or draw it, or sing and dance it, then we can't express any inconvenient ideas anymore and we'll all be doomed. Without a safe haven for art and theater, counternarratives and innovative ideas will be suppressed.

I find this a difficult dilemma. My Dutch and not-very-religious-brain whispers that anyone should be allowed to draw a cartoon. Jokes and humor are a way of questioning the status quo, of positing an alternative story. This is an important weapon in the battle to continually challenge the existing balance of power and to keep the debate alive. It's like the jester, who can say anything and everything without risking punishment. That freedom exists in a realm reserved for this purpose: that of art, lyrics, drama. At the same time, I empathize with the pain that people feel at such jokes. And just because something is not forbidden, doesn't mean you necessarily have to do it. We all know that feeling of making a remark and then thinking: "Oops, I went too far." You wouldn't hang just any cartoon of your manager on an office whiteboard with your name under it. And you wouldn't laugh at every cartoon drawn of you or someone you love.

Jokes as a signal and predictor of trouble

Jokes can be intended as jokes, nothing more, nothing less. Just for fun and laughs. But they can also be signals of important things going unsaid, because we find it too scary to say them directly. In that case, jokes are used to hint at something while also giving us a chance to laugh away the tension. If you notice that similar jokes keep being made, you should look for a way to start having the underlying conversation. This can be about anything, but it's often about discontent concerning ranking, decision-making and the division of privilege.

The Resistance Line: a diagnostic tool for the level of inclusion

In my earlier books, I explained how unspoken issues will eventually lead to problems and resistance. For completeness' sake, and because it is so important, I'm going to include a summary of this topic in this book as well. For a detailed description of it and more information on how to handle resistance, please see my book *Deep Democracy*.

The Resistance Line

▶ *The resistance that people show when things that need to be said remain unsaid. This Resistance Line was developed by Myrna Lewis, founder of the Lewis method of Deep Democracy.*

IMAGE: BASED ON AN IMAGE BY SUGGESTION & ILLUSION, FROM: WOW! WHAT A DIFFERENCE!

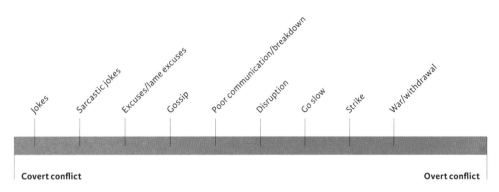

When people feel ignored and minority standpoints are denied airtime, friction grows. You can sense it in many ways, as if it's in the air. People start to complain to each other at the water cooler, but don't speak up in meetings. People say 'yes' to a proposal, but act out 'no' and come up with excuses. These are frustrated attempts to say something urgent that isn't being said. The Resistance Line describes these behaviors. Resistance is active in every layer of society, in all groups and at any age. A new member of the group is best off quickly learning the team, department or organization's favorite rules and resistance tactics. That will make it clear how this group handles conflict.

The Resistance Line can serve as a diagnostic tool for the level of inclusion in a group. If people feel unheard, the number of issues in the group's undercurrent will keep growing. A lot of resistance is a signal that some people's perspectives are being excluded. Because the inclusion level is too low, the wisdom of the minority, and hence the collective, is being underused. The sooner we pick up on the signals of resistance, the better.

There are many reasons why we don't dare say what we think and keep our thoughts to ourselves. The biggest mistake anyone can make is to think that silence equals consent. It's much better to habitually ask if anyone has any other ideas. And to follow this up with the question: "Are there others who can relate to this?" so as not to leave the brave soul who speaks up, alone. Almost always, there are several people who have similar feelings, but didn't want to be the first to speak up. Yet, if people are explicitly invited to put their two cents in, they will often do so. And this goes to show that those who are silent often do not consent at all, but have quite different ideas. You may be unpleasantly surprised at first, but in the long run you'll be glad they contributed. In short, the solution is to talk and to listen. Use the jam circle to learn how to jam with differences.

Kingpins, Harries, obstructers, scapegoats and heroes

A dissenting opinion, a narrative that diverges from the collective story, can be hailed as an innovation and embraced, or branded a threat and suppressed. People can occupy various positions in this arena of power. Allow me to describe a few striking ones.

Kingpins
People who have a vested interest in the outcome of discussions and who hold responsibility for decisions are called kingpins. These are our leaders, parents, and teachers. They're the ones who organize things in the playground. These are the people, who—sometimes skillfully, sometimes clumsily—stick out their necks and set the direction. They're high up in the pecking order and have a lot of influence on the group's thinking and actions. They have the power to define and can either use it to the greater good of the group, or to further their own interests. Others may shrug or shake their heads at them, or even try to undermine them. People need kingpins. They set the frameworks within which we can give our all. Inclusive leaders know how to do this in a constructive way, as I described in Chapter 1.

Harries

▸ *This is the original Harry picture, taken by photographer Hideta Nagai. I contacted him and asked him about this moment. He told me how he saw a starling land awkwardly on the cable and end up upside down. Image: Hideta Nagai*

Harry symbolizes a different take on things, a dissident voice, a new angle. Harry (or Harriet) is that bird that might prompt us to say: "C'mon, get real." Or if we're in the health care profession: "Oh dear, are you okay?" Which is code for: "Come on, get with the program" or "Can I help you get right side up?"

And if anyone were to join Harry and intentionally hang upside down from the wire in order to see things from the same perspective, chances are the rest of us would say: "Just stop. One Harry is all we need."

As long as Harry is the only one, the group knows how to deal with him. We can prop him up and give him some extra attention. But as soon as we're faced with more Harries, it gets complicated. Actively searching for an alternative perspective requires us to engage, to listen instead of sigh. It means we have to view Harry as an enrichment rather than an obstacle. That's what Jam Cultures is based on. No Harries, no innovation.

One reason not to want to listen might be that we sense it will upset the way we've always done things. A few years ago, I was coaching a manager who wanted to learn to listen better. He was in his late fifties and his colleagues had been telling him for years that he was a bad listener. Now his wife had said the same thing. That iced it for him, so he decided to do something about it. We talked about what listening entailed and I saw and heard that he understood. Nevertheless, he then suddenly jumped up from his chair and exclaimed: "I'm not gonna do that!" When I asked why, he said: "Because I might have to change my opinions." Yes, this is a scary process, and it's time-consuming and causes uncertainty. Yet that's exactly why it offers so much opportunity!

If we don't listen to Harry's ideas, the Resistance Line kicks in. At which point people will feel too unsafe to speak up.

Obstructers

From an inclusion standpoint, every angle is welcome. However, sometimes people just keep pushing and pushing, about everything. Notorious obstructers. The best practice is to listen very intently to such people and include them in the conversation. But let's look through the lens of the jam session metaphor. If someone just keeps tooting their horn and ignoring the

Ethical dilemma: is Harry crazy or brilliant?
Sometimes, Harry-type ideas and behaviors are so unusual that we can't tell whether they're brilliant or crazy. If these ideas don't cause any problems, fine. But if they do, we need to take action.

As you know by now, inclusion doesn't mean anything goes because we need to keep everybody happy. It's okay to set boundaries. We have to set boundaries and provide love and leadership. So, sometimes it might be better for everyone involved if we stop listening and stop integrating, because there is a point at which more acceptance just makes things worse. Everybody is welcome, but not every type of behavior is tolerable. This is a very touchy situation, of course, which hinges on power. After all, who decides whether someone's behavior or ideas are within bounds? And who decides what the next steps need to be? Some things are defined by law: punishable offenses lead to a fine, firing or prison time. In addition, there's etiquette and common decency, although these are not set in stone, as we will see in the next chapter. Psychiatrists, medical doctors and other experts can assess whether someone is healthy, whether a child with special needs can be mainstreamed and whether an employee can handle a certain job. Yet, these assessments are also open to various interpretations, because they're created by humans.

Still, keeping someone on the team out of pity benefits no one, not even Harry. If you're Harry and they put up with you, you won't exactly feel like your ideas count. That's not inclusion. In this case, it would be better to find a different solution that will ultimately be better for everyone involved.

other musicians, then it's time to talk about whether he might be better off in another band. If it's someone who plays solo quietly in a corner without bothering anyone, the best approach might be to let them continue without paying them too much mind.

Scapegoats

Projection is as old as the human species itself. We project onto others the traits that we disapprove of, either personally or as a group. This makes us feel like we've gotten something off our plates. Those who we project onto are called scapegoats. It's an abuse of power that often targets minorities and people with dissenting opinions. In the past, the same mechanism led us to burn witches. They were accused of using black magic to bring adversity upon the group. And besides, they stood out like a sore thumb anyway. The therapeutic action of writing all bad things on a piece of paper and burning it is based on this principle, too. It's less bloody and cruel, but the thought process is the same.

Suppose your company's corporate strategy really stinks and everyone is affected by it. This is increasingly blamed on Peter, who is gradually excluded. After all, it was always Peter who said we had to do things differently. His complaining didn't help, did it? Here we are, up the creek without a paddle and he's the reason why. He always was hard to get along with anyway, don't you think? As our discomfort grows, we get more annoyed with Peter. We continue labeling him and soon we're really assailing his character. Peter's bad news and needs to go. He's demoted or fired and that buys us six months of grace, because we no longer have to think about our strategy. But soon, we'll need a new scapegoat, because our problems haven't vanished. At the same time, everyone gets warier and warier in the knowledge that anyone could be the next scapegoat. So we shut up. This happens a lot more often than you'd think.

The Beast, the seven-headed dragon, giants, trees that can talk, wolves: these are all symbols of the unknown that we're so frightened of. Monsters need to be slain. If we don't have the get-up-and-go to do that, we'll start to offer sacrifices. And we'll have to continue to do that faster and faster, because the monsters keep getting bigger and the chopped-off heads keep growing back. Scapegoating is magical thinking. We apply it everywhere, in every area of life: we believe our relationship will improve if we move to a bigger house, or if we have a child, or find a different job. None of which addresses the problems in the relationship itself.

Heroes

Someone who stands out, a person who does or knows something special, can be maligned, but might also be worshipped! Experts are turned into gurus, artists become icons. We sometimes take leave of our rational minds and ascribe these people almost mythical powers. Because such heroes have charisma, they attract followers, who unquestioningly swallow anything they say. Fans may even copy their hero's dress or imitate the way they talk. We attribute to them positive aspects of group dynamics, which have absolutely nothing to do with the person behind the guru. We want to touch our icons, get close to them, feel the magic and take a bit of magic with us.

This hero status is something others attribute to you, so it's an assigned status. However, you can also (try to) create this status for yourself. Based on the motto 'fake it 'til you make it,' you can present yourself like an icon and hope that others will be fooled and start to treat you that way. But if someone bursts your bubble, you'll take a hard fall. That's what happened to Dutch-Israeli singer Dotan, who was exposed for having enlisted the aid of at least 140 troll accounts in order to boost his online reputation and following. Or you can play the expert and hope people will start believing it. If you know how to back up this fake status with the real stuff, you've successfully boosted your image. That's good marketing. If you fail to deliver, you'll damage your reputation beyond repair. There's a great movie about this topic, called *Kumaré*. I highly recommend it if you're interested in these dynamics.

Scapegoating

Scapegoating usually starts small, but can quickly mushroom:

- Our meetings never end on time. That's because of Hasan. He loves to hear the sound of his own voice. Actually, all Muslims are long-winded.
- Everyone on the team is working hard on this. It's strange that we don't have any results. Too bad Jenny is always joking around. That's what you get when you hire a millennial.
- It's Giuseppe's fault that the project isn't getting done on time. He doesn't know how to stick to the plan. Come to think of it, I don't know a single Italian who understands time management.

If you don't step in, this blaming of one individual can quickly get out of control. It harms the scapegoat first and foremost, of course, but it ultimately damages the organization as a whole. Particularly when other employees realize they might be next in line. A business that's rife with negativity and fear does not function well.

The danger is that people can project too much onto their hero and lose their own ability to think critically. Allowing one individual to hold too much power is not good for our collective intelligence. But we knew that already.

Privilege and Sources of Power

As I illustrated earlier, we're continually ranking each other. If you think you're the exception to the rule, I can only say wake up. Those who score highly tend to be privileged. The privileged find it easier to climb the social ladder. It's a human game with an uneven playing field and we're all players. Even if we don't know it.

Privilege

You can earn privilege by working hard. For example, I'm writing this from a great location on the island of Ibiza. I can afford it because I've worked hard for it. At least, that's what I tell myself. It's true, but at the same time, I have to admit I also got here thanks to privilege that I've enjoyed all my life, privilege that I never had to lift a finger for. I was born healthy and grew up in a warm, stable family. Both my parents had paid jobs, so I could pursue the hobbies I liked. My parents took me on trips and supported me financially while I was in college. All this gave me a great start in life that I could expand on and pass down to the next generation. Which is why I can afford to pay for extra tutoring anytime my children need it. They're privileged because I can see when they need help and have the means to pay for it. Not all children have these advantages. Are my children grateful for this? Nope. To them, it's really awful: not only do they have to attend school, they also have to spend extra hours on tutoring! They have to work much harder than kids who can't afford tutoring.

There are several videos on YouTube that explain what privilege is about. For example, there's a video of a group of teenagers who get to race against each other for a $100 prize. Before the race starts, they're lined up and presented with a few statements. Kids to whom the statement applies can take two steps forward. The rest stay where they are. For example, take two steps forward if you're parents are still married, if you grew up with a father figure in the home, if you had access to extra tutoring, if you never had to worry where your next meal was coming from. When the coach is done with these statements, some of the kids are already halfway to the finish line. Others have not been able to take any steps, or only a few. That's a great visualization of inequality based on privilege. It shows the position we're in through no fault or merit of our own.

Everyone has to work hard to achieve something, but some of us have a head start. Privileged folks are often unaware that so many people start the race at such a disadvantage. In life, this is seldom as starkly visible as in that video. Privileged people are often shocked when their eyes are opened to this, but some get pretty angry, too. What do you mean privileged? I've had my share of setbacks in life. I know what it's like to overcome adversity! Sure you do. But other people have had to contend with much, much more.

White privilege

White privilege refers to the fact that white people are privileged purely because their skin happens to be white. Some aspects of this privilege are trivial, while others are more significant. But if you add them all up, it's a lot. Let's name a few aspects of white privilege: nude tights, the right type of shampoo in every supermarket and almost every commercial features white people. What's more, your role models, e.g. Disney princesses, have white skin. In Western countries, almost everyone in power—politician, CEO, teacher—is white. And then you have the less innocent examples, such as the cultural archive I talked about earlier, with its deeply rooted notions that white people are superior to black people. Essentially, the problem is that most of the power in our society and in many organizations is distributed unevenly. And our society seems—both consciously and unconsciously—hell-bent on keeping it that way. We're playing a game with winners and losers and that's what's got to change if we want to take big strides in diversity and inclusion. Let's start by giving people the same pay for the same work, and by opening up jobs and vacancies to everyone. Let's organize the job market in a way that neutralizes our mindbugs and our current position in the pecking order. Let's stop talking and hedging, let's clone less and look beyond our personal preferences.

Own, play and share your rank

The privileged among us had better enjoy it. There's nothing more annoying than people who deny or downplay their privilege. It's wonderful you have a swimming pool in your backyard, so just enjoy it and don't pretend your housing situation is the same as someone who lives in the projects.

The same goes for ranking. Those of us who are in leadership positions, should lead. Own it! If you're the CEO, don't act like you're 'just' a member of the team. That's a disrespectful attitude comparable to saying you're your children's best friend. No, you're not. Their best friend doesn't set their curfew or their allowance. Nor does their best friend 'force' them to be tutored. Don't be like that manager who pretends to the janitor that they're all equals in the company. Treat everyone as equals in terms of their value as human beings, but don't make belief you're on an equal footing. The manager manages a budget, the janitor doesn't. The manager has the power to make definitions and decisions, with access to a network of other powerful people who are out of reach to the janitor. With this power and position comes the responsibility for making and keeping it safe for those who do not have such advantages. In other words, a word of admonishment to everyone: own the position you have, in whatever area of life or work and share this by involving others. Play the game so that everyone benefits and share your privileges. *Own, play and share your rank.*

Building on the work of Arnold Mindell and Julie Diamon, Shakil Choudhury distinguishes between social power and personal power in his book *Deep Diversity*. Social power is the power others accord you when you enter a room full of strangers. These are first impressions, based on characteristics like skin color, sex, wealth, social class, age, attire and religion. There's little you can do about most of these impressions. You may be ranked higher in one context than in another. In rural areas, people may have different ideas about what increases your status than in the big city.

Personal power is about your personal capacities, your self-confidence, your ability to speak well and integrate, your ability to size up people and your expert knowledge in a particular field. It's quite possible to have a lot of social power, but to be unable to put this to use because you lack personal power. Or the other way around: you may lack social power, but increase your standing by virtue of personal power.

By the way, most people don't mind that some people have better jobs, larger homes and better-looking partners. As long as this happens for reasons we con-

'A country is only as strong as the people who make it up and the country turns into what the people want it to become … I don't believe any longer that we can afford to say that it is entirely out of our hands. We made the world we're living in and we have to make it over.'
– James Baldwin

sider fair. And with privilege comes responsibility, we feel. In times of crisis, when we don't have enough to eat, when we come under attack, when consumer demand plummets, or when we're consumed by stress and fear, then we expect our powerful, privileged leaders to take the lead. They have to take risks to protect the weaker among us. Quid pro quo. Or as Simon Sinek, whom I also quoted in Chapter 1, puts it: "Leaders eat last." Unfortunately, this is often not the case. When things go wrong, our leaders often only protect their nearest and dearest, their friends and family, their fellow managers. Or worse, they simply run and hide.

Give back and share

If you or one of your parents or grandparents were given a disproportionate advantage in life, it's only reasonable to give it back when the error becomes apparent. Even if you've worked hard to preserve your privilege and feel you truly earned it. Even if you never took anything from anyone, but it was just passed on to you. And even if the error was made generations ago. If it becomes clear that the division is unfair, you should just give it back. You shouldn't be ashamed or angry about it. You can be sad and think back on how wonderful it was to enjoy such privilege. Still, now that you've redistributed the privilege more evenly, you can continue to enjoy what's still yours. If you're the one who finally gets some privilege back, embrace it. Especially after all those years of complaining, nagging, harping, coaxing and threatening. Try not to rub it in or sulk because you should have gotten it sooner. However difficult that may be. Obviously, you have all the right in the world to be livid about the unfair division and all the times your parents and peers couldn't join the game. It takes an awful lot of

The daughter-effect

High-level board members and CEOs with daughters are more motivated to implement Corporate Social Responsibility (CSR) and achieve equal rights for women and men. This remarkable conclusion is based on a study carried out by Henrik Cronqvist, expert in behavioral finance, in 2018. On average, businesses run by CEOs with daughters score almost twelve percent higher on a commonly used CSR rating than businesses whose CEOs have no kids or only sons. Why? Because women tend to be more concerned with other people's well-being and daughters apparently cause their fathers to act more like women in this respect. So say the social scientists. It's a remarkable finding, yet we shouldn't exaggerate this daughter effect, according to social psychologist Jeanine Prime: "Men have always had daughters and yet there's a deep-rooted inequality between men and women." Ben Tiggelaar, a popular Dutch writer, speaker and behavioral scientist, mentioned this research in one of his newspaper columns. He concluded: "The daughter-effect shows first and foremost that it really takes a lot before a man will seriously start thinking about issues that women find self-evident."

strength to simply say "thank you" and not to make nasty jokes. Yet, you've got your advantage now. So, let's get back on the ball and continue to play.

I once used the metaphor of marbles to explain the principle of privilege to my children. There are many marbles, or privileges, that at some point must be redistributed. That won't make you popular with the haves, but sometimes it's necessary to create a more equal, inclusive workplace, family or society. You can either wait for someone to point out that you own way too many marbles, or you can start sharing your marbles with others out of your own accord. You can use your privileged position to drastically change someone else's position by giving them some of your money, attention or time. Or you redistribute the privilege by sharing your knowledge, network or contacts, or by restructuring systems, procedures and patterns to make them fair, so that the marbles will never again get divided so unevenly. Just share whatever you have more of than others, for whatever reason. That's inclusion, too.

Outside aggression: they'll take it all away from us

We don't welcome everyone with equal enthusiasm. We're not too thrilled with our new co-workers from the company we just merged with; our upcoming competitor; refugees on the border, or new neighbors on our block. We're not always breaking out the champagne and shouting: "Great to have you here! Please tell us what's special and different about you!"

#MeToo

In October 2017, #MeToo ignited a worldwide revolt against sexual harassment. For a full year, one story after another broke, featuring famous and less famous women. Counselors had their hands full, not only listening to people report inappropriate sexual behavior in the workplace, but also fielding a ton of lame jokes and complaints about "all those women and their hysterical #MeToo".

The #MeToo debate is rife with everything I've discussed so far:

- Prejudice about how men should act sexually: macho and focused on frequent sexual conquests of many women
- Prejudice about what we expect women to be: sweet, pleasing, proper, modest and absolutely not slutty
- Ideas about innate drives: 'sorry hon, I couldn't help it, it was my testosterone and the beer talking'.
- Notions about childrearing: those adolescents have such a strong sex drive, so cut them some slack.

The effects of power and ranking: power eroticizes and attracts women; high-ranking men fancy themselves unassailable and grab whatever they can get their hands on. This seems partly true, by the way. After all, it's much easier to kick a stranger in the crotch if he goes too far than it is to whack your boss (or your teacher) over the head, because you depend on them in so many ways.

"What are your strong points? What do we need to make allowances for?" More often than not, we squint suspiciously, make jokes about the newcomers' appearance and whisper behind their backs about how we can take them on. Sometimes, people even literally say they're afraid that the newcomers will take everything away from them. This sentiment is based on a notion of scarcity, in which we've already divided the pie and we have to re-divide it now, making one party relinquish their carefully saved piece to someone else. And this someone else should be mighty grateful for this personal sacrifice.

It's obvious that the #MeToo debate is about much more than lust and drives. It's about power and dependence, both in the sexual game and in the entire debate that erupted afterwards. It has now reached the level of a wider battle about who gets to define what normal sexual etiquette is. Women are getting more of a say in many areas and are taking the opportunity to actually engage in norm-setting, assuming the power to define. It's no longer the case that the male story is by definition the only true story. The female story is gaining traction and becoming equivalent to the male version. This makes many men angry and insecure; they can now suddenly be accused of misbehaving.

I expect this debate to eventually lead to new rules and policies. In the meantime, it's all very confusing and emotional. No one knows who can do what anymore. This makes all of us feel unsafe. Anthropologists call this a liminal phase, a period in which old norms and standards are no longer valid while the new ones haven't crystallized yet (see also *The Corporate Tribe*). In such a phase, some people heave a sigh of relief: change, at last. Others feel nothing but regret: in the old days, things were better. This is a normal process. It's part of change. You could call it a bit of a wild, worldwide jam session that has woken people up to differences. We've been struggling with all the emotions released, and explored all the viewpoints expressed. We're slowly heading towards a new phase, in which we get to set new rules. As we saw in the Jam Circle on page 73, power plays a big role in this. As I write this, we're in that phase where we have to find a way to get from sharing our stories to new policies and new laws.

'Everything in the world is about sex except sex.
Sex is about power.'
– Oscar Wilde

IMAGE: UNSPLASH

In this battle, we deploy all our ranking techniques and sources of power.

First of all, the power of location:

- We were here first and therefore have more rights to the lockers at eye level than the newcomers.
- We were here first and we've always organized this block party in this way.
- We were here first and this is how we conduct team meetings here.
- It's fine if you want to be part of our society, but Black Pete is ours, so keep your hands off.

Another source of power is the power of numbers:

- Sure, it's great that you list all your ideas and wishes, but we're the majority.
- We're not going to be shouted down by some loud minority.

We can also use the power of language. All we need to do is to speak some dialect that the others can't understand. Or we can use some obscure jargon so our negotiating partner doesn't have a clue and will have to agree.

There's a more inclusion-oriented approach to working together. Let's not treat it like a finite pie, but like a world of opportunities. We're expanding the band, with more musicians, who have their own instruments and their own musical style. How can we turn this into a new mix? What can they add? And yes, the newcomers will also have to join in and integrate. The trick is to hear, see and appreciate what their talents are and rank them accordingly.

Old habits and traditions are under pressure or under attack from strangers.

Aggression in your own group: the crab basket
There's no need to close off a crab basket, because any crab that tries to escape is pulled straight back down by its fellow crabs. This is a great metaphor for the people in your workplace who can't stand it when others rise in rank. This mechanism—in which people pull each other down by the ankles and no one is

Old habits and traditions change over time due to inside and outside influences.

allowed to rise to the top—has some overlap with 'the sticky floor': the difficulties that disadvantaged groups experience in moving up from low-paying, low-ranking jobs. Like the glass ceiling, the sticky floor keeps people from climbing the corporate ladder. The crab basket metaphor is often applied to women, but is not exclusively feminine, of course. If a man starts paying more attention to emotional matters at work, he's often pulled down by his coworkers: "What's gotten into you? Don't be such a wuss." The existing, low-mobility group tries to keep you down. It's interesting to note that we only pull one other down by the ankles as long as we can still take someone on. If the power differential becomes too big, the group has to let the 'climber' go and things return to normal.

The power of the crab basket is oppressive, and painful for those who get trapped by it. I'm speaking from personal experience here. Over the past few years, I've made big strides career-wise. For years, I taught courses for small groups of people, eight to twelve at a time. Soon, these groups became larger and larger. As my audience grew, so did my popularity and this started snowballing. In the leaps and bounds I made, I had to leave behind some of the people I used to work with. I no longer co-authored papers with them, for instance, but chose to write articles with others. I shared the stage with other people. In short, I developed a new peer group. In this process, I experienced the crab basket. I was told I was arrogant, I had sold out to commercialism, I was selfish, I was acting like a diva because I no longer shared my phone number with anyone and everyone, I had become dopamine-addicted, I acted like the Sun King because I had arranged for a make-up artist prior to a photo shoot, and so on. This has not been fun and has created a lot of tension in some of my relationships. I deal with this by checking with myself what old pain each of these comments triggers in me. I check whether there's a kernel of truth in what someone says, or whether it says more about them. And then I just get back on the horse. I've learned that growth and changing peer groups can be a great adventure, but it also involves pain. Every leap forward means I gain new people and lose a few old ones. Thankfully, some relationships are rock solid. There are also people whose growth keeps pace with mine, or who are happy with their own station in life and not consumed with envy.

How to see the power of power

Ranking is a delicate balance between being yourself and adapting. The trick is to accept your ranking, whether high or low, and use that as a jumping-off point for playing the game with the people around you. To jam, we need to know where everyone's at and to have the courage to take the stage at times. Make sure that everyone, regardless of their formal or informal place in the pecking order, has the room to express their opinion about issues that matter to them. Be sure our powers are used for our benefit rather than our detriment. Talk about rules and behavior that exclude others, but do so without any intention of undermining or overthrowing the pecking order. People need hierarchy. It's about jamming from different ranking positions in order to achieve the best possible results.

Questions to reflect on and discuss with others
Plenty of food for thought, I think. Here's a list of questions you can explore, either by yourself or with others. Share your insights on social media, so we can all benefit: #jamcultures.

- How often do you think about who has the power to decide the rules of the game?
- How readily do you talk about the rules of the game? To what extent are you prepared to change your habits and traditions? I mean traditions like the ones in your family, workplace and religion.
- Do you think there should be limits on freedom of expression? Can anyone make any joke?
- Do you use your privileged position for the greater good? And what is that greater good?
- What types of minority stress do you experience?

Quota, yes or no?
Should we impose quotas? This is always a thorny issue. Should we legally enforce inclusion and require businesses to hire x percent women, x percent people with a non-white skin color, and x percent people with special needs? Ideally, more diversity comes about naturally, because people believe in it, think it's only fair, or expect it increases quality (as described in the four Whys of Diversity and Inclusion on page 30). However, the reality is different. Quotas might help to change the status quo. Sometimes, quotas are necessary, like when attempts to achieve change through dialogue never get beyond the expression of good intentions.
If you decide to go the quota route, it's essential that you also address the skills needed for inclusion. A quota should be a means to an end, never an end in itself. Make sure the women, Hispanics, Young Turks, people-people, and employees with special needs get a good, official position and a role in your organization, so that they're not just token figures.
Something that can help is to approach any quota from the majority rather than the minority perspective. In other words, don't say we have to hire a minimum of 40% women, but we want a maximum of 60% men in our most senior positions.

- In what way might dominance blindness be affecting you?
- What ranking point system is used in your family? In your team? In your workplace?
- Were you ever excluded as a child? As an adult? How did that feel? How did you reconnect with the group? How did you get included again?
- Did you ever exclude others? Why? Would you do that again?
- Where do you notice exclusion in society? In your workplace, in your department, on your team?
- What is a good reason for excluding someone?
- How would you answer these questions from a workplace perspective? And from the perspective of your professional role?

Do something

Reflecting and talking are important, but so is taking action. Below I've provided a few ready-made ideas to put into action. Clearly, this is not intended to be exhaustive. Add your own ideas and make the list longer. Share your insights on social media, so we can all benefit: #jamcultures.

- Count your blessings: list all the ways you are privileged and realize how easy you have it.
- Share your privileged position with someone unexpected, i.e. someone other than a family member or a friend. Do something for someone who is unable to do that for themselves. Happiness will be your reward.
- Talk to someone who clearly ranks higher or lower than yourself. Show a genuine interest in how they see you.
- Have people in positions of power, status and authority explain why a workplace where everyone can be themselves is important. And make sure these people openly take action against intimidation and discrimination.
- In debates on racism and sexism, white men often take the floor first. Know your place. Realize that men, or white people, are not in a position to speak about these topics with authority. The debate should center on the thoughts and feelings of the people who are the topic of the debate. They might be less used to taking the floor, particularly about sensitive subjects. Give them room. At the same time, don't hesitate to broach the subject of racism and sexism with your peer group. Stand behind the minorities, support them and use your ranking to get their story out.

- Dare to take the step from discussing wrongs and obstructive mechanisms to creating new, more useful rules. Sure, this requires guts and courage. And yes, this will cause shifts in the current ranking and the power to define. That's what happens during change, when you do what's needed to create that wonderful, magical flow.
- Play the Switch It Up - mind game from page 99 at your workplace for a few days and discuss the results.
- For men only: have daughters! (;-) read about the daughter effect on page 126).

References

Braun, Danielle & Kramer, Jitske (2016). *The Corporate Tribe: organizational lessons from anthropology*. London: Routledge

Choudhury, Shakil (2016). *Deep Diversity: Overcoming Us and Them*. Toronto: Between the Lines.

Hofstede, Geert, Hofstede, Gert-Jan & Minkov, Michael (2012). *Allemaal andersdenkenden. Omgaan met cultuurverschillen*. [All Dissenters: Dealing with Cultural Differences]. Amsterdam: Business Contact.

Kramer, Jitske (2014). *Deep Democracy. De wijsheid van de minderheid*. [Deep Democracy: Minority Wisdom]. Deventer: Management Impact.

Liswood, Laura (2009). *The Loudest Duck: Moving Beyond Diversity While Embracing Differences to Achieve Success at Work*. Chichester: John Wiley and Sons Ltd.

Sociaal Cultureel Planbureau. 2018. *Economische zelfstandigheid vrouw krijgt in relatie weinig prioriteit. [Women's economic independence not a priority in relationships.]* https://www.scp.nl/Nieuws/Economische_zelfstandigheid_vrouw_krijgt_in_relatie_weinig_prioriteit

Solnit, Rebecca (2008). *"Men Explain Things to Me"*. Essay in *Guernica* magazine: www.guernicamag.com/rebecca-solnit-men-explain-things-to-me/

Stuurman, Siep (2017). *The Invention of Humanity: Equality and Cultural Difference in World History*. Harvard University Press.

Tiggelaar, Ben (2018). *Waarom je beter een baas met een dochter kunt hebben – 52 inspirerende lessen voor werk en leven*. [Why You're Better Off with a Boss Who Has a Daughter]. Utrecht: Tyler Roland Press.

Trompenaars, Fons (2004). *Riding the Waves of Culture: Understanding Diversity in Global Business*. London: Hodder & Stoughton General Division.

I based these ranking exercises on Arnold Mindell's writings, including Mindell, Arnold (2002). *The Deep Democracy of Open Forums*. Charlottesville: Hampton Roads Publishing.

The documentary film *Kumaré* comes highly recommended if you want to learn how people turn someone into a guru and how you can turn yourself into a guru using this knowledge.

You can find a repeat of the original Doll Test here: https://www.youtube.com/watch?v=ybDaogSuAcg

Joris Luyendijk has written several books. He also lectures in theaters. His bubble lecture is highly recommendable: https://www.youtube.com/watch?v=UELv5hQ5iSk

Understanding white privilege through a $100 Race: https://www.youtube.com/watch?v=4K5fbQ1-zps

3

TRUTH

How to deal with multiple truths

Challenge
the truth

JAM
CULTURES

Different sounds fill my ears.
I whistle a new tune. I surf on
strange thoughts and taste my
novel knowledge. Fresh words
open up my feelings. Mysterious
insights mix with my common sense.

I am watchful to the eyes that
challenge me to see beyond my blindness.
To hear what speaks beyond my whispers.
To taste how confusing thoughts can move
my lips.
I long for new flavors
and miss the old ones already.

Known letters form unknown words in
wound-up silences. I mutter
new ideas. Air escapes
whistling between my teeth. I
giggle. I sing my new tune and
laugh out loud.

Jitske Kramer

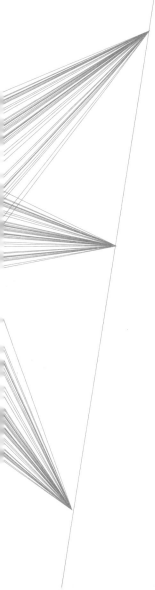

Anyone who refuses to shake hands with a woman ...

... doesn't respect women. Someone who doesn't show respect doesn't belong here and should just go back where they came from, get out of here, find another job. However, in some countries, someone who touches a woman just like that shows a lack of respect. Someone who does that would be an outcast there, and be told to leave, go back to where they came from, find another job.

We need stories to believe in, for the meaning, direction and structure they provide in our chaotic world. Not all of us believe in the same order, in the same dividing lines between good and bad, pretty and ugly, true and false. The more diversity there is, the wider the options. How should we deal with all these truths? How can we question the status quo yet create a truth we can agree on? How can we be inclusive? These are the questions I'll tackle in this chapter. Talking about these things is important, but taking action is even more crucial. Inclusion means creating space for passion and personal action - a freedom that is far from self-evident. Inclusion, democracy, speaking up ... all of these take hard work and hinge on our willingness to challenge our own truths.

There is more than one truth

The absolute truth doesn't exist. I strongly deny this. Things that are true in one culture are not necessarily true in another. But if many people say something is so, this becomes the group's set of values, its truth. And if what we say is true, then what others say must be untrue. If this is my normal, then the other set of values is abnormal. Some people and cultures ascribe great value to universal, scientific truths while others see truth as contextual and situational. When I was working in India, the general manager that hired me, would often contradict himself. He would tell me one thing in his office and something else entirely when we were on the production floor. When I asked him about this, he simply answered, "That's just my other reality." What I tell someone in a particular setting affects my story. People who are looking for the

Ursus Wehrli
– The Art of Clean Up.

There are so many different ways of experiencing and ordering the same reality. Culture orders our world. It gives our lives meaning.

IMAGES FROM: THE ART OF CLEAN UP, URSUS WEHRLI, CHRONICLE BOOKS, 2013.

absolute truth would call this lying. Others might call it foregrounding different aspects depending on the context.

We believe what we hear most often, particularly when we hear it from our parents, teachers, (religious) leaders and best friends. We also interpret these constructed truths as facts. Sometimes we even say this: 'women have poor spatial awareness, that's just a fact'. Sometimes, we say it slightly less directly: 'Those people are not refugees, they're just economic migrants, they really are'. Or we say it in an even more roundabout way: 'Let's just give every unemployed person over 50 their benefits and forget about them ever finding a job again, because that isn't going to happen. Let's just face facts here'. Many people find it hard to distinguish hard, demonstrable facts from the stories we tell each other. The dominant group has great defining power: by saying things loudly and repeating them often, it can determine what we accept as the truth. And because all of us have a tendency to clone and to seek out people who hold opinions similar to our own, our filter bubble keeps getting bigger and more closed off to outside influence. With less and less room for fresh perspectives and different truths. We get stuck, and we all know what that leads to.

Different takes on the notion of truth

There are three ways of looking at the truth: as an absolutist, a relativist and a pluralist.

Absolutism

You're a proponent of absolutism if you think that there are absolute truths that cannot be called into question. This goes hand in hand with the assumption that whoever believes a different truth is an out-and-out liar, has not yet seen the light and needs converting, or is rotten to the core. For example, God is good and ubiquitous, so whoever does not believe in God is a bad person who will not go to heaven and—in the most extreme forms of absolutism—has no right to exist. Or let's take another example: heterosexual love is natural and acceptable and therefore homosexual love is unnatural and unacceptable. Or: animals have the same rights as humans; hence, meat eaters are murderers.

Feeling the truth
Anytime you work with other people and you're all in 'exactly the same' situation, everyone ends up having a different experience. And everyone's experience is true. Such experiences can vary even more widely when everyone involved is from a different country or language background.

Not only do we all hear and notice different things, we each assess the same situation differently and form different opinions about it. What's more, cultural frameworks and filters can even cause us to feel differently about the situation. Culture has much more impact on us than we tend to think.

From an absolutist point of view, you judge anyone who thinks differently as inferior, or at least ignorant. You measure everything by your own yardstick; your standards are the norm (egocentric and ethnocentric). The dissident minority in the group has only one way to survive: adapt. For them, it's the only way to be seen or heard. Absolutism demands that others assimilate and excludes those who don't. Challenging the truth is not done.

Cultural relativism
In the early twentieth century, absolutism reigned supreme. The basic idea was that there were civilized countries where educated people lived, and the rest of the world which was populated by 'savages'. The educated believed the savages were significantly less intelligent. This is one of the reasons why well-meaning Westerners would set out, often with the bible in hand, to spread civilization to these poor, underdeveloped regions. At the same time, there were people who disputed this absolutism, among whom were the first anthropologists, who insisted that 'different' did not necessarily mean 'lesser'. Anthropology became the mother of cultural relativism. Relativism holds that truth depends on the context. Relativists argue that there is no single truth and that our actions and behavior are not determined by our biology. Rather, it's our circumstances and our culture that determine what we consider normal and how we go about things. Hence, different cultures have different truths, based on different intrinsic logics - and that's fine. Different does not equal inferior and diversity is a fact and an enrichment. It's not something that needs to be erased in favor of one, absolute truth. Everyone should be allowed to be themselves. We are able to work alongside each other despite our differences. This is the anthropological turn I wrote about in Chapter 1 on Difference.

During my anthropology studies, I learned to view the world through the paradigm of cultural relativism. During my time in college and in my first jobs, this was the reigning truth in anthropology. Eventually, these ideas also came under attack, because if you're a radical cultural relativist, you can only understand behavior in a very specific cultural context. You can't judge the other if you don't fully take that context into account. That's the reason anthropologists like to live in another culture for an extended period of time; if you're immersed in a culture, you get to know it inside and out. The problem, however, is that relativism makes it hard to critically discuss moral frameworks. For example, a hard-core cultural relativist would not criticize Trump's policy of separating families of illegal immigrants at the border, but would reason that this is part of American culture at this point in time and therefore can't be judged. It's part of US cultural history and therefore there's an internal logic to the policy. If you get lost in relativism, you can't raise any questions about anything. Even defending universal human rights becomes problematic, because who thought these up and do they even apply to everyone?

Pluralism, or critical relativism
Ideally, we'd see everything in context while remaining critical. This way of looking at humanity is called pluralism, or critical relativism. This school of thought holds that even though culture should always be seen in context, some topics lend themselves to application of universal truths or human rules. After all, we're all on this planet together and we're interdependent in so many different ways. It is what it is and we'll just have to deal with it. We can only resolve our biggest issues if we work together. That's why I believe we should strive to make life worth living for as many people as possible, based on our similarities and with respect for our differences. Because of our differences, we shouldn't be looking for commonality necessarily, but rather for a mix that benefits the group as a whole. We should be looking for compatibility in society, at home and at work. Instead of a large, grey plain, we can cobble together a patchwork of ideas. This requires us to learn from each other and to adapt to each other, but not endlessly. In my view, people are not prisoners of their culture (as in absolutism) and how we should view their behavior is not completely context-dependent (as in relativism). There is such a thing as universal values. But even if we share certain values, we can differ in terms of which values we prioritize and how we express them. That's pluralism.

Inclusion and truth

Inclusion is about working together to complete the puzzle. It's about jamming and achieving the best possible result for everyone involved. It is a process that's never done. We need to keep moving to stay alive. Inclusion means we have to recognize that every person can see only part of reality. We need others to help us see the bigger picture. We can only open up to others if we take a critical look at our own assumptions and behavior patterns. We should realize that challenging someone else's truth is one thing, but challenging your own is quite another. Truly, deeply accepting that there are multiple truths leads to the challenging job of creating new synergy. This spiritual quest is essential to resolving complex issues and a precondition for co-creation.

► *Take a different perspective. Anthropologists make the unfamiliar familiar and the familiar unfamiliar.*

'To hold different opinions and to be aware that other people think differently on the same issues shields us from the Godlike certainty which stops all discussion and reduces social relationships to an ant heap.' – Hannah Arendt

Inclusion and Activism: Radical Nuance

Activism is to express your support of a particular truth through direct, vigorous action, like waving banners that call for more effective climate action or equal rights for women. Often, activism is necessary to make a minority voice heard in the noise of the majority opinion. At the same time, it's an absolutist expression that leaves no room for other voices and can therefore cause polarization. That creates a dilemma for us if we want to foster inclusion and nuance...

That's just the way we are

You know the saying *When in Rome, do as the Romans do*?

Although there's no single, universal, absolute truth, there are truths that hold true in particular local communities. For example, when you join a company, there's a dress code, a code of conduct and a particular way in which consultation is organized.

Thankfully, there's order

People form cultures and cultures form people. Every group of people has to come up with an answer to universal questions like 'How do we deal with the differences between men and women?', 'How do we provide feedback to each other?' 'How do we plan things?' The answers to these questions differ from group to group. The results are what we call culture. Culture constitutes our thoughts on what we consider valuable—our values—and the ways in which we think those values need to be expressed—our norms. And then we build structures and make rules that fit in with these norms and values. This helps us deal with the multitude of possibilities and brings order to the chaos.

Language is the vehicle of culture

When we discuss a situation, we use language. Our language shows how we think about something. Language is not neutral; it's full of judgments, ranking and emotions. Our choice of words speaks volumes: do we call someone a manager, a leader, a CEO, a foreman, a co-ordinator, a facilitator, a director, or a mentor? These are all labels for those who work with a group of people. But every label has a distinctive timbre and denotes a distinctive importance, influence, emotion. Language is known as the vehicle of culture. We can learn a lot about one another by listening to each other's language and choice of words. It makes a difference whether you call someone a refugee, a migrant, an alien, a newcomer or an expat. Suppose you're divorced. Do you call yourself a single mother, a happy single or a co-parent? And what language does your organization use on the forms it sends to its customers? As a whole, our words form our cultural group's story.

Our bodies speak our truths

Our cultural norms and values are also expressed in our body language. Italians make more hand gestures, and different ones, than Japanese, Russians or Americans. There are regional and local differences, too. What's more, bicultural or tricultural people will display a combination of gestures. So I'm generalizing, you say? That's right. Obviously, there are innumerable differences between individuals in a particular group, but there are also noticeable similarities and differences at group level. Stereotypes are not bad per se, as long as we're careful how we use them (see Chapter 1 on Difference).

We have so deeply internalized our culture's codes about what is pretty and ugly that we can feel physical disgust at those who don't adhere to them. In my talks, I often show a photograph of a woman with armpit hair. People in my audience often express disgust, avert their eyes, or shudder. This just goes to show that if a constructed truth is so ingrained in your system, it can be difficult let go of it and open yourself up to a new way of experiencing what you see.

Words, words, words
Why can't we say 'piccaninny' anymore, while 'cheesehead' is still okay? What's wrong with the word 'half-blood'?

How to stand in line

▶ *Everyone in the world will experience having to stand in line at some point. What that line looks like, differs depending on where you are. In the UK, people 'queue' very neatly. In India, everyone jostles for position. And in Thailand, I witnessed a brilliant solution for having to wait in line in the heat: everybody put their shoes in line, and then sat down on a bench in the shade to wait their turn.*

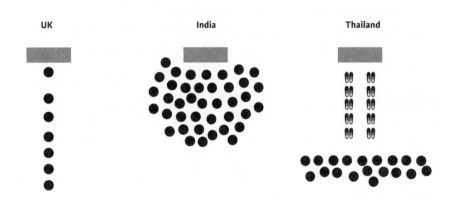

Truths are frozen traditions

Cultural truths are traditions frozen in time. They're ideas and habits we've come to regard as true. We've learned them that way, we share them and hand them down. At the same time, the world is changing fast, we keep meeting new people who have other crystallized traditions. This defrosts our truths and makes them fluid again, which is great because it creates room. But it also creates insecurity. While fluidity enables flow and creativity, it also calls everything into question and jeopardizes what we know. So, it depends on your perspective. Is it fun to doubt whether you want to accept a package for your neighbors across the street who you don't know(a common practice in the Netherlands)? And how quickly do you have to collect a package that was dropped off at your neighbors' house? Would it be acceptable to do this between 6 and 8 p.m., when they're probably eating dinner? And what if it's Ramadan? Can I invite my neighbors to my birthday party then? And is it okay to refuse a Facetime call from my boss when I've just returned from my run and I'm all flushed and sweaty? Oh, and I haven't applied for a job in ages, so what's the right way to respond to a 'We're hiring!' notification on Facebook? Where in today's media landscape can I find news that is at least intended to be objective? How do I deal with privacy? Will there be enough money to pay for everyone's pension? How do I set aside enough time and space to think in a world that just keeps bombarding me with information?

These are just a few examples of the questions we face on a daily basis. Because the pace of change keeps accelerating, there's hardly any time for our new-found answers to freeze into rules and traditions that we can pass down. So our truths remain fluid and in motion. In addition, people often no longer have an overarching authority, such as the church, to turn to for certainties. This can make us anxious, which can in turn erode mutual trust. I will talk about that in Chapter 4.

Groupthink

It is a good feeling to share your interpretation of the world with others. Collective sensemaking is very powerful, far more so than individual sense-making. The collective story is an amalgam of everyone's experiences and there's only a handful that can change that story and the discourse. Going along with the majority vote is much easier. If everyone agrees that a particular restaurant is great, you'll probably want to go there, too. If your experience there also includes a few negatives, you might not even notice them, because you're not expecting any. If you do notice them, you might prefer not to mention them, in order not to stand out. Because standing out would require you to come up with some very good arguments for people to listen to you and not put you down as a whiner or a princess on a pea. After all, the consensus is that the restaurant is great. Even people who've never been there know this. End of story. The same is true of really controversial stories, like that of Black Pete in the Netherlands. The majority says it's always been this way and it's part of the story. It's a story of shared childhood memories and the arguments for maintaining the status quo are emotional. Dissenters will have to tell their side of the story very often and very loudly if they want to be heard. This is due to dominance blindness and deafness, as we saw in Chapter 1 on Difference.

The restaurant story is fairly innocent. Groupthink can also take over in more serious cases, like a large-scale police investigation. There, prematurely reduc-

Guilty, tribal pleasures

In uncertain times, we look to a leader to order the new truths for us. The same applies in organizations. I call this our guilty, tribal pleasures: hankering for a single story, a single song, a single goal, a single label, a single flag, a single totem, a single leader.

ing possible avenues of inquiry can cause tunnel vision. A single-minded focus on a particular outcome can make the group blind to other possibilities. This can lead to wrong conclusions. The same mechanism can be at work in the belief in a business strategy, or in a department that is totally focused on its own interests and has lost sight of the business's overall interests. Groupthink happens when mutual agreement and consensus outweighs the importance of taking a critical look at the facts. Developing a counternarrative ensures diversity in thinking and counteracts groupthink. By interacting, we create room for new stories. This can feel brittle and uncertain, because it lessens that unanimous feeling of 'us' and undermines our sense of righteousness.

Diversity creates breathing room

In a homogenous group, the shared narrative takes up most of the available space, leaving little room for an individual take. Individualist viewpoints tend to stand out. As the group gets more diverse, there will be more breathing room, more space for everyone and more room to be yourself. More difference creates room for individuality.

Peer pressure

The truths we learn from our cultural group are comfortable, too. They provide direction for how we're supposed to live our life and organize our work. They prevent us from feeling stress over every little decision. At the same time, they make it hard to confront the truths in our own group. Groups are seldom charmed by individuals who go against the grain. That's where peer pressure kicks in. Anyone who questions the truths in their own group is likely to run into trouble, and might even be shunned. I discussed this in the section on power and ranking in Chapter 2.

Negative tribalism

The term tribalism often has negative connotations. As a matter fact, it refers to a very natural reflex to protect your own tribe, which was always crucial for our survival. The problem is that our solidarity with our own tribe can go hand in hand with aggression against outsiders. In modern society, this is counterproductive. We live in cities and work in places with people from various ethnic backgrounds, families, religions, and so on. It's impossible to force all these differences into one mold without getting repressive. Tribalism then becomes forced uniformity and fearful fantasies about 'them' without actually having met 'them'. Tribalism clouds the liminal zones and links dif-

How much room is there in your workplace to criticize the way things are organized, without jeopardizing your job or chances of promotion?

ference with negative experiences. Inclusion requires you to juggle different loyalties and to combine different interests. The tendency to withdraw to the safety of your own group is human, but not exactly realistic anymore.

From negative tribalism to inclusion
Inclusion ensures that everyone is heard and thus enables co-creation.

Negative Tribalism – Groupthink	Inclusion – Jamming with Difference
Peer pressure against divergent ideas	Peer enthusiasm about divergent ideas
Doubts and worries are kept inside	Doubts and worries are shared
But-what-if thinking	Yes-let's-try thinking
Calls to adapt	Calls to be yourself
Tendency to withdraw in own group	Actively seeking out others in liminal zones
Illusion that the group is impervious	Awareness of risks and actively exploring risks
Illusion that group opinion is unanimous	Recognition of everyone's unique contribution
Illusion that the group has a single morality	Awareness of the ethical dimension of decision-making
Decision-making is self-evident	A clearly laid-out decision-making process
Dominant and controlling leadership	Inclusive leadership
Approach outsiders based on stereotypes	Approach outsiders with curiosity and openness

Getting to know yourself through others

Inclusion asks people to see beyond their own context, but that's harder than it sounds. I like to use examples from all sorts of different cultures to help people get to know themselves. You only think of yourself as normal because you look at others as strangers. It follows that anyone who looks closely at their own habits—without immediately getting defensive—might find their own habits quite peculiar too. Take the Dutch birthday tradition, for example, which foreigners sometimes rename 'birthday terrorism'. Or the way Dutch people eat raw herring with raw onions. Let me be clear: this is not about whether we should get rid of these traditions, but about understanding how people from another culture might find them strange.

▶ *Getting to know yourself through others. An unexpected encounter at the Brussels' gay pride parade.*

IMAGE: VIXEN. MICHELLE LAMBRECHTS

The inverse is true too: if you spend more time thinking about traditions or behavior that seem weird to you, they become more normal. Actually, it's not all that strange. This is the invention of humanity I wrote about in Chapter 2: realizing we all have similar human needs. By seeing and hearing each other, our opinions can change and vary. Some may find that hard to accept because they've learned to be consistent and predictable. Besides, we already get bombarded with so much information that exploring the unknown can be too much to ask.

Intuition gets in the way

Our intuition can get in the way of a more open approach, because it's informed by our unconscious judgments and possible mindbugs. And we cherish our intuition. We want to be able to rely on it, because otherwise things can get a little scary. On the one hand, intuition is that gut feeling that we have to rely on—something's fishy here—and on the other hand, we need to be aware that those gut feelings are colored by judgments and stories handed down to us.

Truths as mental slavery

Like I wrote in Chapter 2, Power: the invisible chains of culture can keep you imprisoned in a frame. The thing is: we don't mind. It's comfortable and that's why we adapt as well as we can. After all, outside our little cocoon there are all these things going on that we'd rather not let in.

Somewhere in the interior of Uganda, I showed people pictures of my home in the city of Utrecht. One of the snapshots showed bikes chained to the railing on a bridge spanning a canal. At least four times, the people looking at my pictures asked me in surprise whether there were black people in my town. I didn't understand what they meant. Why? Because the bikes were locked. The first time I thought I had misunderstood, but then the coin dropped: the idea was that white people don't steal. Locking your bike must mean there's black people around. Such an internalized story about a truth that is actually detrimental to yourself is known as mental slavery.

Mental slavery is believing in a dominant narrative that degrades and discriminates against (groups of) people. Anyone who goes along with the story by acting in accordance with it and talking about it as if it is the truth, keeps the chains in place. It's the mindbugs that are seen as the truth in the conscious story and hence shape and influence institutional regulations. Women are simply more interested in taking care of kids than men. Or, our employees are just not smart enough to do that. Breaking out of such deeply rooted truths brings about major change, as we saw from the #MeToo debate. If one group is liberated, it means another group has to face the music.

Don't be naive

All day long, we're bombarded with stories intended to influence—or manipulate—our view of reality and our notions of truth. Those who can influence your thinking, have you in their power. If you stop thinking for yourself, you'll soon fall prey to all kinds of manipula-

My purse!
You're a woman. You're walking on the street. You're alone and you see a group of dark-skinned guys approaching. Unconsciously, you clutch your purse a little closer.

You are responding to your gut feeling, but is it justified? Dare to question your own intuition.

The truth about positions of power: a provocative story

Anthropology professor Arie de Ruijter likes to provoke his audience. With a huge grin on his face, he starts his story: "Do you know what a woman's value is?" He answers his own question: "She can walk and she can lie down. Because she can walk, she can gather food and do work. Because she can lie down, she can reproduce. But there's one big problem. Because she can walk and lie down, she can also walk off and refuse to lie down. If she walks off, there's no food. If she refuses to lie down, men can't have sex with her. These are two big downsides. To safeguard their position, men had to domesticate women. They did this by coming up with marriage contracts and taking away most of women's rights. This is how they secured their male position of power, which they otherwise would never have had. Because men know full well that women need very few men to reproduce. And that dead animal men give them once in a while after a successful hunt is nice, but not strictly necessary either."

What positions of power and rules were instituted in your workplace out of fear of losing something?

tion. World leaders try to achieve this by calling other people's stories fake news and by spreading disinformation and propaganda. Protesters talk about conspiracy theories. Managers flock together for strategy sessions and roll out new values in the workplace. Inclusion means constantly being on guard and realizing that there's a flip side to every story. It also means realizing that we have to decide together what the story is that makes most sense to us as a group. We can only do this if we take ourselves and the other seriously and listen to everyone's worries, fears, wants and ideas.

3 TRUTH

Hunt for alternative views

You seize every moment to comment on how strange and stupid you think I am. I fantasize about hitting you where it hurts most. I don't act on it. I stay quiet, because I don't want any trouble. I only talk about you behind your back. I always have the right excuses not to confront you face to face. My anxiety for rebuff is holding me back.

Are there any other views? I hear the question, but keep my mouth shut. I'm sitting at the big table, staring out the window. I know why things keep going wrong. I feel a silent revolution in my chest, but I don't make a move. I just sit and watch as we make an embarrassing mess of things. We both fail to mention the elephant in the room. And keep smiling our phony smiles and make our stupid jokes.

Do you maybe disagree? The question rushes through my vains. You say "penny for your thoughts." I mumble something under my breath. You look at me with a glimpse of genuine attention. I think you might be listening. But I don't know for sure. I take the chance and speak my words. I hope you hear me.

Jitske Kramer

IMAGE: UNSPLASH

Actively looking for alternatives

Actively listening to other people's opinions requires not only some skills and useful methods—which I will describe later in this chapter—but also a certain amount of curiosity. If you're not willing to connect, you'll just talk at each other rather than to each other.

Not everyone is equally adventurous. An adventurous spirit is one of the competences tested in assessments for people who want to work internationally. What employers are looking for is a willingness to seek out variation and change in your life. It's about how eager you are to put yourself in uncomfortable and unclear situations, even when you're not sure you have the right skills to deal with them. Less adventurous people often have a hard time working in a foreign country, particularly if they're also rigid in their judgments and behavior and don't find cultural differences interesting.

An adventurous spirit, or lack thereof, is difficult to change or learn. But within the limitations of your comfort zone, you can develop your curiosity about how others think and act. That doesn't mean you have to applaud others' opinions; you can still disagree with them. You don't even have to fully understand what the other is saying, as long as you can show some empathy. Pushing yourself a little in this respect is a must in today's society and work environment.

Differences between conservative and curious attitudes

Conservative attitude	Curious attitude
I prefer routines and habits.	I'm curious about people's cultural backgrounds.
I feel most at ease in clear, predictable situations.	I feel at ease in uncertain and unclear situations.
I tend to feel overwhelmed when faced with too many signals that I don't immediately understand.	I love trying new things, looking critically at the way I work and improvising when needed.
I do understand other ways of behaving, but I don't like to try them. I'd rather stick to my own ways.	I accept that things sometimes work out differently than planned.
I use only the elements in a situation that I'm comfortable with.	I like integrating new experiences into my behavior.
Diversity makes me think: Oh no, that's not going to be easy.	Diversity makes me think: Cool! All those differences. I wonder where we're going to end up.

Anthropological view: amazement and wonder

Looking at human behavior from an anthropological perspective is all about amazement, wonder, doubt and listening. It means looking at cultures and organizations from both an emic and an etic angle. The suffix emic stands for taking an insider perspective: looking at the way people inside the culture experience it. The other suffix, etic, stands for taking an outsider perspective: exploring how outsiders look at it. Actively looking for alternatives requires you to put yourself in other people's shoes. In practical terms, you can use the Triple Perspective Model for this.

▶ *Looking at each other.*

IMAGE: UNSPLASH/MARTIN BEKERMAN

Triple Perspective Model

Do I understand my own position? Can I put myself in someone else's position? Do I understand the dynamics between us?

Us

Interaction: how we
affect each other.
Miscommunication.
Similarities and differences.

Me

Thoughts, feelings,
behavior, interests, goals, intentions, self-image, perception of
the other. Cultural framework:
good/bad, pretty/ugly, true/
false.

Other

Thoughts, feelings, behavior,
interests, goals, intentions,
self-image, perception of
the other. Cultural framework:
good/bad, pretty/ugly, true/
false.

See the difference between debate and dialogue

To get even more practical, we need to take a look at the difference between entering into a dialogue and holding a debate. Both types of conversation are suitable for exploring shared truths from various angles. Both have pros and cons, so it's good to be aware of which one you want to use, and when.

Debate

In a debate, the participants are out to win by showing that their 'opponents' are wrong or that their arguments are weak. Chances are the debate will get heated very quickly when it centers on essential truths and participants' ideas, which is what it is all about in diversity, intercultural friction and conflict.

Dialogue

In a dialogue, the participants bring presuppositions to the table and talk about these. It's about temporarily setting aside all focus on solutions, decisions and concrete actions and devoting time instead to determining exactly what everyone means. Wants and needs are defined and shared and judgment is postponed while viewpoints, opinions and arguments are treated as optional, though meaningful and relevant—even if you don't agree with them. In a dialogue, putting forward opinions is less important than asking relevant questions. What is essential is to carefully listen. It's about looking at thought patterns: both your own and others'. It takes guts to allow in doubt about your own reality and sensemaking, all the more so if you feel you have a personal stake in the issue.

In other words, dialogue is not geared towards proving you're right, but towards examining the ins and outs of a particular issue. Which assumptions and beliefs lay hidden beneath a point of view; what are the unseen dimensions and blind spots? Dialogue gradually uncovers how our cultural lens colors the world. It doesn't set out to establish who's the winner and who's the loser, but seeks to establish a connection that fosters deeper understanding, which leads to finding similarities and differences. Whether the win-win results of dialogue can be maintained in practice, depends on how a team deals with it in practice.

Being able to determine quickly whether a conversation is still a dialogue or has veered off into a debate is an important skill. Another one is being able to switch between dialogue and debate. Especially when the search for alternatives is getting bogged down or has completely ground to a halt, it can be helpful to jar things loose by polarizing the discussion. Let some sparks fly. Such debate should always be followed by dialogue, of course. Also, the debate should remain acceptable and not turn into a free-for-all that undoes everything you've achieved.

Debate	Dialogue
Geared toward action, thinking on your feet	Geared toward insight, thinking slow
Persuade, take a stand	Understand, listen
Oppositional thinking ('Yes, but …')	Cooperative thinking ('Yes, and …')
Focus on answers	Focus on questions
Attack and defend	Explore and check
Viewpoints and arguments	Principles, norms and values
Pass judgment	Defer judgment
Solution-oriented	Aimed at uncovering underlying reasons
Risk: pseudoconsensus, muscle-flexing	*Risk:* legitimized abstraction, woolliness

Music is created in the silence between the notes

- We listen to what is being said, how it's said and who says it. The question is whether we're also attuned to what is not said. Often, the most important things are left implicit. There are different types of silence; there's the silence of hope, the smoldering silence and the silence that's full of possibilities. We also know the painful silence, when we know what's going on but don't dare say it aloud. Or the threatening silence, when we do hear what's being said (and implied), but don't act on it.

- In a September 2018 speech, the Dutch minister of Foreign Trade and Development Co-operation, Sigrid Kaag, urged her compatriots not to remain silent about the insidious danger of exclusion, but to name it and talk about it. She warned her audience that the exclusion of certain groups in society was slowly growing and would infringe on freedom. By downplaying the initial signs of exclusion and bullying, by not actively opposing these tendencies, we all allow our fellow human beings to be treated unjustly, she argued:"In the uproar caused by our fear of the other's voice, the silence can grow into a collective muteness. And in that deafening silence, we can no longer hear the signals of judgment, exclusion and stigmatization." Especially then, and especially now, counter-arguments and a counternarrative are needed.

- Jamming is also a matter of using the silence between people. Music is created in the silence. It requires courage of leaders and team members to listen to the silence and put into words the unspoken problems in the air.

Whose truth? Achieving a win-win situation

If you've managed to actually get every opinion, viewpoint and idea on the table during your brainstorm sessions, away-days and campfire talks, it's time to lay down some agreements. That can put everyone up in arms again, because the question that's pertinent when agreeing on methods or solutions is: Whose truth do we consider more true? Yours, mine or some kind of synergy between the two?

Either/or thinking is for lazy people

Either/or thinking is always an option, of course, but it's a lazy approach. It doesn't require any energy. You don't have to work on finding a solution that everyone is happy with. You don't have to think of moving over. The whole preamble has been for nothing. You just go back to using the old power arguments: we were here first, we are the majority, or he's the leader. Then, the whole exercise of listening creatively and openly to everyone's point of view has been futile. Inclusion as window-dressing. Creating grassroots support has then been nothing but the incumbent powers' manipulation strategy.

How many black dots do you see?
There are twelve black dots, but you can't see them all at once. Our brains are simply incapable of that. Just as in life, many things are present simultaneously, but we can't see them all at the same time. What we can do, however, is be aware of this. And be prepared to really listen and believe others if they point out things we haven't seen. We see more together than alone.

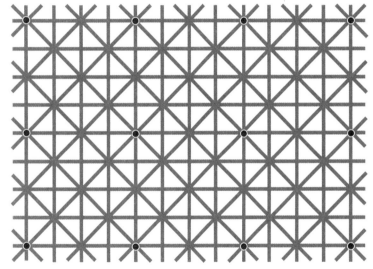

IMAGE: BASED ON AN IDEA BY AKIYOSHI KITAOKA

Simple answers

Once the full complexity is visible, what often follows is a call for simple solutions, preferably laid down in one-liners, slogans and soundbites. Simple answers give us a sense of security. They're nice and clear, unambiguous, easy to digest. But many issues, and especially complex ones, require us to think long and hard, to include multiple viewpoints and think through long-term consequences. This leads to 'it's both' thinking.

'It's both' thinking

While it requires more work, 'it's both' thinking is worth it. It's all about making the most of everyone's uniqueness. How can we accommodate everyone's individual sound while still creating a harmonious whole? We can only do that by listening extremely well and then deciding who is going to do what and when. Jamming is possible only if we lay down some ground rules and agree on the key we're going to play in. What we need is a few frameworks and overarching principles that create space for everyone involved.

To achieve this, we need good, inclusive leaders who safeguard the space for difference while guiding the process of reaching deals and solutions with courage and creativity. Leaders like this need the guts to give direction without knowing what the outcome will be. They need to be able to find certainty in the process, while being ready to make decisions along the way that will turn things on their head and will not go down equally well with everyone. Such leaders also need the creativity to keep looking for new options and the wisdom to ensure that minority viewpoints are reflected in every decision. In Chapter 5, where I write about Courage, I will discuss in greater detail what good leadership entails.

Confirmation bias: our tendency to see what we already know People tend to see new signs and events they come across as confirmation of their existing narrative. It requires active thinking for new information to penetrate into your current story.

Unfortunately, we've mostly been preprogrammed to think either/or. That type of thinking is deeply ingrained in us. We continually ask ourselves—without even being aware of it, most of the time—is this good or bad? It's like we're constantly working out what I call the multiple choice quiz of life. I've identified the right answer, so all the other answers must be wrong. This is how we're raised and trained. This makes it hard to flip our perspective. It's difficult to stop eliminating the wrong options in favor of the one right answer and instead conduct an open-ended search for a new answer. And to realize that this is not so much about finding the best solution, but getting *the most* out of the solution chosen.

In Jam Cultures, the leader of the decision-making process does not steer the process based on the dominant truth, but works from a position of not knowing. This requires them to think on their feet and to improvise in search of shared truths. It's a process-oriented rather than content-oriented approach. Instead of practicing a piece and performing it twenty times in a row, it's about creating a new piece of music togeth-

3 TRUTH

er. It's about jamming, albeit in a framework of clear, practical ground rules and codes of conduct to prevent the session from descending into cacophony. There should be room for different rhythms, but all should be playing to the same beat and all players should be allowed to contribute. It's about finding similarities and shared needs and creating combinations of different ideas.

Five routes for dealing with difference

There are roughly five routes we can take to deal with difference. Logically speaking, different situations call for different approaches. The route you take depends on how much value you attach to your own interest and needs; how much value you attach to others' needs and to maintaining a good relationship; your assessment of your own position of power; how much value you attach to dialogue; and your personal preferences. The five routes are in line with the ways in which people deal with oppositions: complementary; corresponding; contrasting and hierarchical (see p. 77) and the rationale behind absolutism, relativism and pluralism (see p. 141). Your preferences might be reflected in the route you choose for forging solutions.

1 My way

Although you understand where the other is coming from, you're not prepared to make any concessions. It's my way or the highway and you can afford to think this way. This is a good strategy when your own core values are at stake and you are ab-so-lute-ly sure that your (visionary) idea is the very best.

In the business community, large corporations with a strong market position often have this strategy. You are only hired if you agree to a particular way of working and clear procedures. Businesses are not always aware that they're taking this route, but their very restrictive competency profiles and their culturally colored interviewing style neatly filters out groups whose culture does not conform to the dominant business culture. This means a lot of talent is overlooked and imbalances in society are perpetuated. Be on the lookout for mindbugs and unconscious bias.

Harmony is not the same as absence of conflict
One of the biggest misunderstandings is that 'it's both' thinking is all you need, that it makes everything fine and does away with all conflict. Sorry, but that's not true. Dialogue does not erase conflict; in fact nothing does. Conflicts are not an exception to the rule of peace and harmony. They are the rule and they keep rearing their head. The existence of conflicts is a normal state of affairs, while harmony is nothing but the ability to resolve conflicts.

Whose way?

My interests and needs

The other's interest and our relationship.

My way
'I can afford to lay down the law and make people conform to my way.' My way or the highway.

The other way
'I see how important this is to you and I don't mind one way or the other.' Choose your battles.

Stop. No way
'I'm calling it quits.' Our differences are too big. The effort required outweighs the advantages.

Compromise
'Let's meet in the middle.' A solution that satisfies exactly no one.

New way: synergy
'We're going to bridge our differences, and preferably put them to good use.' Swapping out 'either/or' thinking for 'it's both' thinking. Synergy. Creativity. Inclusion. Third way.

I once spoke with the HR manager of a US-oriented company that had also adopted typically US labor relations. His board of directors and he himself, too, were of the opinion that if people didn't feel at home in their corporate culture, they should just clear their desks. They kept this up until their very talented Dutch employees were so fed up with the lack of vacation days and the target-driven culture, that they actually did leave and started working for the company's biggest competitor.

At team level, you see this approach taken in the more powerful, influential subgroups. Everyone talks about integration, but what they actually want is for people who think differently to assimilate. This only works if 'the other' doesn't mind adapting and if the assimilation demands are doable. Many team members who are made to feel different in various ways will either leave the team or fail to show their full potential. In this situation, you have diversity, but no inclusion.

It's easy to demand assimilation, but adapting can be hard, time-consuming and even detrimental in the long run. It's wise to discuss such matters and ask whether demanding adaptation is the best way. I was once told by a Dutchwoman of Surinamese descent that her Dutch manager had told her to call him by his first name. She said: "The first year, I couldn't get myself to do it. The second year, I managed to say his name, but every time I did my stomach squeezed tight. It was only after three years that I was able to call him by his first name without it feeling inappropriate and impolite." Would it have been so awful to let this woman address her boss as Mr. Such-and-such?

If you decide to impose your way anyhow, then at least ask the other what they need to go along with that. Invest time and effort in exploring how to minimize the damage or hurt done to the other.

2 The other way
In some cases, you can simply adapt to the other's preferences. *Choose your battles* and be prepared to be flexible. If something is not terribly important to you, but it is to someone else, than you can also choose to adopt the other's ways. Clearly, this requires some flexibility on your part and the willingness to change your behavior and way of working. It can be very nice for the minority on a team to see that the majority is willing to accommodate them in some respects.

Assimilation carries the risk losing yourself. While refusing to assimilate irritates others, adapting too much means giving up your own identity. A moderate degree of assimilation can be a very good strategy. Sometimes, it's simply good to do something for someone else. It does raise the question: what do I need to be able to let this go? And that means you might have to talk about it.

3 Stop! No way
This route has only losers, particularly if we can't actually go our separate ways. In a country where people are born with all sorts of different

Toothbrush
During my stay in Botswana I noticed that my host family used my toiletries and wore my clothes without asking. Although I understood full well this was due to different ideas about property and privacy, I still decided to hide certain things. I couldn't stomach the thought of sharing my toothbrush with the whole family. No way.

'The trouble with other cultures is that people don't behave the way they are supposed to – that is, like us. The solution is to stop expecting them to.' – Craig Storti

backgrounds and skin colors, you cannot and should not send anyone away, and definitely not if they're citizens with a Dutch passport. Some people want to have absolutely nothing to do with Muslims, or Ajax soccer fans, or meat eaters, or dog owners, or tourists or whatever. This is just not possible. You can't totally ignore that horrible Jake and Jenny at the campground. You can't tell your child that his playmate needs to leave because you can't stand him. In such situations, you can have all sorts of emotions and needs, but you will have to find some way of putting up with a modicum of coexistence.

And sometimes there is room for two sides to go their separate ways. In these cases, deciding to stop working or living close to each other might be the best option. Sometimes, two parties conclude that their differences are too big to work together. In other cases, your collaboration never gets off the ground, or it's such a struggle that the effort outweighs the benefits. In all these cases, stopping can be a smart move, particularly when there's an alternative. Someone who leaves the team does run the risk of damaging their reputation; they can be seen as bad team players. That's why you should do everything in your power to help the one leaving avoid loss of face. Exits should always be handled correctly, anyway. People use rituals for that. That's best, not only for the person leaving, but also for yourself, your team and your organization.

When you decide to call it quits, you should really cut loose instead of halfheartedly trying to muddle through from a different angle. And if you do decide to cut things off with someone, don't expect other people, coworkers, customers or friends to cut things off as well. If you're on the receiving end of a breakup, have the courage to let go.

4 Compromise
In the middle, at the crossroads of the image, you see the compromise. Actually, to reach a compromise, everyone involved does something they don't want to do. A compromise makes no one happy. Everyone meets everyone else halfway. A badly conducted talking shop session can result in ideas that are unrecognizably watered down from their original versions. Sometimes, you have to settle for a compromise because there's no time to fully explore a real win-win situation. Sometimes, a compromise is the highest attainable outcome after an emotional argument. But it's never an ideal to strive for.

Not either/or, but and/and

I have no idea how you could get as good a deal as I got in the loudness of opposing interests. My fist comes down on the table so hard it upsets the cards. I hiss "it's my way or the highway." You don't say a word, just stare back at me. The tension, the deadlock of not knowing and the threat of defeat take our breath away. We gasp.

I want to find the key to synergy. I want to breathe in and out. I want black and white. Thick and thin. God and no God. To make my own decisions and be guided. I don't want any compromises. No water with the wine. I want to fight for the best possible outcome. I want to get past the tyranny of always having to choose. I want to celebrate, dance, sing, float. I want there to be winners only.

All our cards are on the table. No more secrets. We know each other's beautiful and each other's ugly. We decide to fight for the other. I fight for you. You fight for me. Both of us battle to secure the best for the other. We put each of our interests first. No winning or losing. Just winning. We believe there is always more. Not either/or, but both and/and.

Jitske Kramer

5 New way: synergy

Every other route is based on linear thinking, where differences and oppositions are regarded as either/or choices, combined with a power struggle or negotiations. As I said, these are sometimes good, but none unlocks the energy and creativity that a multicultural team can potentially release. In order to make this transition, you have to give up your either/or mindset and adopt 'it's both', a way of thinking that allows you to bridge or even utilize differences. 'It's both' is an inclusive mindset. Getting rid of the either/or dichotomy allows you to consider new options.

This inclusive and creative mindset allows you to think of new ways in which all team members can happily and effectively work on team and organization-wide goals. Opting to work on a new, collective way to achieve goals, or one that enables everyone to be themselves, is often the best solution for the long term. It draws on the power and strengths of everyone involved, which unlocks progress and innovation. This will require both the minority and the majority on the team to change. Later in this chapter, I will discuss two methods that can help you find new ways to work: Deep Democracy and Polarity Mapping. These are not the only two instruments available (obviously). My reasons for mentioning these two in particular is that I have achieved good results with them in my consultancy work.

Cultural appropriation

On the topic of synergy and new ways of collaborating, I'd like to digress briefly on the notion of cultural appropriation. It's a term that keeps popping up in the media, but that's ill-defined, often used bluntly and seldom warmly received.

If someone accuses you of cultural appropriation, it means they feel you are taking over, stealing, or claiming as your own, a cultural element (a custom, symbol, piece of clothing, tradition, language), without consent from the group it originally belonged to. This is not an inclusive, win-win situation, but rather a matter of pinching someone's cultural heritage and traditions. One example is native Americans who stand up against the use of Indian costumes for parties. Cultural appropriation of characteristics associated with a marginalized group is often seen as institutional racism. In other words, these are some serious, emotionally loaded accusations.

When I first heard the term a few years ago, my first response was: what nonsense! This thwarts creative, cultural exchange. After all, creating something new involves combining all sorts of ideas, your own and others'. Everything we eat is the result of mixing and matching ideas and ingredients. Music is full of cross-over genres. And just because Islam has settled on the crescent moon as it symbol, does that mean this symbol is now patented? Moreover, culture doesn't belong to anyone, so you can't appropriate it either. As writer and columnist Tommy Wieringa wrote: "You can cherish culture, revere culture, deform it, destroy it or return it irreparably 'improved', but it's not your property." Culture is shaped and used and belongs to the commons.

My secondary response, after I had read more on the issue, is more nuanced. Let me explain using an example from the fashion industry. In 2015, the British fashion label KTX used a traditional Inuit print on one of its pieces of clothing. They had taken the print from an old photograph from 1902, showing a member of the Nunavut tribe. When Salome Awa found out about this, she raised the alarm. The picture was of her great grandfather. He was a shaman and had asked his wife to appliqué the two hands on his parka to protect him from someone who wanted to push him into the cold ocean water. Salome criticized the British fashion label not only for using a symbol that was sacred in her tribe, but also for infringing on her great grandmother's copyright. The Fashion Law website made the news public under the headline: *'KTZ Under Fire for Copying "Sacred" Inuit Print'*. The quotation marks around the word 'sacred' just fanned the flames, because these showed that the whole argument wasn't taken very seriously.

This incident lays bare all the sensitivities surrounding cultural appropriation: using cultural elements with a

2015

▶ *Model on the KTZ Fashion Show's catwalk in London on January 11, 2015 in London.*

1902

▶ *1902 photo of Salome Awa's ancestors' original design.*

deeper meaning without consent, lack of respect for artistic copyright and the power imbalance of a dominant group toward a marginalized group.

We can't just sidestep cultural appropriation. Equality also means treating each other as equals when it comes to rights and responsibilities. It's not okay to use any symbol or tradition we like for commercial gain. If someone takes offense at the use of their traditional costume, you should defer to that. At the same time, I hope that whoever puts in a claim keeps a sense of proportion. After all, Halloween is about dressing up in stereotypical costumes. How strict do you want to be? Culture consists of ideas and stories and different stories influence each other.

Telling stories about each other, in movies and plays, is actually a really good way of getting closer to each other. The whole concept of intellectual property is a moot point in co-creation projects. Also, I hope we can stay away from a legal claim culture. Inclusion, jamming and diversity require us to create an atmosphere that's conducive to cultural exchange, one that enables cross-pollination. What we're looking for is a co-creation in which ideas can freely flow, based on good intentions and mutual respect. In the same way that voodoo rhythms from West Africa found their way into funk, blues, pop, jazz, and that, through hip hop, are now inspiring my own son to create his own music.

New Ways with Deep Democracy

So, how do we arrive at a good win-win situation? How do we find a solution that includes the existing diversity up to and throughout the convergent phase of decision-making? You want to keep everyone on board, but hard choices have to be made. You can't decide two things at the same time. How do you go about this without making people unhappy?

One answer to these questions is the Lewis Deep Democracy method. This method was developed by Myrna and Greg Lewis in the Johannesburg business community in the 1990s. The end of Apartheid meant that existing structures and hierarchies were collapsing. Groups that had long been trapped in the dynamics of violence and exclusion now had to start working together as equals. To guide this process, the Lewises started exploring other ways of organizing the decision-making process. This led to the development of the Lewis Deep Democracy method. I learned about this methodology in 2007, decided to specialize in it and wrote *Deep Democracy: The Wisdom of the Minority* in 2014. These days, I work with a team of licensed Deep Democracy instructors and train hundreds of people in this method every year (see www.deepdemocracy.nl).

The method is based on the notion that for a group to function well, it needs to listen to and value every voice, viewpoint and idea. Decisions are only sustainable if the group manages to integrate the wisdom of the diverse minority into the majority decision. If the group fails to do so, there's a great risk that the minority will in the long run undermine the decision (see: Resistance Line, described in Chapter 2). Deep Democracy is about ensuring that the minority can truly accept the majority decision because it incorporates their viewpoint. Below you'll find a short summary of the method, so you can get a feel for it.

Deep Democratic decision-making consists of five steps:

1 Collect all views
Invite everyone to share their opinions, ideas and viewpoints. Note, this also applies to ideas that run counter to your own! Every perspective matters. Listen to all of them with an open and neutral mind.

2 Actively look for alternatives

While discussing ideas, you often see the broad contours of a proposal taking shape. Our tendency is to go along with these proposals and quickly move on to decision-making. To counter this tendency, explicitly ask if anyone has any other views.

3 Spread the alternative

Someone who brings a new perspective to the table is often met with laughter or sighs of 'There he goes again!' or 'We were almost done and now it's back to the drawing board.' *Actively protect people who speak up from being singled out this way. Prevent scapegoating (see p. 121) by asking whether others can relate to what was just said. You'll find that there're almost always others who agree and who only dare speak up if actively invited to do so. This way, an alternative is spread and the responsibility doesn't stick with the individual who brought it up.*

These three steps are continually repeated during the conversation. They help the group to put all the different ideas on the table and to jam during the exploration phase. Once everything has been examined and said, it's time to move on to the decision-making phase. The group takes a vote on the proposals it has worded. Everyone gets to vote once. If the group has thoroughly explored its options, there's usually a clear majority. If the vote is unanimous, you can move on to implementing the decision. If the vote is more or less split, you may have rushed the decision-making phase and you should return to Steps 1 through 3 one more time, asking everyone to explain their reasons for voting for or against to clarify the various options. Once the vote has resulted in a clear majority, it's time to move on to Step 4.

4 Add the minority wisdom to the majority vote

In this step, you go to the people who voted against the proposal or abstained from voting. You repeat that it's a majority vote and acknowledge to those who had favored another outcome that it hurts to lose: 'I'm sorry you lost your vote'. Then you ask every single member of the minority what they need to be able to go along with the majority decision: 'what do you need to come along?'. Once you've collected all this wisdom, you repeat the majority decision and add in the wisdom from the minority. This new proposal is put to the vote once again.

If three tries is not enough to secure a clear majority, chances are something's going on that has not been put on the table yet. There's an issue at play in the 'undercurrent'. Time for Step 5.

5. Conflict resolution

Many things can be at play when groups get stuck in their communication. Often, this has to do with emotions, relationships, ranking, (unconscious) dilemmas and oppositions. If so, a conflict may well be brewing. In that case, the Deep Democracy decision-making and communication skills discussed in Steps 1 through 4 are not enough and we need to shift to different ways of exploring our views. How to deal with conflicts is a topic I discuss in more detail in Chapter 4, when we zoom in on Trust.

Deep Democracy provides various tools for conducting difficult conversations. If you're not going to read up on it, at least take note of three questions that can be a game changer in such a process:
*   Is there anyone who has a different idea?
*   Who can relate to one or more aspects of what was just said?
*   What do you need to go along with this decision?

Decision-making

As Deep Democracy shows, inclusive decision-making depends on very careful exploration of every possible angle (Steps 1-3) and very careful decision-making (Step 4). Naturally, you could use other decision-making methods, too. But what I love about the Deep Democracy method is that it makes the tensions that arise during Step 4 so clear, so explicit. Groups know this is the moment of truth, when all options jell into the best, most feasible solution at that time. At that moment of creation, every aspect of power and ranking I talked about in Chapter 2 comes into play. Who is in a position to decide what the group is going to do, and what is the norm? In Jam Cultures, the members of the group ideally look beyond their personal interests and egos, and vote for the benefit of the group as a whole. That's real jamming. And yes, it's an ideal that isn't always attainable.

The following questions can help you to organize decision-making processes in a way that ensures all voices are included as deeply as possible into the convergent phase of the process.

*   *When* are the decisions made? In an official meeting, or behind the scenes, in the margins of the process? Is the meeting truly an opportunity for negotiation or purely a symbolic moment when an informally-made decision is formalized? People who are more relationship-oriented tend to organize things more informally than people who are task-oriented.

- *How* is the decision-making process organized? Do team members find it important to reach unanimity, consensus, a compromise or a democratic majority, or does the leader have a veto? The extent to which people assess and experience a power differential will influence their preference. From an egalitarian and individualistic point of view, every voice in the group has equal weight, but it is also possible to attribute more weight to the opinion of those with a higher status—based on their expertise, experience, age or seniority.
- • *On which basis is the ultimate decision made: logic or emotions? Which arguments are decisive: numbers, emotions, gut feelings? As a team member or manager, are you influenced primarily by objective arguments, for which you put aside your personal feelings? Then you'll probably focus more on local, realistic arguments, principles, rules and consistency. Or are you sooner influenced by subjective arguments, for which you use your personal feelings to find out how honest and truthful they are? Then you're likely to focus on friends, the situation, ideals and the practicability of rules.*

New Ways with Polarity Mapping

Not every issue can be neatly resolved and closed off. Particularly in the arena of diversity, many issues are polarized and pose unresolvable dilemmas. If we treat those as solvable problems, we will get stuck. A polarity (or dilemma; I use these terms interchangeably) has two sides that are interdependent, but we can't choose between them.

When it comes to polarities, there is no solution. It's like having a choice between only breathing in or only breathing out. What we *can* do, is make room for both sides of the coin. Polarities must be managed carefully. You have to know when the balance is leaning too much to one side and when to the other. It's a constant weaving back and forth between the one and the other, to make sure that both sides are accounted for. Just like you breathe best if you first inhale fully and then exhale completely. Compromises are a bad idea because they make you dizzy and cause hyperventilation. And if you're forced to choose, you'll die. The only way to deal with a polarity is by making ample room for both sides.

We all struggle with oppositions, dilemmas, paradoxes and polarities. They regularly rear their head in our lives, especially in a diverse environment, because people from different parts of the world have different ways of dealing with human polarities. If you have a diverse team, these diverse ways of dealing with polarities will clash. Again, there are many methods that can help you deal with this. In *Dancing with Dilemmas, authors* Steven Olthof and Allard Everts give an exhaustive overview of the various options. Personally, I like working with Barry Johnson's polarity map from *Polarity Management: Identifying and Managing Unsolvable Problems.*

Making room for oppositions: don't choose, but facilitate both sides. In other words, not 'walk the walk' or 'talk the talk', but 'talk the talk and walk the walk'.	
Task	Relationship
Autocratic	Participatory
Stability	Change
Talk	Action/walk
Think	Act
Individual	Group
Hierarchical	Egalitarian
Competitive	Co-operative
Expressive	Neutral
Perfectionist	Easy-going
Loving	Business-like
Internal control	External control
Rational	Emotional
Fixed	Fluid
Universal rules	Situational
Process-oriented	People-oriented
Variety	Homogenous
Reality	Imagination

Polarity mapping

Before we can tackle a polarity, we have to map it out. We need to list the pros and cons of both sides and consider how we can include as many positives and as few negatives as possible. Barry Johnson has developed a matrix for this. It's simple to grasp and easy to fill in for all sorts of polarities.

The trick is to try to stay in the top half of the matrix. Johnson says that choosing Side A or Side B exclusively is invariably going to be too much at some point. That's when you'll dip down into the bottom half. As soon as you're down there, you need to cross to the other side. And as soon as you get a dip on that other side, you need to cross over yet again. This creates a figure-eight movement, the symbol for infinity.

Barry Johnson's Polarity Map

▶ *Barry Johnson's Polarity Map*

	Highest purpose	
Green actions To create or hold on to the upside of side A. What? By whom? When?	The upside of 100% Side A / The upside of 100% Side B	**Green actions** To create or hold on to the upside of side A. What? By whom? When?
Side A		Side B
Red flags Clear signs we're getting into the downside of side A	The downside of 100% Side A / The downside of 100% Side B	**Red flags** Clear signs we're getting into the downside of side A
	Deepest fear	

The left and right side of the diagram each represent a side of the polarity. The top half is reserved for all the pros, the advantages of choosing a particular side of the polarity. Fill in the advantages for both Side A and Side B. The bottom half is where you list the cons, the disadvantages of choosing one side only. Fill in the disadvantages for both Side A and Side B.

Then, fill in your highest purpose. This expresses what the polarity is about: what do we get if we know how to manage this well? If we take our example of inhaling and exhaling, our highest purpose is 'life'. Then, you do the same for the deepest fear associated with this polarity: what happens if everything fails and we get lost in negativity? In the inhaling-exhaling example this would be 'death'.

The result is a relatively general polarity map, in the sense that this map will be recognizable to many people and would likely be filled in similarly all over the world. Next comes customization, that is, the 'green actions' and the 'red flags' in the diagram. This is where you answer what the green actions on the upside of A and B look like for you, or for your team. What do I see in *your* behavior, what do you say, what do you do? What does it look like when you (or your team) are in the top half of the matrix? For example, we smile, we ask each other questions, we end the meeting on time. Then you do the same thing for the red flags: what *personal* red flags do you notice when you're sinking into the downside of the matrix? For example, I find myself checking the time, we start interrupting one another, we start snickering to cover up that awkwardness, I slam the door. Once you've filled in all your green actions and red flags, you've written your personal instruction manual for this polarity. Anytime you get lost in the bottom left quadrant and you become aware that you are showing your typical red flag behavior, all you need to do is to start acting according to the green actions you've defined for the top right quadrant. At some point, you'll end up in the bottom right quadrant and show the red flag behavior you wrote down there. As soon as you become aware of this, you cross over to the top left quadrant behavior, and so on. Walk through this figure-eight symbol a couple of times and check whether your personal actions more or less cover all the bases. Add and refine where necessary, until you are happy with your instruction manual. Now print it, hang it up somewhere and act accordingly.

The Power & Love Polarity

Using power and love is a deeply important part of inclusion. On the one side, there's power, with an emphasis on decisive boundary-setting. On the other, there's love, with an emphasis on togetherness and connection. We need both, it's not a binary choice. It's one of the basic polarities we must manage. Earlier, I discussed this in slightly different terms, as the inclusion paradox: be yourself (power), yet adapt (love). In the following polarity diagram, the main

Highest purpose
Life, participation, inclusion, wholeness, independently together, human.

Goal-oriented. Boundary setting. Performance. Results. Defiant. Dopamine. Endorphins. Eagerly. Getting stuff done. Growth. Innovation. Different. Add on. Be yourself. Openly discuss and deal with power imbalances. Fight and take on suppressive systems and institutions. Get rid of obstructive patterns. Productive power to change. Seek progress.

Relationship-oriented. Connecting. Loyalty. Trust. Holistic. Oxytocin. Serotonin. Respect others. Acknowledge. Listen. Make whole what has been disconnected and fragmented. See the whole human being. Opening up to others and building trust. Heal unhealthy and broken systems by joining differences and people. Be silent together. Reflection. Feeling good is more important than progress.

Side A – Power
Focus on interests, Differences, Goal-oriented, Differentiation, Get-the-job-done energy

PowerLove

Side B – Love
Focused on context, Similarities, Relationship-oriented, Integration, Sensing, Empathic energy

Abuse of power. Undermining. Suppression. Superhero syndrome with pompous drive to save the other ('if not me, then who?'). Reckless. Soulless. Destructive. Denying or actively breaking ties with others. Build separation barriers. Impose solutions. Tyranny. War. Hurt others rather than be hurt. Losing connection with everything and everyone around. Isolation. Lonely.

Collusion and entanglement. Denial of different and conflicting interests, ranking and power positions. Denial of ongoing latent conflicts. Oppressive harmony. Lily-livered peace. Boxed-in status quo. Sentimental. Apathy. Total unity without any room for difference or opportunities for change. Denial of personal power and competencies. Undermining of personal development. Hidden and veiled power. Polite racism by denying difference ('we're all people'). People become the victims of underground power imbalances.

Deepest fear
Death, exclusion, fragmentation, paralysis, loss of identity, dehumanization.

issues have been broadly filled in, based on my own knowledge and experience and drawing on the insights I gleaned from *Power and Love*, Adam Kahane's great book, and Simon Sinek's leadership lessons in *Leaders Eat Last*. It's up to you to add or change what you want, and to fill in your own green actions and red flags. The result will lay out exactly how you can deal with this important inclusion polarity.

How to challenge the truth and find new ways of working

The gift of inclusion is that it challenges everyone's truths. Asking questions, eliciting diverse opinions and discussing underlying intentions and needs creates room for other viewpoints, ideas and ways of seeing. Together, diverse truths generate better solutions and decisions.

The skill you need for this is a flexible gaze. Fortunately, this is a learnable skill. We can all develop an ability to set aside our own cultural lens for a while and to defer judgment. This allows us to see things not only from our own perspective, but also from someone else's, which enables us to develop a wider perspective, a helicopter view or a metaperspective. This ultimately teaches you to ask questions rather than start a fight. And that's an important step in the right direction.

Clearly, a curious, exploratory attitude helps, as does the realization that your truth is one of many. Another helpful realization is that not every issue is an 'either/or' choice that can be resolved by opting for one or the other. Contradictions, polarities or dilemmas are 'it's both' issues. Such issues are best dealt with by allowing both extremes to exist, so they can reinforce and balance each other out. Truth is a dynamic aggregate of constantly changing viewpoints. That's life.

Questions to reflect on and discuss with others
Plenty of food for thought, I think. Here's a list of questions you can explore, either by yourself or with others. Share your insights on social media, so we can all benefit: #jamcultures.

- What are your absolute truths that are beyond question?
- Do you dare put your own opinion up for debate?
- Can you accept that there are multiple truths?
- Do you see a different opinion as an obstacle or an opening to new opportunities? Is this always the case? When is it not?
- What do you like about tribalism? Do you have guilty, tribal pleasures? What are they?
- People with new ideas bring change, innovation. Sometimes they're hailed, sometimes they're shunned. For whom or what would you be prepared to risk exclusion from the group?

- How often do you listen to what goes unspoken?
- How would you answer these questions from a workplace perspective? And from the perspective of your professional role?

Do something

Reflecting and talking are important, but so is taking action. Below I've provided a few ideas that are ready to be put into action. Clearly, this is not intended to be exhaustive. Add your own ideas and make the list longer. Share your insights on social media, so we can all benefit: #jamcultures.

- Go to a museum, a performance or a concert that you never would have picked yourself, preferably with someone who is a big fan of the thing you're going to do. Put yourself into your companion's shoes, with gusto and without judgment.
- Arrange to meet someone you can't stand. Have a candid discussion about your similarities and differences. Make sure you listen.
- Go looking for where you're wrong in a complicated issue that's close to your heart.
- Fill in your personal green actions and red flags in the Power-Love Polarity Diagram. Put your actions into practice.
- Ask does anyone have another view? at least three times a day and follow up by asking: who can relate to this? Listen to the responses, without trying to make your own point.
- Schedule time to solve complicated issues. Reserve one hour per week, at a time that suits you. But make sure you do it every week.When a decision is made, ask the nay-voters what they need to go along with the decision. Find a way to include this wisdom.
- Organize your decision-making process with great care, so that it's crystal clear who does and doesn't have a say, and in what issues.

Inclusion principle: Challenge the truth

- Dare to put your own opinion and the group's norm up for debate.
- Have candid conversations about differences and similarities.
- Actively try to uncover where you're wrong.
- Accept that there are multiple truths.

Inclusion principle: Hunt for alternative views

- Don't shun deviating viewpoints.
- Respectfully say what needs to be said, without fear of being rejected or losing your position.
- Personally involve people with a stake in the matter in your decisions.
- Listen sincerely to their opinion.

Inclusion principle: not either/or, but and/and

- Don't regard a different opinion as an obstacle.
- Have an 'it's both' mindset and keep your eye on the common goal.
- Work from your own preference and add the qualities of others to the mix.

References

Everts, Allard & Olthof, Steven (2017). *Dansen met dilemma's. Op weg naar wederzijdse winst. [Dancing with dilemmas: Toward mutual benefit]* Self-published by A&S.

Johnson, Barry (1996). *Polarity Management: Identifying and Managing Unsolvable Problems.* Amherst, Massachusetts: HRD Press, Inc.

Kahane, Adam (2010). *Power & love. Een strategie voor blijvende verandering. [Power & Love: A Strategy for Permanent Change].* The Hague: Sdu Uitgevers.

Kramer, Jitske (2014). *Deep Democracy. De wijsheid van de minderheid.* [Deep Democracy: The Wisdom of the Minority]. Zaltbommel: Thema.

Kramer, Jitske & Braun, Danielle (2018). *Building tribes. Reisgids voor organisaties.* [Building Tribes: Travel Guide for Organizations] Deventer: Management Impact.

Lewis, Myrna (2008). *Inside the No: Five Steps to Decisions That Last.* Florence, Oregon: Deep Democracy Institute.

Article on the Inuit Print: TFL, November 27, 2015: http://www.thefashionlaw.com/home/ktz-under-fire-for-copying-sacred-inuit-print

October 2018 article on cultural approriation by George Nicholas, on Sapiens.org, a digital anthropological magazine: https://www.sapiens.org/culture/cultural-appropriation-halloween/

Tommy Wieringa's newspaper column *"Onze andere levens"* [Our other lives] in *NRC*, February 2, 2019.

TRUST

How discomfort
releases energy

ENJOY THE UNKNOWN

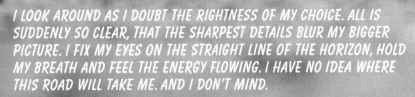

I LOOK AROUND AS I DOUBT THE RIGHTNESS OF MY CHOICE. ALL IS SUDDENLY SO CLEAR, THAT THE SHARPEST DETAILS BLUR MY BIGGER PICTURE. I FIX MY EYES ON THE STRAIGHT LINE OF THE HORIZON, HOLD MY BREATH AND FEEL THE ENERGY FLOWING. I HAVE NO IDEA WHERE THIS ROAD WILL TAKE ME. AND I DON'T MIND.

I SLIP AND SLIDE FROM DECISION TO DECISION. THE WIND RUSHES THROUGH MY HAIR. EVERY SOUND VIBRATES IN MY BONES. I TASTE THE SHOCK OF NOT KNOWING. I BURST OUT LAUGHING WITH EVERY STEP I TAKE. I'M DANCING. I'M ALIVE.

THE BUTTERFLIES FLUTTER IN MY BELLY. I HESITATE, WALK ON. I RUN THROUGH OPEN PASTURES. I FRISK THROUGH FIELDS OF SUNFLOWERS, BRIMMING WITH CONFIDENCE. I TASTE THE SWEETNESS OF DESIRE. FIELDS OF POSSIBILITIES MAKE ME SMILE. THEY MAKE ME ROCK. I JAM MY WAY THROUGH MY ANXIETY, I FEEL CERTAIN WITH UNCERTAINTY. I BLESS THE UNKNOWN.

Jitske Kramer

Trust is the foundation of all collaboration ...

... and every society. Without trust, a team can't function and an organization can't survive. Without trust, a group can't look in the mirror. If there is no trust, we don't develop ourselves, but grow estranged and distant. We build walls and break up into factions and divisions. Without trust, there can be no meaningful contact, no good talks, no working together, no inclusion, and no opportunity to jam.

Trust is at once essential and confusing. We all know what it is and we all need it, but find it hard to put into words. Trust can be based on relationships, results, previous successes, experiences, warmth, politeness, institutions and laws, predictability, someone's expertise, openness, rules (or a lack of them), family ties (or lack of them). Trust is about something you can't control; it's about dealing with uncertainty.

Trust is about your relationship to the unknown. The more diversity we are surrounded by, the more possibilities exist and hence the more uncertain we become. One of the first things you hear from people on diverse teams is that their members don't trust each other enough. I believe the trick is to teach yourself how to enjoy the unknown. That's what this chapter is about.

Trust as a choice

There's a big difference between blind trust and conscious trust. Blind trust means believing the other will always be honest, consistently speak the truth and never betray or cheat on you. This is also known as being naive, because humans aren't by nature all good. Just ask yourself: can you be trusted one hundred percent all the time? Are you always completely honest with yourself, are you always true to yourself, do you always do as you say and say as you do? Let's face it. It's hard enough to be faithful and loyal to ourselves, so being trustworthy to others is even tougher.

▶ *In 2017, French street artist JR organized a grand pop-up picnic on both sides of the border between Mexico and the US. When we meet, we get to know each other. When we meet, trust can take hold. As JR said: 'People eating the same food, sharing the same water, enjoying the same music, all around the eye of a dreamer. We forgot the wall for a minute.'*

In other words, trusting people is not the same as putting yourself completely in their hands. And yet, we generally like a relationship to be as unreserved as possible. Conscious trust is about taking a calculated risk, a leap of faith, even as you realize there will be setbacks and disappointment. You know that leap is necessary, because if you don't take it, you'll thwart your own development and your relationships with others. So, how exactly do we give and earn trust? And how do we do this swiftly? For this, we have to understand that trust is not an elusive mystery, but a set of agreements based on reciprocity.

Universal needs in a conversation

If we look at these reciprocal agreements at the level of conversation, we find that people have similar conversational concerns but different ways of dealing with them. This can lead to inadvertent miscommunication and distrust. And that's on top of all the ways in which we already differ to begin with.

Min-Sun Kim, a Korean-American communication sciences professor, has studied the cultural differences that influence how we converse. Cutting across all our differences, she argues, we share the same interpersonal needs. In what she calls the *conversational constraints theory, she* defines five universal constraints we all share during conversation.

1. *Clarity*: Do people understand what I'm saying?
2. Other people's feelings: Am I not hurting or offending anyone?
3. *Avoiding negative evaluation by the other*: Do people see me how I want to be seen? Do I come across as trustworthy?
4. Space: Do I occupy too much (or not enough) verbal and non-verbal space? Do I talk too much, or am I too quiet? Am I infringing on someone's personal space? Am I too distant?
5. *Effectiveness*: How do I get what I want? How do I ensure I won't get turned down?

It turns out that people are constantly considering these elements while talking to each other. However, the ways we deal with them vary widely. Individually, we each have our strategies for easing our conversational concerns; culturally, there are a great many norms that dictate how we're supposed to deal with them. Some people try to achieve clarity by getting straight to the point, continually recapping and candidly expressing their opinions. Others believe clarity is best served by voicing thoughts very cautiously and meticulously, while taking care to ask their interlocutor questions so that no bases are left uncovered. Talking to someone who ensures clarity in a different way than you expect can make you irritable and distrustful of the other's intentions. Before you know it, someone starts ridiculing the other, mocking the other's way of speaking and in fact breaching trust.

As diversity increases, we are faced with an ever wider variety of ideas on how we should tackle our problems, how we should communicate. On these matters, like those we discussed earlier, there's more than one truth. Some people may feel they 'minimize the space they take up' by allowing a maximum two-minutes of speaking time, while others feel that even ten minutes would be a modest allotment. It helps to become aware of those differences so we can refrain from judging each other. Otherwise, we may find ourselves thinking: 'if he knew what he was talking about, he would waffle less and get to the point.' Or, 'he's got so little to say on the subject, he probably doesn't know his ass from his elbow,' or, 'how arrogant he is to take up so much time,' or, 'wow, he's really non-assertive and insecure, he can't be a good leader.' Jamming does not mean that everyone has to act the same or that everyone gets to talk exactly the same amount of time. It does mean taking into account that others have different ideas and allowing each other enough room to express those. It's the inclusion paradox in action: be yourself, yet adapt.

▶ *Five universal conversational constraints*

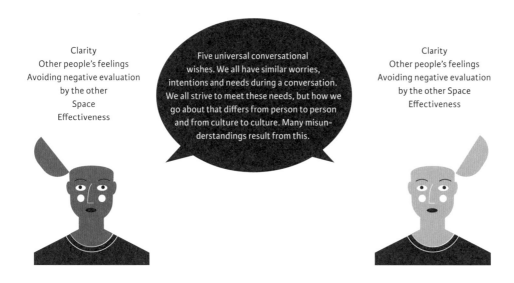

Clarity
Other people's feelings
Avoiding negative evaluation
by the other
Space
Effectiveness

Five universal conversational wishes. We all have similar worries, intentions and needs during a conversation. We all strive to meet these needs, but how we go about that differs from person to person and from culture to culture. Many misunderstandings result from this.

Clarity
Other people's feelings
Avoiding negative evaluation
by the other Space
Effectiveness

IMAGE: SUGGESTION & ILLUSION, FROM: WOW! WHAT A DIFFERENCE!

Cultural differences in what we look for and what we show

People all over the world look for similar signals indicating whether someone can be trusted. However, the sheer diversity in how we prioritize these criteria and in how we express this prioritization, render us unable to 'read' each other. In other words, we don't see the signals we're looking for and we don't send the signals that the other expects. We don't like depending on people whose actions are hard to read. The feeling that the other is unpredictable feeds our distrust. It's easy to react to this lack of trust by imposing demands, expectations and desires so as to control and constrain the other. That's why we need to make sure we can keep connecting in the here and now, even if some of those reciprocal agreements we need are not yet entirely clear.

The same set of criteria are used all over the world to determine whether someone is trustworthy. Yet, from culture to culture, they are prioritized differently. In random order, they are: authenticity, honesty, craftsmanship, safety, expertise, commitment, open sharing of information, transparency, modesty, predictability, support and help, friends of friends, position in the work-related network. And all of us have different criteria in our Top 3, which means we often don't send the right signals for others to check their criteria against. For example, I might be doing my best to stress my expertise, while you want to know who I know, whether our networks overlap. If I don't mention anyone you know, you might conclude we don't have any mutual acquaintances. However, you could also assume that I haven't mentioned them because I found it less relevant to do so at this point. The latter strategy builds more trust.

How to trust not-knowing

Our formal education, and for many of us our upbringing, teach us that we should know, master and control most things, if not all. We can insure ourselves against nearly anything, even bad weather while on vacation. Corporate managers seem to think that anything we can't measure, we can't monitor, and therefore it doesn't exist. In business, as in life, we want to get a grip on erratic human behavior and preclude all risks with an arsenal of rules, regulations and laws. This is what causes the well-known problem of regulatory burden. And because we try so hard to achieve absolute certainty, it's no wonder we

In Jewish tradition and law, there are many cultural norms pertaining to business trust. In an Orthodox Jewish store, it's not done to ask what a product costs unless you intend to buy it. Asking the price means that you want to negotiate and you're confident you'll be able to make a deal. Jewish diamond traders deal in precious diamonds sight unseen. They hand each other diamonds in sealed envelopes. It's a sign of trust. If you scam a negotiating partner, you'll be shunned by the entire community.

feel disappointed when things don't go according to plan. Before you know it, we feel betrayed by the system, our co-workers and our clients. This fuels our mistrust and the feeling we need more rules to patch up the holes.

What to trust: the rules or your relationships? Watch out, this is not an either-or question, but a polarity best tackled with a Polarity Map (see p. 173) or by using the Deep Democracy method (see p. 170) and saying: 'There's no rule for this, so what do you need to trust me?' Ultimately, trust is found in not knowing and in the vulnerability of admitting this to yourself and others. We expend a lot of energy calculating, predicting and interpreting signals and preparing a plan B in case something falls through. We want to shield ourselves from, and prepare for, disappointment. We talk about creating trust as if it's a structure, a flat-pack kit that we can simply put together if we read the instructions and have enough people on board. But trust is not a structure with a blueprint we can follow or a checklist we can work our way through. Trust comes from daring to let go and act, knowing that you can rely on yourself, others and the world. To achieve this with your co-workers, you'll need to invest time in learning each other's language and fine-tuning communication until you arrive at a shared story. Just as Kyteman and his band didn't prepare for their jam session tour by practicing melodies, rhythms or chord progressions, but by agreeing on a musical sign language that gave them the flexibility to seek out and trust the flow.

Being in sync with yourself, the other, the message and the rest of the world
When push comes to shove, some people put their trust in God or the universe; others trust themselves, or their fellow humans. And some assume all uncertainty will somehow be cleared away in the fullness of time. If we trust all of these things, we're in sync. We're tuned in and synchronized with everything in and around us. The luxury of being in a flow is that you don't have to think or fret, because deep down you know someone will catch you if you fall. You stop looking for contradictions and incongruences. You no longer worry what people say about you behind your back. Your brain can relax and focus on the now. That's real trust. And that's why it's such a shame when our trust is betrayed. We tense up, brace ourselves, don't dare take the leap. And unfortunately, we can even carry this experience with us into the next situation, where we meet another person and don't dare trust them either. Trusting the unknown is not easy; we fall flat on our face sometimes, but it's more than worth it to keep trying.

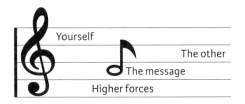

Trust: who goes first?

You get trust by giving it, not by asking for it. However, you'll only want to give it to someone who you trust not to abuse it. That's an interesting stalemate. Before people ask a question or put forward an idea, they want to make sure leaders and teammates won't make a fool of them or punish them. Leaders play a particularly important role in these dynamics. Inclusive leaders lay down the frameworks and standards for a safe space in which everyone can jam, even when—or especially when—the going is tough. Leaders' conduct is reflected by the group they lead. If they call for trust, but express distrust, their mixed message sets the stage for trouble and can even do irreparable damage.

Trust is built *during* the process of tuning in to each other. It comes about in the act, not in the preparation or strategy-setting. In other words, we need to keep working on and talking about our mutual expectations and needs. We need to continue to act, with love and power, based on the assumption that the other probably means well. In the belief that this process will benefit all. It's about surrendering to the relationship rather than trying to control it. It's about surfing the wave, about jamming. It's about letting go, without guarantees, while keeping your eyes and your ears and your heart wide open.

'The best way to find out if you can trust somebody is to trust them.'
– Ernest Hemingway

Blissful ignorance, comfort and shock

We don't mind if people are a little different from ourselves. We understand, of course, that we can't all be the same. Besides, that would be pretty boring. Still, there are limits. When we experience difference, we're challenged to leave the safety of our routines. We're nudged out of our comfort zone. We have to leave the place where we feel safe, where we understand how things are done, where we have a lot in common and there's no need to question anything. This is hard, because we're forced to leave the area where we know the routine, culturally speaking. While we may sometimes find our comfort zone boring, we have to admit it's also pleasant. And we definitely want to have the option of retreating there.

Once we step outside of our comfort zone, we enter our so-called stretch zone. This is where we experience a healthy sense of tension and excitement. Wow! That's great! Did you see that? You should really try it! There's another side to the stretch zone, though: a slight discomfort because you don't know exactly what's what and you can't predict what's going to happen. However, it's still comfortable enough there for you to take risks and start exploring. It's the zone you're in when you've just started a new job or taken on a new role in your organization. You're eager to get started, perhaps, but you're slightly nervous about whether it's all going to work out.

If the differences grow more pronounced, you might start to panic inside, thinking things will go wrong. You might get frustrated and start wondering whether you can still get back to your comfort zone. You fear you might lose your position, ranking and privilege. Welcome to the panic zone.

Diversity and inclusion take you out of your comfort zone. They take away the status quo of your blissful ignorance, your ability to blindly rely on a self-evident truth. This puts you in the stretch zone. After all, when truths are called into question, anything becomes possible. Questioning truths can trigger emotional knee-jerk reactions, which differ starkly from person to person and situation to situation. It makes us 'anxiously ignorant.' In this state, we're aware that we don't understand everything that's happening; we feel the differences, but haven't come to terms with them. They can make you curious, but also fearful or angry. We don't want to end up in the panic zone, but it's fine to be in this stretch zone. This make you 'consciously incompetent.' Hopefully, this leads to 'thoughtful sensitivity,' where you learn to get more of a grip on your ignorance. In thoughtful sensitivity, you can use your empathy and reflection to regain confidence in yourself, the other and the situation. Thoughtful sensitivity is the opposite of 'spontaneous sensitivity,' in which you're not on the lookout for differences but simply sticking to your own routines. That's more comfortable, though not very open to other options. Working with a lot of differences, in a diverse environment, means you're in a continuous stretch. It's doable and even fun and energizing if you dare to trust that things will work out. Somehow. One way or another.

Comfort zone and beyond

Consider yourself invited to enter your stretch zone more often and for longer periods of time.

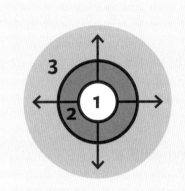

1 Comfort Zone
Safety, comfort, stability, normal, easy, habits, routines, recognizable, security. A bit boring at times. Monotonous. Aimed at conservation rather than change. At times, reserved towards the unknown.

2 Stretch Zone
Healthy tension and excitement about the unknown. Actions aimed at change. Learning, new, exciting, willing to take risks, dreams, adrenaline, challenging, expectations. School of hard knocks, willingness to continue to get back on the horse you fell off of.

3 Panic Zone
Disbelief, stress and anxiety obstruct any actions that might lead to change. Freeze. Tense, discomfort, stress, worried, tired, frustration, longing for 'normalcy', judgmental about anything different or new. Negative.

Patient information leaflet: there is no miracle cure

I regularly come across quotes on the internet that say things like 'Miracles happen outside of your comfort zone'. That's where the magic happens, the one-liner would have us believe, where life begins, everything is wonderful, and everyone has fun. Sadly, it's a fairytale. We'd love it if miracles happened and we didn't have to go through any pain to make a gain. Alas. Being *outside your comfort zone is a lot of hard work.* Innovation and renewal invariably go hand-in-hand with letting go, feelings of loss and the need to part with our old ways.

Note: Too much safety stifles change

People often argue that it's not safe enough to start taking action. This might be true, and if it is, we need to take swift action to create more safety. However, I think we frequently invoke this argument when there is no basis for it. There's often an overdose of safety that keeps us in place. It's nice and comfortable that way. It might not be 100% ideal, but at least we know what we're up against. Better the devil you know, right? Privilege is something people build up over the course of time. Teams insist there are never any underlying tensions. Things are just chugging along. It's a security blanket, but the real intimacy and passion are long gone. Nothing new is added to the mix. Tensions are circumvented, irritations are swept under the proverbial carpet. People turn a blind eye to most problems; to the point that it gets suffocating.

If we're too comfortable, we don't feel any urgency. Why would we strive for more diversity? Why go looking for alternatives? Anxious ignorance doesn't sound very appealing. Yet, it's that slight hint of unsafety that makes our blood flow faster, accelerates our heart rate and makes us take action. This stretch, this mildly uncomfortable zone, is where we can jam. Sometimes, when I'm feeling particularly cynical, I suspect some leaders of creating an abundance of safety and comfort in their team to stifle any inconvenient questions. They seem to like it when people just go about their day-to-day without any resistance and simply do as they're told.

Too much panic for too long is unhealthy

We can't live in the panic zone; we can only survive there. Real uncertainty takes a physical toll. If we can't relax anymore, we remain uneasy and generate stress hormones. If this continues for too long, we get sick. The fact is that in our fast-paced, ever more diverse world, we encounter more and more unexpected differences. So we need to make sure that we can feel comfortable with them, even if we can't know everything. Such trust is hard-won. It takes time and effort.

Culture shock

We can get thoroughly upset when cultural differences are too all-encompassing or too big. This is known as culture shock. What's happening is that your way of ordering the world suddenly doesn't work anymore. The other acts so differently, that you can't read their signals and you need to think about every little thing that you'd normally handle on automatic pilot. This causes stretch, no matter what. You wonder whether to hug this new customer or shake their hand. Stretch causes a healthy dose of stress; it puts us on alert and allows us to learn. However, it can also make you panic. You don't just wonder whether to shake someone's hand, but you freak out about it: 'WTF? Am I supposed to shake this new customer's hand, or hug them???' Whether you feel stretch or full-blown panic depends on you, the situation and your interpretation of the context.

Different stages of culture shock

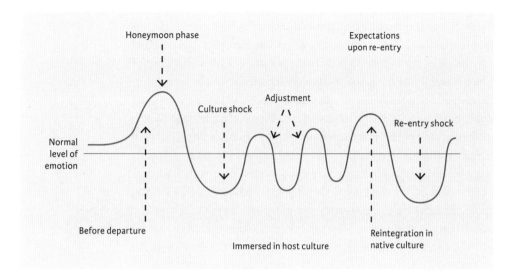

This diagram is used to illustrate what happens emotionally when you move abroad for six to twelve months. Similar processes occur when you get a new job or begin a new relationship.

As you can see, you have emotional ups and downs. When you are up, you regain control of the situation, you're better able to understand the cultural codes and you feel more like you belong in the new group. You trust more. Until you find you're not fully 'one of them,' or have not really grasped the cultural rules. Then you're down and you tend to trust people less.

Culture shock has various stages. I will describe them below as they apply to expats, but they hold equally true for long-term backpackers and refugees. Refugees often arrive with sky-high expectations, but are rudely awakened by reality. Because they arrive uninvited, their host country expects them to be cheerfully grateful. Culture shock occurs when there are major changes in the workplace, too. Those changes come in a series of waves, some big and others small. In other words, it's perfectly normal to have a hard time during such changes. Getting accustomed to each other and to new situations is never easy. Nevertheless, this process bolsters your trust in yourself and others, because you know it's part of growing together and taking on new challenges.

When you start planning a stay abroad, your feelings are neutral. You aren't feeling many new emotions, because your regular life is still going on. As your departure date draws near, the honeymoon phase sets in. Anticipation is sweet and once you're there, everything is new and exciting. You meet so many interesting people. But then you hit your first dip and it hits hard. You start to get irritated with all these different habits. You'd really like to eat a hamburger, shop at the stores you know, hang out with your friends and speak your own language. Or just get behind the wheel of a car without taking your life into your own hands. And actually, it's really smelly everywhere. You sense you don't quite belong, you miss home, you're disappointed in your ability to understand the cultural codes and the language. Perhaps you thought you spoke the local language passably, but now that you're there, you find yourself struggling to grasp the finer points. You bothered to read up on the habits and business etiquette in the host country, but now you've encountered dozens of troubling customs that make no sense at all.

To deal with the fear evoked by this dip, we either take refuge in drink, drugs and sex, or we start projecting, blaming our discomfort on everyone else. It's definitely not your fault, you think. You're trying. If this happens, you'll have to take a good hard look at yourself and carry on. You need to switch from anxiously ignorant to thoughtfully sensitive. You have to consciously explore, to experiment with your behavior and take note of people's reactions. Suddenly, you start to understand the unwritten rules and improve your command of the language. Then you notice that you are invited to people's homes! Until your next dip. This is how you keep getting tossed back and forth. And all the while, your understanding of your new foreign posting increases. You get better at connecting with people. You slowly become consciously able and chug along with the general flow of things. You've integrated or assimilated, or you have found a way to deal with the inclusion paradox: to be yourself yet adapt (see p. 57).

'Fear is curiosity that hasn't come out of the closet yet'
– Loesje

When you return to your familiar situation, your native culture or your old job, you're hit by the shock of re-entry. You think you're going to reintegrate seamlessly in your old comfort zone back home, but unfortunately, that's fiction. Two things have happened in your absence. One is that your old friends, neighbors and aspects of your culture, such as TV shows and the latest news, have changed, because while you were away, the world kept turning and your old, familiar place changed, too. Two is that you have changed, so you don't quite fit in as you did when you left, or at least not without a struggle. This re-entry shock is often severe, because when you left and entered your host culture, you were a welcome stranger who was helped to adjust to their new surroundings. Now that you're back, your old environment responds to you as if you're being needlessly complicated. You're back, right? So what's the problem? At the lowest point of their post-return depression, people often decide to leave and go abroad again. If you continue this cycle, you end up traveling the globe, and—if you're unlucky—never again quite feel at home anywhere.

It is absolutely true that outside of your comfort zone is where things happen. There's more laughter there, but there's also more tears.

Mutual shock

Culture shock works both ways. If you're shocked by others, they're probably shocked by you too. This thought is both reassuring and disconcerting. This would be a good question to ask when you're out drinking with your co-workers on Friday night: how many people did you shock this week?

IMAGE: SHUTTERSTOCK

You're not lost. You're here. And I'm here with you.

'We are not lost, we are right here', wrote Margaret Wheatley in *So Far From Home*. When you've lost your way in the wilderness, there's only one decision you need to make and that is: when to accept that you're lost. In full panic mode, this is what will allow you to find yourself again and accept that your usual habits and maps no longer provide the information you need. Not denying this helps you get a grip on the fear, enabling you to think more clearly and face the situation. Once you've found yourself again, you can start to look around and make new plans. It allows you to take stock of your options and make decisions based on them. You can decide that you are not lost; after all, you are here, in this place. This provides the internal calm you need to find new paths in the wilderness, in the chaos of your daily existence, on your own mental map, in your way of dealing with diversity, in the common search for new means of coexistence. In the wilderness of diversity, *you* are the steady factor. You are here, even if you don't know what's going to happen. And if you don't have a clue yourself, it helps if someone else comes stand by your side and says: 'You're not lost. You're here. And I'm here with you.' What I am referring to here is the concept of holding space from inclusive leadership, as I described in Chapter 1.

The zone of discomfort: clashing ideals

While working together based on connection may sound warm and fuzzy, there's also a thornier side to it. After all, to stretch our comfort zone we need to reconcile differences, which requires us to acknowledge them first. We have to be transparent. We have to work through the pain to the location of discomfort, while making explicit all unspoken obstacles. In Botswana, they have a great saying: *Ntwa kglo keya molomo*, or 'dialogue is the best way to wage war.' Inclusion means you don't get nervous about oppositions and conflicts. And if our dialogue makes clear that we need to restructure procedures, change structures, products and services, or want to appoint different leaders, then we need to ensure that we make these changes carefully, without creating a panic. Even if that causes discomfort.

*Do we have to rehash this again?
Yes!*

When we're falling prey to weariness about a particular topic and the majority starts sighing that they're done with it, we need to press on. The problem may have been discussed umpteen times, but it hasn't been solved yet. That's why it keeps rearing its head. The majority may want to take a break from this process, but the people suffering from the problem—the minorities who keep bringing it up—can't take a break from the stress they feel, can't simply forget about the situation for a while and blend in. Continually being matter out of space, being misunderstood, takes a lot of energy. It causes minority stress, particularly when the story is crystal clear but nothing is done to address the issue. There are so many examples, like the endless public debate on the glass ceiling in Dutch businesses, on special education vs. mainstreaming, on sheltering the homeless, or the underrepresentation of women and minorities on TV.

It's good to realize that leaning back and doing nothing from a dominant position is a luxury. It's a privilege. And with privilege comes responsibility.

Matter out of space

Anthropologists have their own term for things that deviate, that fall outside the normal, regular, daily order of things. We call that 'matter out of space'. This is stuff that is good and valuable in and of itself, but causes discomfort when it appears at the wrong place or time. An apt symbol for this is a weed, which is really nothing but a lovely little plant in the wrong place. A manager who wears shorts to an official board meeting would count as matter out of space in most organizations. Shorts are great for a day off in summer, but not for the boardroom.

Likewise, when a woman is named partner at an accountancy where the other fifty partners are men, she may also be perceived as matter out of space. What are we going to do with her? Does she need a separate restroom? What topics do we discuss when she's around? Does this mean we now have to buy home decoration trade show tickets in addition to our skybox tickets to soccer matches (haha)? People and things that fall outside of the usual order cause disarray. Some people have a hard time dealing with this and are tempted to pursue a strategy of fragmentation (see p. 57) rather than inclusion. The latter entails that the regular order will be replaced by a new one. Some might consider this a fun challenge, but others will find it difficult and painful.

Safe space: daily safe space to jam in

In Chapter 1 on Difference, I wrote that one of the main responsibilities of an inclusive leader is to create a safe space for people to jam in. Inclusion-based action opens the door to opportunities and, hence, to uncertainties. Not only is it unclear where we're headed and what decisions we need to make to get there, but it's far from certain how best to communicate this and who calls the shots. This is why managing uncertainty and anxiety is considered a key competency in intercultural and international contexts. It's important to keep an eye out for this all the time and to facilitate a way of working together that provides enough certainties for people to deal with change and difference. This is also known as psychological safety. If workflows, ownership and boundaries are clear, then the demarcated zone will be safe enough to work on inclusion. It's essential to create time and space for important conversations and real connection at regular intervals. We can create certainty by making explicit subconscious expectations and rules on participation and decision-making. It helps to make clear who has a say in what, what the status of a proposal is and how much room for influence there is. Is this proposal just a matter of testing the water or is it a mere formality? Clarity creates safety.

An inclusive environment always has a certain degree of uncertainty, but because that's the norm, you start to feel comfortable with it. You get used to it. It no longer causes tension. It's just like having to address a huge audience. The first time, you think you're going to die, but by the tenth time it just causes a short spike of healthy tension. In urban planning, shared space is the term for a public square without traffic lights. You can only cross this square safely if you pay close attention to all other road users. The idea behind shared spaces is that they involve people in creating safety by making them co-responsible. Because people have to be more careful, they make more eye contact with others in traffic. Safety becomes a joint effort; pretty much the same way it does in what I call jamming.

If Westerners make contact with Muslims for instance—and I don't mean living on the same street and just nodding hello at each other, but really talking with them—their presence will become more and more normal. We'll start to understand our differences and similarities better. Our intercultural awareness will grow. Differences will no longer be stressful by definition, because they will no longer make us feel insecure in advance. The same can be said of all other cultures and subcultures we don't know well, from preppies to hipsters, nerds and transvestites.

I don't have all
the answers
To all your whats
and whys
I see how doubt is hurting
How you agonize
I feel your body moving
And will help you stabilize.
– Marnix Pauwels [translation
by Jitske Kramer]

Liminality: in the meantime

In some cases, change is not gradual, but rather a sudden upheaval. This happens, for instance, in a corporate merger, or when a new system is introduced that changes everyone's workflow. Or when you're confronted with new supply chain partners, innovations, or participation processes. Anthropologists call such times of change 'liminality'. It's that no-man's land between two boundaries: it's neither this, nor that; the old order is gone, the new hasn't taken hold yet. The space of no longer and not yet. In liminal territory, old certainties are called into question, we learn new languages and customs, shift balances of power and create new stories and identities. This is exciting and fun. The sky is the limit. It's also scary, because anything is possible. It's easy to step into the pitfall of judgment and prejudice during this phase, because it's human to point the finger at someone else instead of changing yourself. It is also the phase that is most suited to learning, talking, trying to make sense of things, creating new meanings together. This is how the new reality is shaped, step by step, decision by decision.

IMAGE: UNSPLASH

YOU ARE NOT LOST
YOU ARE HERE
... AND I AM HERE WITH YOU

This process can take a day or several years, depending on how big the change is and on how you lead. Now is the time to show inclusive leadership. Not only is it key to create that daily, safe space, but someone also needs to shoulder the burden of this extra tension.

Holding space: extra attention at those special moments

I already mentioned it when I summed up the characteristics of inclusive leadership: when conflict arises and people don't know what to do, leaders need to step up and absorb part of the tension. Holding space means making room for what's going on, particularly when things are tense. It means examining the matter, however painful or sad, so that the next step and the solution can present themselves. In other words, it's not about focusing on a solution, but making visible where we're at. It's about getting every viewpoint, emotion and power issue on the table.

This isn't always an easy role to play. Sometimes, leaders can't do it alone and need help from a professional. This can be someone from within the organization or outside of it. Someone who can help organize campfire talks about topics that go beyond the everyday, creating space for transformation. Often, it is not the leader, the chief, who leads such sessions, but a consultant, inspirational speaker, coach, facilitator or trainer. In tribal terms, a magician. How do you deal with cultural clashes? How do you respond to people's various knee-jerk reactions to the unknown? Think back to my explanation of culture shock and the jam circle with its phase of opening up to everything there is, to create an open-mindedness that allows you to listen to all the differences in wonder and uncertainty.

People can react in surprisingly many ways to insecurity. Below you will find an overview of six types of reactions, each followed by tips to deal with them. Obviously, this overview is not exhaustive, but it does make some suggestions of how you might handle the dynamics of uncertainty. If you look closely, you'll see that this is a different take on how people deal with differences (p. 77), the types of fragmentation (p. 57) and the question of whose approach will win out (p. 163). And remember, no one expects, or should expect, the leader to have all the answers. It's a shared problem, after all. This entails that leaders do not necessarily act as truth seekers or judges who have to decide who is right and wrong. Don't choose sides or play favorites, but create space for everyone's emotions, thoughts, ideas, concerns, wishes and beliefs. Be sincere and independent.

From there, solutions will start to emerge. To help this process along, you can use the Deep Democracy steps or the Polarity Map from Chapter 3 on Truth.

So, here are six typical reactions to insecurity, followed by tips on dealing with them:

1 Attacking

People with strong convictions often go in attack mode when they feel uncertain. These convictions can pertain to many different things: religious beliefs, opinions on how work flows should be structured or dogmas on the position of women. Attack is a frequently used reflex from people in a majority or power position. 'This is how we do things. End of story!'

Characteristic behavior: Aggression, anger, tears.

💡 *Tips*: Stay calm. Repeat what you've heard. Acknowledge the other person's feelings and their right to feel this way. Take a short break. Check with others what is afoot. Listen and empathize. Realize that emotion is also a way into dialogue, that it is simply part of the process.

2 Resisting

People who become defensive want to prevent others from interfering in their business, their personal space. If you feel assaulted by difference, you'll get defensive. In that case, debate might only have an adverse effect and prompt everyone to entrench themselves even more firmly. A dialogue—truly listening to each other and staying open to being influenced by someone else's thoughts and feelings—would be more productive, as it will help to clarify people's underlying intentions and needs.

Characteristic behavior: Defensiveness, 'yes, but', 'no', sticking to your own ideas, refusing to listen. Defensiveness readily leads to blaming others and expressing prejudices and stereotypes in a recriminating way.

💡 *Tips*: Acknowledge the criticism as the individual's personal truth. Explore their personal needs. Listen and empathize. Temporarily change the subject. Take a short break and talk to everyone involved. Focus on the desired common objective.

3 Denying

People who are in denial simply act like there are no differences and there is no clash. They insist on staying blissfully ignorant, keeping their head in the sand. Some take a more active approach and explain away the differences. More emotional types might freeze. They can see the differences, but have no idea how to deal with them and cling to what they know. That's panic.

Characteristic behavior: Acting as if nothing's wrong, laughing to relieve the tension, acting relaxed but showing tension in the eyes, withdrawal, staying silent during conversations, deflecting attention by quickly changing the subject.

 Tips: Allow 'deniers' to take the time they need. It's fine for someone to seek safety in this way. Invite them to 'come back', seek contact. Listen. Compliment them on their calmness. Ask questions. Draw a connection to the changes, the others' needs. Start a conversation about dealing with uncertainty. Talk about how you yourself deal with this. Help 'deniers' to connect to the team.

4 Isolating yourself (and the other)

People who isolate themselves take maximum distance from the other by avoiding contact. In society, this is expressed in cultural ghettos: the habit of remaining safely among 'our kind of people'. Sometimes this is translated into actual physical isolation, as in gated communities, security fences and walls. Isolation in teams is recognizable in employees who have their own separate lunch table or in subgroups who always take on the same type of task.

Characteristic behavior: Actively excluding others. Not inviting some people to meetings or team events. Deliberately refraining from seeking some people's opinions and withholding feedback. Not acknowledging certain people's presence. Throwing them out of e-mail groups or blocking them on social media.

Tips: Initiate contact. Listen. Set limits: you are a team, so exclusion goes against your inclusion goals and kills your safe space. It's essential to seek dialogue and stay in touch. Speak with the excluded people, too. What's their story? Ensure that both groups start talking again as soon as possible. Don't let things get out of hand. Perhaps there are options for living alongside each other (as I discussed under No Way on p. 164), but maybe not.

5 Adapting

Adapting to the others' standards prevents a lot of conflict. It's a knee-jerk reaction you see a lot in people in minority positions. Too much adapting can get painful after a while. Your cultural identity and its associated qualities are ignored. This causes tensions that can erupt unexpectedly. In a team, it may be pleasant when a 'different' group adapts to the majority, but not seeing or listening to certain team members is risky in the long run.

Characteristic behavior: Acting like nothing's wrong, *smooth sailing.* Possibly, subtle forms of saying yes and doing no. Making little jokes, meting out little jabs and gossiping.

Tips: Look closely to determine whether the adjustments are a conscious choice or based on fear. Stay aware of the power of the majority, dominance blindness and minority stress. Be aware of your own position: do you belong to the majority or the minority? Be on the lookout for sadness and pain. Ask everyone to name their needs and concerns. Continue to jam.

6 Neutrally mediating: engaged, yet independent

Someone in the group notices the tension and starts mediating in a way that brings the different parties closer, but without showing their own true colors. It's fine to play this role to get and keep communication going. Still, in the long run, it starts to get uncomfortable when someone stays emotionally disengaged from the conversation and dynamics. What does the mediator think and feel? It's important for everyone in the group to be emotionally involved, to empathize, otherwise the group may, at some point, start to perceive the mediator as matter out of space and an easy scapegoat to blame everything on.

Characteristic behavior: Having an active, exploratory mindset, engaging with everyone, asking questions, creating agendas, making observations about process. Keeping opinions or emotions out of the conversation and staying out of conflicts. Connecting with both the nays and the ayes in a debate by taking both camps equally seriously: asking questions and giving them time and attention.

Tips: Use your powerful, connective ability and invite everyone to express their own ideas, emotions, judgments and needs. No one is always neutral. Get involved. Make emotional connections with the issue and the people, while remaining independent by examining and taking on board everyone's viewpoint.

How to talk in a Safe Space or while Holding Space: The Check-In

Borrowing from Deep Democracy, the Check-In is a great way of talking in a safe space or while holding space. It's a preamble, without any of the characteristics of a dialogue or debate. Everyone is asked to share their thoughts and feelings regarding a particular talking point, phrased as a question. This is called 'sharing and dumping': you say what you want to say without anyone interrupting or asking for clarification. Once everyone's had a turn, the moderator summarizes it all: these are the themes that are relevant in this group. It's important to avoid calling on people to speak in the order they happen to be sitting in. People decide for themselves when they're ready to talk. You're the moderator, so you go first. Suppose you want to know what people think of the leadership in your organization. You first ask the question: What do you think of the leadership in this organization right now? Next, you answer this question first. This creates openness and sets a good example. Openness begets openness, but reticence shuts people down. If your answer stays on the surface, the next person will probably stay on the surface, too. Once everyone has checked in, you need to summarize what has been said and then ask: Does someone want to respond to what has been said, or does anyone want to add to or clarify something they've said, or does anyone want to ask someone a question, or is anyone upset, or glad or sad about anything, or want to make an observation about anything? This opens the door to dialogue and possibly debate, too.

Zone of Discomfort: clashing ideals

It always gets tense when you make explicit what has been unsaid for a long time. We've been beating around the bush for ages, we've done everything we can to make and keep it unmentionable, but now the time has come. This is the *zone of discomfort*, a term formulated by Dutch sociologist Jan Kooistra, and popularized by André Wierdsma, professor emeritus of Organization and Co-creation at Nyenrode Business University. It's a wonderful term that denotes the discomfort we experience when plucking up the courage to speak frankly with each other about thorny issues. It's uncomfortable and it takes a lot of effort to talk about these with people from every rung on the corporate and social ladder, with every kind of ranking present and in the knowledge that privilege and pecking orders may start to shift.

In the zone of discomfort, people question the status quo. The dialogue is not just about the rules of the game, which are based on judgments like good or bad, ugly or pretty, true or false. It's also about what we find good or bad, pretty or ugly, true or false. That's why it's called the zone of discomfort: because re-evaluating deeply rooted assumptions and principles that we can barely articulate is stressful and arduous. At times like this, when our ideals clash, it can feel like our diverse opinions and ideals just drive us apart. The debates that make us feel this way are on issues like freedom of expression, God's existence, men who won't shake a woman's hand, banning face-covering women's garments, gay marriage, the global division of wealth, abortion, sustainable energy solutions, more strictly controlling big finance and curbing salaries and bonuses for top-level managers.

It takes courage to openly discuss the principles we want to live and work by and to really listen to every voice, regardless of the speaker's ranking, status or current privilege. It requires courage to freely speak our minds and if we can't speak freely, to say so. Seen in this light, defining your organization's core principles and the conduct conducive to it, is not something you cram into a late Friday afternoon meeting.

The zone of discomfort is where deeply rooted and seemingly self-evident truths are put up for discussion and change. It's where you're challenged to stay open, curious, in dialogue and to question your own truths, even when your core values are under attack. The bigger the discomfort, the greater the odds that people will resort to power play and start excluding others from the conversation in subtle and not-so-subtle ways. Some are not invited to the table for meetings and others made out to be liars. The excluded are sometimes accused of spreading fake news or made the target of a smear campaign. Only those who are seen as credible by the dominant group get a chance to speak their mind. And credibility depends on whether you stay within the bounds of 'the real story', within the existing, received principles; credibility will be your reward if you rub elbows with the incumbent powermongers and if you continue to shore up the dominant narrative. The minority voice, the dissenting opinion, will get less and less airtime and the resistance line (p. 117) will kick in. The public debate will feature only socially desirable and politically feasible opinions. The people who are still involved in the conversation will think less and less independently. Instead, they will respond more and more to what they think is acceptable, in order not to be shut out or ostracized. They will self-censor to prevent exclusion.

Inclusion is not a fashionable marketing strategy. It is not a short-term training course. Actually, fully taking diversity on board and making it part of the decision-making process is an emotional job that involves sensemaking, legitimacy and power. It is a conversation that goes beyond language. You need to collect insider information to understand the context, history and relationships that implicitly determine the meaning of principles. The zone of discomfort requires you to stay true to your own ideas, while also staying in contact with others. In other words, it requires you to stick to the existing cultural rules and principles while at the same time daring to question them and allowing others to do the same.

When we expose our own deepest, invisible thoughts and feelings, we enter the zone of discomfort. Here, we need to slow down, to take time to process our own feelings and others'. This type of conversation has to take place outside of the regular order and workflow. I call it a campfire talk; it's where a joint transformation becomes possible. The closer our reflections on ingrained thinking and behavior gets to our core identity, the harder it gets to jam. Some manage to create new synergy, but sometimes the most you can get out of the dialogue is mutual empathy and respect and ways to cohabitate. The story you write together won't be a shared one, but a story in which your differences can coexist.

'Those who know do not speak. Those who speak do not know.'
– Lao Tzu

Independently, together. Inclusion at this level is not easy to achieve, but it's fantastic for those who do.

Continuing to act: temporary work agreements

Perhaps you hope to completely resolve all big issues in one go at every level of standards, emotions, principles, procedures, regulations and structures and then to roll out this solution step-by-step or in a waterfall process. I've got bad news for you; it won't happen. There will always be uncertainties. This is known as dynamism. Seen in this light, change is mainly growth. Jamming means taking action based on uncertainties.

This can be an unnerving idea for classic organizations with top-down leadership and a penchant for checks, balances and control. Inclusion is about the dynamics between people and those processes are erratic and unpredictable. To deal with this sea of uncertainties and to create some semblance of order in all these fluid possibilities, André Wierdsma invented the concept of the Temporary Work Agreement, or TWA: in your explorations, you don't have to come up with the Absolute Truth, but with something that works for the time being. Finding the One Truth is next to impossible anyway. To deal with difference and attain a balanced whole, you don't need to find eternal solutions. Temporary solutions are fine, as they're enough for everyone to get on with their work. TWAs are always *temporary*; meaning we can change them. TWAs are *working* agreements, which means they're pragmatic; we're all working on the same thing. And lastly, TWAs are *agreements*; meaning that people support their wording and feel it leaves enough room for all who sign on. Based on this interaction and a continuing series of small decisions, we slowly build trust in each other.

Courageous conversations in the zone of discomfort

Use the inclusive skills from the previous chapter, such as frequently asking: 'Is there anyone who has another idea?' and 'Who can relate to this?' Discuss the rules of conduct and ethics, talk about knowing and understanding and about principles and sense-making. The following practical questions can help. Replace the blank (___) with the value or theme under review, like *trust*, for example.

- How does ___ (trust) play a role in your personal life?
- What examples do you know of ___ (trust) in your workplace, your own job, your life?
- Do you have a role model, someone who is good at showing ___ (trust) in your organization, or outside of it?
- What kind of behavior goes with ___ (trust)? Try to be as explicit and clear as possible. How can you display this kind of behavior (more)? How can you encourage others to show this kind of behavior?
- What kind of behavior do you need to stop showing in your personal life if you want to increase ___ (trust)? What do you need to stop in your role at work? How are you going to do this? How are you going to call others out on this?
- What procedures and structures foster ___ (trust)? What procedures and structures obstruct it?

Make a list of actions.

We're all more than familiar with the notion that everyone in the organization 'needs to be on the same page'. Granted, this is important, because it means the story is the same everywhere. Yet, it's madness to delay action until everyone is on the same page. Even if we're not all there, André Wierdsma argues, we can start to take action. That keeps us moving forward, gets us unstuck. Although it's true that you can't undo an action, in the sense of what's done is done, you *can* change course by acting in different or unexpected ways. When that happens, people will be more prone to go along with it if the emphasis is on the temporary nature of those actions. This means that even if we're not on the same page yet in terms of story and thought processes, our actions already are.

The risk of fear and uncertainty

In Chapter 1, on Difference, I talked about how people are prone to call for strong leadership in times of uncertainty. The scary thing is that they often end up with a strong leader and that this is usually not someone who acts out of a sense of equality and humanity. A perfect example is found in the book *Fascism: A Warning*, written by former US Secretary of State Madeleine Albright. She was born to Jewish parents from the Czech Republic. They fled the Nazis to England, returned to their home country after the war only to flee again from the Communists when Madeleine was eleven years old. In her book, Albright draws parallels between 20th century fascism and 21st century methods of seizing power. Her examples include:

- a call for a mythical, 'pure nation';
- political slogans aimed at creating a rift, such as 'build that wall', 'drain the swamp';
- denouncing intellectuals, journalists and academics (e.g. climate scientists) as rabble rousers, conspiracy theorists and fake scientists;
- sow doubt in the shared, public discourse (social media, newspapers, TV), which makes it difficult to see the difference between facts and rumors, lies and manipulation;
- claim victimhood for the dominant group, e.g. Trump trying to make his electorate believe that white American men are the real victims of the #MeToo debate;
- fear mongering by calling immigrants drug criminals, terrorists and rapists;
- make people feel their jobs and income are at risk by saying that 'they' are here to 'take our jobs' and 'live it up at our expense.'

Whenever such polarizing sentiments appear, it's particularly important to combat them by continuing to talk about what connects us and by telling those who think they're lacking something materially to do a reality check. Unfortunately, casting doubt and spreading negative gossip is much easier than spreading a constructive, positive story that leaves room for contradictions. Just think of school or the company restaurant, where rumors are rife. It's fun to create a stir. It gives us an excuse to raise our voice and call each other names. And we all know, where there's smoke, there's fire... But let me turn that sentence around: if we don't take a stand against the smoke, we'll indeed have ourselves a fire, sooner or later. Not the type of fire I'd like to see, however.

How tension can lead to conflict

If we can't reach an agreement and if we stop discussing our differences and similarities and the irritations that arise between us, things will get worse. The mutual trust will erode and might, in the long run, disappear altogether. In Inside the No, Myrna Lewis, founder of the Lewis Deep Democracy method, describes conflict's various phases and how to resolve it. The solution is very simple: start talking and, above all, listening. To *yourself, the other, each other. Use the Jam Circle a lot. Open yourself to emotions and everything that's going on. Explore every viewpoint and create ways of dealing with difference. Use the triple perspective and other discussion methods from Chapter 3, on Truth.*

You can observe Lewis's stages of conflict at home, on the world stage and in your workplace. I will use an example from the household arena, because we've all been there, I assume.

1 Tension
You keep running into a certain person and every time it happens, you feel how different the two of you are. Yet, your differences feel exciting and attractive. The other challenges you, pulls you out of your comfort zone. Everything feels new, refreshing and fun! Soon, your new significant other asks you to come along on a Saturday trip to the farmers' market. Normally, you would never go there, because it feels so pointless to endlessly chat with the farmers who sell there while tasting all their cheeses and sausages. You just want to get the whole grocery shopping thing over with as quickly as possible. But now your partner has invited you to the farmers' market, and you're happy to go along. Everything feels fun, even that!

I grab my hand

I free myself from the toxic web of thoughts. I grab my hand
and walk. I run. I flee from the words that turn and spin me.
I cry out at every syllable that oppresses me with maddening
precision.

I grab my hand and walk. I keep walking. I feel the tears,
but I'm not allowed to cry. I grab my hand and walk. One by one,
I rip the prying judgements from my soul. Letter by letter, word
by word, I shake the accusations off.

I fight against the smothering grip of control. I grab my hand
and walk. Step. By. Step. In panic and hurt to the very bone.
And suddenly. One morning. I start forming new sentences.
Word. For. Word.

My new open end.

Jitske Kramer

However, this doesn't last forever. You eventually grow tired of the shopping expeditions. You don't understand why you have to tag along. But apparently, you're expected to.

And you do want the other to keep liking you. So, in order not to hurt the other, you come up with ways of dealing with it, without saying what's bothering you. For instance, you can only get your hair done on Saturday morning, or you have to help a friend move house. Or you find a place to sit down and have a coffee instead. If this requirement to go to the market starts to irritate you and you get upset that you can never plan anything else on that day, it's high time to raise the subject with the other. If you don't do that, you'll enter phase 2.

2 Double messages

Your irritation keeps growing and because it's not something you openly discuss, you start sending double-edged messages. When the other asks you to come shopping, you say, 'Of course,' while your facial expression and body language tell a different story. You don't want to be a whiner, so you suck it up and go along. Before long, however, you start coming up with more and more reasons why you can't do the Saturday morning shopping. Or your significant other notices that you are constantly on your smartphone while you're at the market, supposedly together.

Still not ready to raise the issue? Wait 'til you hit phase 3.

3 You talk, but without the other

You're disgruntled and you argue, but in your head only. 'Oh no, is it Saturday? Another market day. Oh, crap. I guess I'll just have to play along. If the other can't see that I hate it … Why do we ALWAYS have to spend our Saturdays this way? Is there really NOTHING better to do? It's ridiculous. And selfish, too.'

You start making funny faces while discussing on the phone where and when you'll meet for your weekly shopping trip. You start talking about it with others. You gossip about the other, but then feel guilty about it. Meanwhile, it's getting harder and harder to communicate normally with the other. Your feelings about the market visits are contaminating other matters. For example, the other asks you to make dinner, and you find yourself thinking: 'How dare you ask me to cook dinner? I've already spent my time going to that stupid market. You're asking too much!'

Your Saturdays together are getting less and less pleasant and there's more and more grumbling. In the meantime, you're now also expected to visit the in-laws. On top of all the other expectations... Raising the issue is getting harder and harder. You should probably have said something sooner.

4 The conflict proliferates

You've allowed so many irritations to stack up, transferring the original feeling to so many other issues, that you've lost sight of what the original problem was. Your irritation at having to go to the market has spread into a fuzzy, unclear soup of pent-up dissatisfaction, irritation, judgments, needs and emotions. This is a tense phase, because the original conflict about a concrete matter has now gotten tangled up with many other images and stories that you two have about each other.

Talking has now become really scary. Things might go wrong.

5 We polarize, invent caricatures and talk in stereotypes

Because you've forgotten the root cause of your dissatisfaction, you start inventing caricatures to make it appear logical to yourself. Neutral oppositions such as male vs. female or young vs. old are charged with meaning and personal emotion: 'Of course, he only thinks of himself, typically male.' Or, 'For heaven's sake, always with the nagging, always creating trouble, that's women for you.' Or, 'So, a real Johnson: just like everyone else in that family.'

This mechanism occurs widely. In another scenario, you might find yourself thinking:
'There's an American for you, they're so superficial.'
'Those good old boys from the country club are gaming the system.'
'Of course he has no sense of humor: he's German.'
'Such a typical CEO, always the big ego.'
'What do you expect from a sales rep? Actual product knowledge?'
'He's a Roman Catholic. They can't be trusted.'
'They're Jewish, right? I guess the war is to blame again.'
'There we go again. Another angry Arab.'
And so on.

Once you start mixing your personal anger with caricatures, it gets really nasty. You're simply looking to confirm your bias, so you will definitely succeed. Alienation continues to grow and in your mind, the other stops being human and slowly turns into an object, an intangible cog in the great machine. You don't know how to even begin to repair this.

The conflict has reached a critical level, particularly if it involves entire groups of people. Polarization of conflicts happens in societies, families and organizations alike. Polarization means that we have turned an original, tangible conflict into a polarity, with a made-up 'us vs. them' issue and unclear ownership. At first, we could still see who owned the problem, but now it's completely unclear who should be held accountable for what and who can take decisive action. It's become too emotional, too widespread and far too vague. Everyone's behavior has become more irrational and, from an outsider perspective, more illogical.

Mutual trust is at an all-time low. We think: it's no use trying, they never listen to anything anyway. Even mediators encounter distrust: politicians are in it for themselves, democratic process is just for show, they'll do what suits them anyway, no one has our interests at heart. This is how we often end up feeling in the midst of a polarized issue: helpless.

The only good way to combat this is to rediscover what we have in common. We need to step out of the compulsive, oversimplified thinking of an imagined black-and-white opposition and look at it with a new set of glasses. We need to lift ourselves out of the polarization flow and pinpoint the underlying, shared issue. To return to my example of 'going to the market', we should ask: How do we make sure we get healthy food on the table? Or, how do we make Saturdays a fun time for both of us? Bart Brandsma, a Dutch philosopher and expert on polarization, puts it simply: 'We have to stop putting our mutual relationship in focus and at stake and concentrate on the actual issue we need to solve.'

6 Separate

If we can't find any commonality, then we've reached the end. You're exhausted, you're done, the other doesn't listen. Actually, no one listens. Clearly, it's not your fault! You've lost sight of the root cause of the conflict and your own role in it, too. It's all gotten way out of hand. We're going to wage war, or lawyer up for a bad divorce. We want the other to back off, leave the house, get fired. We want the other thrown out of the country, their passports revoked. We want to build a wall.

If you want to try and find a new way of coexisting this late in the day, both parties will have to dig deep and be prepared to discuss the underlying issues. The question now becomes whether separation is even possible. If you have a big mortgage based on both your incomes, it can be practically impossible. Not to mention the kids, if you have them, because they bind you forever. Not everyone can just pick up and move to escape the neighbors they keep quarreling with. Likewise, you might want to quit your job, but will you find another position in the same industry if you leave on bad terms? Can you really afford to leave that professional partnership? And on a world scale: can the UK really cut all ties with the EU? Can the US truly isolate itself?

A big mistake people make in a conflict, is to think in terms of winning and losing. When you do that, everything is riding on the outcome. It may be hard to set aside your desire to win, but it makes a huge difference. The question shouldn't be whether it's going to be your way or their way, but what might work for both of you. Inclusion is not a finite but an infinite game.

You also need to realize that people have a harder time giving in when there are deep, meaningful principles at stake than when it's about sensemaking or insignificant rules. To come back to my example of the Saturday market: maybe the other insists on going to the market to buy organic food or to support local farmers, while you are a fan of supermarkets and find all these organic, vegan superfoods a bunch of bull. If that's the case, the issue never was about how you spend your Saturday mornings. It's not just about behavior, but also about what that behavior signifies. It's about principles and meaningfulness. That makes it a zone of major discomfort, particularly this late in the game.

There are just three options left:
- Separation is possible and it's what one party (or all) want. If so, find a mediator, come to an arrangement, go about it as politely as you can, leave each other alone and greet each other as you would any other human being if you happen to cross paths.
- Separation is not possible (different groups of people live in the same neighborhood), but we can re-establish some form of contact, to find what we have in common and to see that we all perceive reality slightly differently, that we all have a share of the blame for the conflict and that we can learn from each other. In this case, we can start working on resolving separate issues. Experience has shown that in order to do this, you need to go through every phase of the conflict, in reverse order. You might even end up liking

each other again and remembering what you had in common. In this complete transformation, the enemy becomes human again and we end up seeing each other in a genuinely different light.

- Separation is not possible (different groups of people live in the same neighborhood), but we can't find the courage, willingness and energy to work it out. The only option to prevent further escalation is to establish a minimum of contact and to ask everyone involved what they need to be able to coexist in peace. The two sides will run into each other and/or need each other now and then, so what will make this arrangement livable? Such a dialogue will produce 'lukewarm' communication, devoid of new insults and barbs that can rekindle the conflict. It requires everyone to practice restraint, which is obviously not easy. Chances are the whole thing will erupt again if there's a new incident. Little things can suddenly escalate into big conflicts if the polarization and underlying conflicts have not been resolved.

Talks we avoided: organized arguments

If yelling is the only option, then that's where we have to start. Let's have a *screaming session, or as I've also called it: 'the talk we avoided'. It's a way to deal with the chaos of conflict in the most structured way possible. I've described this type of organized argument, developed by Myrna Lewis*, in *Deep Democracy.*

Below I will describe this conversation model, which fits in the fifth step of the Lewis method of Deep Democracy as outlined in the previous chapter . I've portrayed an argument between two people, but with a few modifications this can also be applied to two groups. By the way, you can likewise decide to have this type of argument at an earlier stage, before it's almost too late. It can even be used in the first phase of conflict: why would I or wouldn't I join the other in going to the market? Particularly when the conflict is relatively new, an organized argument can provide new insights and can even make it fun to discover where you differ and what you have in common. An organized argument works as follows:

1 Set the safety rules

If things haven't escalated yet, you can skip this step. However, sometimes, you need to start by creating the right conditions for a talk. Dialogue can only happen once both parties realize there's more than one truth and that one side's perceptions, emotions and opinions about something are not more valid than the other. Only if both sides are willing to learn from each other can they both benefit and find a good way to deal with their differences. At this point, you may need to reach some very practical agreements, like 'we are going to talk without yelling' or perhaps 'this is our chance to really let go and yell all we want'. You may want to set a time limit for your talk, or the opposite: not talk on the clock, for once.

2 Say it all!

Say it all. Say everything you've been thinking but not saying, but take turns. No interrupting each other, no ping-ponging. You agree who gets to go first and the other listens, does not cut in, comment, defend or correct. Once the first speaker is completely done and has said everything they want to say, it's the other person's turn. Once the second speaker is done, the first can speak again. Continue until everything has been said. Don't sugarcoat your criticisms; pour your heart out. You may find this part of your argument to be painful and, at the same time, funny and a relief. Don't get scared or flustered when you feel that things have just gotten worse now. There are two more steps to take in this conversation.

3 What hit home?

This is the most essential step. Some things that were said, either by yourself or the other, didn't have much impact. But other things really hit home, getting you in the gut or giving you new insight (aha!). You may have gotten goosebumps, started to laugh, had to fight back tears or felt anger well up. Reflect on why that particular remark had such a strong effect on you. After you've thought about this for a while, share your insights with the other and vice versa. Take care not to fall into the trap of reverting back to 'attack mode', e.g. 'When you said I don't do enough household chores, I was hurt because you never see all the things I do.' That's not the idea. Instead, phrase it as a sentence that says something about yourself, e.g. 'When you said I don't do enough household chores, I was hurt because I realized how quietly I go about the things I do and how little I've stood up for myself in that regard.'

4 Resolve the issue

In the last step of this process, we look at how all these insights can help us find a way to deal with our differences. We take our insights back to the original issue, the reason for this talk. What are our thoughts on this issue now that we've heard each other's viewpoints? What needs resolving? Come to an agreement. You'll find that some practical problems can now indeed be worked out. At the same time, some broader issues have been broached that need to be explored more deeply. One talk won't solve everything. We all know it's not that simple.

When conflicts become intractable and deepen into polarization

If dealing with difference and diversity was easy, we'd have very different conversations at the water cooler and the 6 o'clock news would change completely. Instead of looking to resolve conflicts, we stoke them. Give us just a whiff of controversy, let alone a brawl or a riot and we're all over it like flies. We love a good fight! We enjoy gawking at anger, particularly if we're not the focus of it. And we love talking about it, too. So what if that remark made that meeting tense? It did spice things up! Did you hear what he called her? Polarized conflicts support an entire industry of talk shows, reality programs, tabloids, songs, comedy and newsmagazines.

Obviously, intractable conflicts and polarization aren't so fun if you're the target, or if you get caught in the crossfire. Usually, we only end up in that situation when we've neglected to seize one of the many opportunities to start a dialogue. We've stayed silent, perhaps for fear of starting something that might spin out of control. But just look at where that got us! Talking is essential, as it determines whether we can deal with difference. After all, peaceful coexistence is achieved by continually finding good solutions to conflicts. And talking is how you do that.

Polarities: two seemingly contradictory aspects that are inextricably linked. You can't resolve a polarity by choosing either side; you have to find a balance.

Polarization: oppositions that can't tolerate each other and that have an impact on people's identity. Polarization can take on extreme, or extremely violent, forms.

In his book *Polarisation*, Bart Brandsma not only describes the polarization process, but also defines the different roles people play during that process. He lays out the type of talk we need to have in each particular phase in order to get unstuck and meet each other halfway. I like his refreshing way of looking at conflict. For an in-depth analysis, please read Brandsma's book. Below, I have summarized a few of his lessons, because understanding conflict better can help improve the quality of our jam sessions.

Conflicts result from similarities

We tend to think that conflicts arise from our differences and that our clashes are the result of divergent ideas, beliefs, visions, interests, customs, cultures or religions. This is not so, according to Brandsma. The root cause of conflict lies in what we have in common, because we are all alike and want the same things. If everyone wanted something else, there would be little tension and everybody would do their own thing. But if people want the same thing, there's a potential for scarcity and that's what causes us to clash. People want material, practical things like jobs, income, a roof over their head and food, but they also have symbolic wants, such as appreciation and social status. Jealousy is the result of everyone thinking they are pursuing their own, original needs, while this is not the case. Even if the dinner table is full of special desserts, my children will both want that last brownie. It's enough to drive you crazy. According to Brandsma, this is because we are constantly influenced by that which the other finds appealing. That is the be-all and end-all of the marketing industry and the rise of influencers on Instagram. Others model our desires, but are therefore also in the way of what we want: there's just one last brownie, one CEO role, one keynote speaker, one talk show host... We like to think we're unique and original, but we're nothing but copycats. And our copycat behavior is what causes conflicts.

How talking can fuel conflict

As a conflict escalates, the solution at any point is to talk. But that talk must be a real conversation in which every participant opens up, allows him or herself to be moved and shares personal feelings and ideas. We can only achieve shades of grey if everyone takes responsibility for their own share of the conflict and acknowledges the other's point of view. In a dialogue, we can dig deeper and share our perceptions. However, if our talk turns into a debate, which precludes the possibility of a follow-up dialogue, our different viewpoints will harden (see p. 158). If our arguments get more toxic and personal and if we have descended into polarization, parodying and stereotyping, the debate becomes an emotional exchange. Instead of dialogue, we get stuck in monologues that we use to target each other. Everyone's attitude grows more and more entrenched. As you advance through the various stages of conflict that I described earlier, it gets increasingly harder to engage in a real talk. In fact, having a talk in which neither side is willing to question their own truth, show doubt or let themselves be moved only deepens the conflict. And if both parties enter into such a difficult and emotionally taxing conversation, without finding a solution, things will only escalate. As Brandsma puts it: talking can fuel polarization. If you stop adding fuel to the fire, the conversation about thorny issues will stop and the polarization will collapse. That's why it may be wiser to stop talking and only resume when there's room for nuance. While it's best, generally speaking, to start talking as soon as possible, if a conflict has polarized, it may be wiser for everyone to shut up for a while.

Roles in a polarized situation

That sounds easy, right? Just shut up for a while. Chill. Just wait and only resume talking about the underlying issue when you've calmed down. But everyone knows this doesn't always go smoothly. Managers, board members, politicians, neighbors, family members: we all know how to polarize. Polarization in a team means a lot of people are at loggerheads, but it's even worse when the whole organization—or society at large—is polarized. Where do we start, and how?

Brandsma has defined different roles people play in polarized situations, which are very recognizable and help us to get a bit of a grip on polarization's chaotic processes. All of us have played each of these roles at some point; they're all necessary and all present in any polarization process. Seeing them spelled out will make you more aware of them, which will allow you to consciously choose a role, or question whether the role you are playing is helpful.

In situations with two opposing groups, there's always someone who promotes their own group and will go to great lengths to defend it. Brandsma calls these individuals 'pushers'. In a polarized debate, the pushers claim the moral high ground and put the other down as 100% in the wrong. They provide the activist energy necessary to bring about change. Their conviction that they are morally right gives pushers an incredible amount of energy, focus and the emotion needed to kick-start change. However, pushers can also polarize a debate and obstruct the dynamics. This happens when pushers are focused on convincing everyone that evil lurks on the opposite side and that you have to choose whether you're with them, or against them. There's black and white, without any grey. The pusher has declared sides and is highly visible and therefore vulnerable, too. Toning down their point of view would mean loss of face. In their eyes, flip-floppers are of no use in this essentialist battle.

While pushers are pushing people and putting them on the spot, tension grows among the moderates to take a middle position. The 'silent midfielders' are the group of people who refuse to declare sides, either because the issue doesn't mean much to them or because it means an awful lot to them, but they refuse to get sucked into black-and-white thinking. If the pushers do their job well, the pressure to choose sides keeps growing. Choosing sides is what the 'joiners' do: it is their way of lessening the tension. They now belong to a group, with a strong leader and possibly even some slogans and symbols that reinforce group identity and status. They can stop thinking for themselves and can parrot their group's opinions. This helps them

Then I will stop

When you gobble me up in your assumptions
When my every word creates more haze and
you pull me into your world
When your story dictates who I may or may not be

Then I will stop our us
So I can be me

When you shatter me in your icy reception
When you fling all my soft back in my face
and threaten that "if I don't do this, that then all was for nothing"
When every attempt to talk suffocates me more

Then I will stop our talking
So I can be I

When you say sorry and keep on going
When you perceive my ease, my space, as an attack on you
And put others up against me
When you promise this today and the opposite tomorrow
When you act as if you own my being

Then I will stop my love
So I can be me again

Jitske Kramer

'Love will go away if we can't communicate and share meaning'
– David Bohm

to reduce their own stress. They tag along, but aren't pushers. They typically say things like 'I don't agree completely, but they've got a point.' Joiners have no interest in a rapprochement between both sides. They don't want the pushers to adopt more subtle opinions. The good vs. bad mold will continue to fuel their sense of moral superiority and consolidate their position. Pushers and joiners hold each other captive and selectively listen to stories to make their own moral righteousness resound ever louder.

High time for some real dialogue, don't you think? Exactly, but the problem is that at this stage of polarization, talking only fans the flames. The role that calls for dialogue, is the 'bridge-builder' in Brandsma's terms. Bridge-builders take a neutral, non-partisan stance, have an overview of the extremes and shortcomings on both sides and do their best to arrange a sit-down, in the hopes of facilitating a nuanced, rational talk. Alas, such a talk is an ideal opportunity for pushers to launch back into their monologues. And before you know it, the media will get wind of the controversy and this will only put the whole polarization process in overdrive. If this goes unchecked, everyone ends up choosing sides. If eventually there are no moderates left, we have only big groups of people who face each other in a tribal conflict, civil war, or merger battle that wipes out entire departments. Sadly, the first person to be blamed for this is the neutral person in the middle: our bridge-builder. After all, neither side fully trusts bridge-builders because they refuse to take sides. This makes the bridge-builder a perfect figure to focus anger on. The bridge-builder then ends up in the role of 'scapegoat', the person who can be used by everyone else as a screen that they can project their guilt and anger onto. This is the danger zone for professionals like mayors, the police, teachers, HR departments and externally contracted trainers and coaches.

So, no more talking?

No, indeed. Sometimes it's better not to talk. As Brandsma puts it, polarization dynamics is a many-headed monster that takes on a life of its own in a compelling dynamic of memories, thoughts, discussions, debates, rhetoric and posturing. Polarization is only partly rational, and largely irrational, emotional and uncontrollable. That's why it renders us so helpless. Us vs. them thinking contributes to this elusive phenomenon. Once the situation has grown polarized, it is imperative to listen closely to determine which conflict in the tangle of oppositions has the sharpest emotional edge. And then, to decide whether a talk between the two sides is more likely to fan the flames, or restore calm.

It's important to deny these good vs. bad dynamics a breeding ground and to counteract the tyranny of black-and-white thinking as rigorously as possible. In my experience, one of the measures that is most helpful is to accept that diversity is part of life and that there will always be us vs. them oppositions. It helps not to deny this, but to acknowledge it and to open a dialogue about these oppositions at the first signs of rising tension. To this end, we need to carefully arrange our liminal zones so they are conducive to constructive talks and meetings. We need to be willing to go to our zone of discomfort, and to dare say what we think while maintaining a connection. Sure, we're scared of what might surface. But what's much scarier than that first, awkward conversation, is what might happen if we let things 'run their course.'

▶ *The various roles during polarization, with the corresponding needs for types of talk, e.g. a pusher wants to hold a monologue. It's not necessarily wise to go along with this. Based on a diagram by Bart Brandsma.*

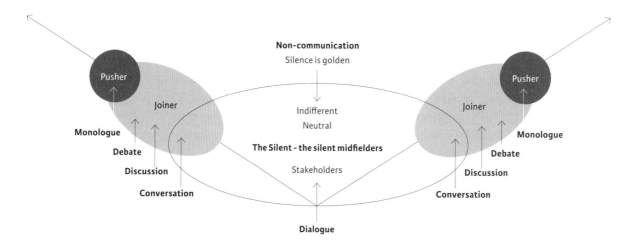

IMAGE: UNSPLASH

Polarizing is learned (and can be unlearned, too)

It is hard to handle conflicts well. It's not at all hard to worsen a conflict, however. Just like it's hard to connect; it takes time and effort, while polarization is easy and takes no time at all. This is how you polarize a conflict:

1. Select an opposition.
2. Add as many ideas, stereotypes and emotions to it as possible.
3. Leave out any shade of grey if possible.
4. Talk about the others as barbarians, 'retards' or animals. De-humanize them.
5. Continue to fuel the fire by adding more images.
6. Stop listening.
7. Regard your position as the truth.
8. Regard all other stances, therefore, as false.
9. Continue to hold monologues.
10. If possible, add some symbolism for extra effect.

And voila!

How to put more trust in the unknown

It helps to acknowledge that inclusion is a huge, emotional challenge. Diversity is not a rational issue. It involves basic emotions like fear and stress. When I meet a group of people whose (cultural) background I don't know and I'm a little nervous about it, I shouldn't act like I don't care. Chances are I'm going to channel my awkwardness into projection. Facing my fears, though, makes it easier to understand what's going on. So, it helps to acknowledge our discomfort.

The more I understand myself and others, the more I can enjoy difference. In order to get there, we need to talk, even when that's hard. And let's be realistic about it: we will never understand each other completely. In any case, the other will not always understand things in the way I want them to understand it. There will always be differences and there will always be a battle for the things we all want, like income, recognition and prestige.

Trusting each other also means trusting that we can see eye to eye, even in the uncertainty of not-knowing or not-understanding. Trusting that we can find each other's beat, despite—or rather, *thanks to*—everyone's individual sound. Trusting that we'll get there, sometimes by not taking ourselves or each other too seriously and seeing the humor in things. And sometimes by earnestly talking with each other. When there is a lot of diversity, we need to make things explicit more so than we're used to. After all, implicit norms are not the same for everyone, so not everyone can see or hear the applicable codes. We need to make things easier. Help each other understand. And show an interest in each other's world. Be open-minded and curious. What does the city look like from a wheelchair perspective? What does a Muslim woman take away from that newspaper article? What goes on in a gay bar? What happens in a Roman Catholic church service? What does management lose sleep over? What does a day in the life of a teacher look like? Ask questions. Investigate. Meet each other, as fellow human beings. And stay true to yourself in this encounter.

'Contrary to earlier announcements, all certainties must be suspended starting today, and from this day forward.'
– Rik Comello

Questions to reflect on and discuss with others

Plenty of food for thought, I think. Here's a list of questions you can explore, either by yourself or with others. Share your insights on social media, so we can all benefit: #jamcultures.

- • How easy is it for you to deal with not-knowing?
- • How often do you divert from fixed patterns and routines?
- • How smoothly do you roll with the waves caused by uncertainty?
- • Do you talk about difference in terms of fragmentation or in words more consistent with inclusion?
- • Who did you shock today? Who was shocked by how you acted or what you said?
- • In what area, in what opinion, have you radicalized? What are your absolute truths?
- • Are you a pusher in a certain polarization? Or a joiner? What does this mean to you? And to the group?
- • If a group maintains a standard that you object to, do you say something about it?
- • How well do you handle conflict? Are there lingering problems you should really talk about? What's stopping you?
- • In your mind, do you have a jar of trust with a limited number of trust shares that can run out, or do you have a never-ending stash of trust?
- • Do you trust yourself? When don't you?
- • What do you need to trust someone else? And yourself?
- • How would you answer these questions from a workplace perspective? And from the perspective of your professional role?

Do something

Reflecting and talking are important, but so is taking action. Below I've provided a few ideas that are ready to be put into action. Clearly, this is not intended to be exhaustive. Add your own ideas and make the list longer. Share your insights on social media, so we can all benefit: #jamcultures.

- Get yourself into trouble and do something that you know beforehand will make you uncomfortable. Depending on what would cause discomfort, go to a country western festival, to the opera, a Christian tent revival, a nude beach, an interior design show, a demonstration, or a public dancing lesson in a busy park. Do something you normally avoid like the plague and would never choose to do. Don't take anyone along, so you have no one to fall back on. Join the group and reflect.

- Wear your watch on your other wrist for a day. Or leave your phone at home for a day. Observe the effects of such a small change.
- Serve your housemates dinner in the morning. Or serve dessert first at dinner and end with soup. Or serve a plate of mealworms or fried crickets. Talk about the effects of this: stretch or panic?
- Think about who you need to talk to but haven't. What do you need to stop postponing? And once you know what you need, go do it. Use the steps of the 'talk you avoided', aka the 'organized argument'.
- Where in your surroundings do you see debates harden? Is it even a debate? Or a discussion? Or is it people taking turns holding monologues? Are they polarizing? If so, don't leave things dangling; start a conversation as soon as the tension builds up. Step in. Be present and prepared to share what hits home for you. And be willing to change your opinion.
- Decide to trust others. Assume they mean well.

References

Albright, Madeleine (2018). *Fascism: A Warning.* London Harper.

Bohm, David (1996). *On dialogue.* London/New York: Routledge.

Brandsma, Bart (2017). *Polarisation: Understanding the Dynamics of Us Versus Them.* Schoonrewoerd: BB in Media.

 Also watch the video on Bart Brandsma's polarization model: https://youtu.be/cKpLzAG-t57U. For more information, see www.insidepolarisation.nl.

Kim, Min-Sun (2002). *Non-Western Perspectives on Human Communication: Implications for Theory and Practice.* Thousand Oaks, CA: Sage.

Kramer, Jitske (2014). *Deep Democracy. De wijsheid van de minderheid.* [Deep Democracy: The Wisdom of the Minority]. Deventer: Management Impact.

Lewis, Myrna (2008). *Inside the No: Five Steps to Decisions That Last.* Florence, OR: Deep Democracy Institute.

Wheatley, Margaret, J. (2012). *So Far From Home: Lost and Found in Our Brave New World.* Oakland, CA: Berrett-Koehler Publishers.

Wierdsma, André & Swieringa, Joop (2017). *Lerend organiseren.* [Learning Organizing] Groningen: Noordhoff Uitgevers.

Wierdsma, André (2014). *Vrij-moedig positie kiezen. Moreel leiderschap in vitale net-werken. [Boldly taking a stand: Moral leadership in vital networks]. Retirement address June 26,* 2014. https://www.nyenrode.nl/docs/default-source/pdf's/pdf's---faculteit-research/oraties-emeritaatsredes/afscheidsrede-andr%C3%A9-wierdsma.pdf?sfvrsn=ea26cb14_0

Otherness

I don't know, I don't think that I will ever
truly understand you. Our otherness sits between us.

Maybe if my cradle had stood, where your cradle ...
But no ... real understanding. No chance. Not even then.

I will try to see you. I - see - you
I will allow myself to be touched by your beautiful,
your ugly, your sweet, your pain, your difference.
To recognize myself, in what I think you might ...
But truly understand. No.

I will try to feel you. I - feel - you
Let us move and be moved by the rhythm of words.
By the time of doing and not doing...
By the time of being ...being ... being ...
Different. Tune in and out and in and out...
Trying to maximize life for you... and for me.
Give and take and take and give... Rhythm.

Always searching. No. Always finding.
Finding what binds us ... what we are together.
What we can do together. What we need to do together ...
because we live in this one world.

And then, of course ... Connection.
A sudden connection in which our souls meet.
New thoughts tumble. Touch me. Touch you. Touch us.

Confusion. Disruption. Searching. Finding ... Crea-ti-vi-ty
Liiiiife. Connection. Wet cheeks. Shiny eyes. Scary.
Because in our moment of true connection,
we enter the space of not knowing.
Not understanding. Never-truly-understanding each other.
Just ... seeing and feeling.

I think. I hope.
That if I try this for you, you will try this for me.
That we will find rhythm. Feel our rhythm.
Independently together. And. Together independently.
Rhythm of life, rhythm of being. Rhythm. Together.
Jamming.

May I find me in you?
Life is not about understanding. It's about feeling
and seeing.
May I feel you in me. Our sameness in our otherness.

Jitske Kramer

5

COURAGE

About jamming in a flow and with extremes

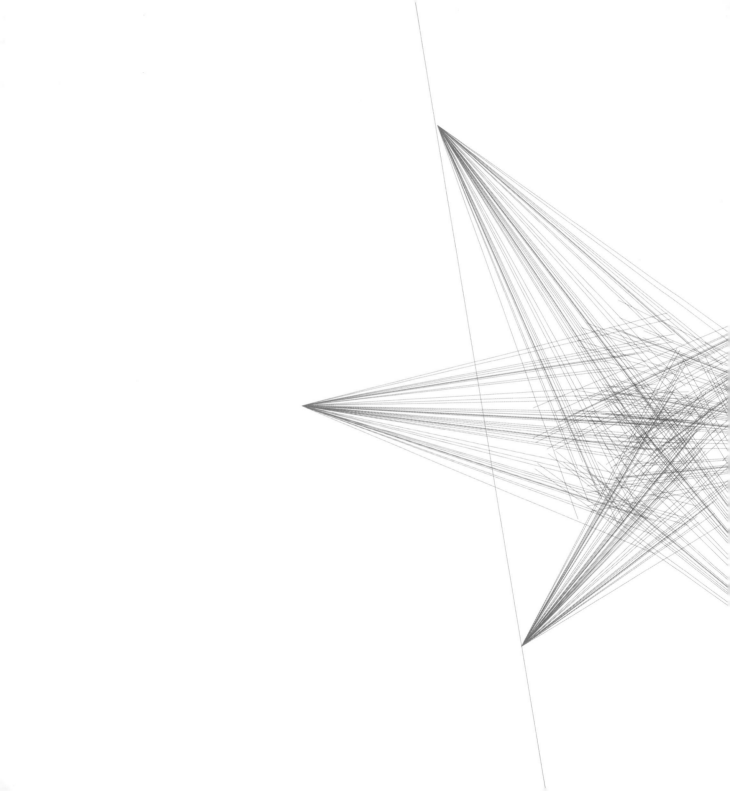

Inclusion is about everyone participating ...

... participating for real, that is. With energy, influence, a say, and meaningful encounters. That takes guts and courage from everyone in the group. It takes courageous leaders who know when to speak up, and when to listen to what others think and feel. And it means the collective needs to have the guts to appreciate and embrace different voices.

▶ *Waterplay during the Songkran Festival in Thailand. This is a New Year Festival in which everyone can soak each other with water for three days. Whole families line the roads with buckets of water, garden hoses and water pistols, ready to soak passers-by. Pickup trucks drive around slowly, transporting groups of people scooping water from barrels in the truck bed and heaving it at people along the roadside. Many add big blocks of ice to make the water freezing cold. They mainly target people holding umbrellas, whoever is still dry and young women on motorbikes. The festival features a lot of music-making, dancing and drinking. I was lucky to witness it once. For three days, people have fun with strangers and friends alike. It's a festival for all generations.*

IMAGE: SHUTTERSTOCK

The question is when are we finally going to get started? After all, we know exactly what to do. How long can people continue to exclude others from the job market? How long can we continue to keep refugees waiting at our borders, in camps with inhuman conditions? How long can we continue to act surprised that women never seem to reach the top of organizations, or that men appear unable to find qualified women to fill these roles? When will we stop denying that there is a cultural heritage and a history, which means that the Dutch (and other nations) should acknowledge their role in the slave trade. History has an impact on our international relations and how we regard each other in society. When will we stop allowing company executives to treat one particular department as less important, or managers to smirkingly compare their PAs' looks at meetings? When will we stop accepting that kids have to stay home because there's no suitable school for them? Or that mergers stagnate because they're actually takeovers, but aren't supposed to be referred to as such? Or that measures to halt climate change run aground because the cost of new technology outweighs the consequences for humanity?

Cultures are formed by every micro-decision. That means everyone can influence them. Every day, each of us can choose whether to greet someone or ignore them, to welcome or exclude them, to speak up against exclusion or look the other way, to act or do nothing … So, what are we waiting for?

Inclusion does not mean making everyone your BFF. You don't have to agree with everyone. You can even choose to keep your distance from people, if that's physically possible. And some degree of competition is healthy. Not everything can be hunky dory all the time. Sometimes, you throw yourself into something new with a passion and sometimes you steer clear of it. If you can't get along, then give each other some space. And seek each other out when and where you can. Or only if you must. Sometimes, you need to drag yourself and each other through the zone of discomfort, kicking and screaming, because we also have to make room for people who have dropped out of society for one reason or another. In all cases, we need to actively look for ways to enjoy each other's differences.

That's quite idealistic, I know. More inclusion requires a strong, energetic story and a generous helping of courage and perseverance. And faith, hope and love, I'd like to add. Because that's what's needed to go from good intentions to action..

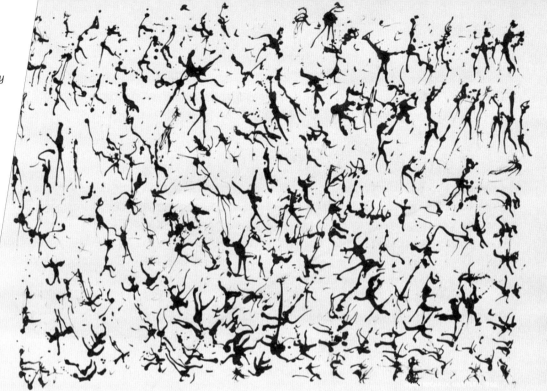

▸ *Rhythmically together.*

Jamming to the beat

Courage comes in many shapes. Let's start with the guts to adjust your own rhythm to some-one else's. This can help not only to establish a new beat together, but also to get into a flow and transcend ourselves. Rhythm is an important aspect of our existence, but one we usually pay little mind to. If we're out of sync, however, we notice it immediately.

In 1999, I was in Laos, where I spent a few weeks in the city of Luang Prabang. Every morn-ing, I went to the same place for breakfast. That would take at least two hours. First, the eggs would be delivered, and then the flour, and then someone would go get the rest of the ingre-dients from somewhere. And then, the careful mixing and baking could start. And finally I would be served my pancake. I would be completely absorbed in this calm rhythm that en-veloped me as I enjoyed the surrounding smells and sounds. One morning, however, a group of Italians arrived, clearly fresh off the plane from Rome. They were hot, tired and had lost some of their luggage. They were very uptight, talked very loudly and gestured wildly. I saw the people around them grow rigid and saw how their facial expressions and gestures froze.

The Italians in turn became even more boisterous. I sat and observed and thought: I could analyze this using various theories I learned in my anthropology classes, but actually, it's like a piece of music.

That's the moment I started looking at groups in terms of rhythmic differences. I had written my MA thesis on the use of drama, music and dance as educational tools in Uganda. However, it was only while watching this breakfast scene in Laos that the puzzle pieces fell into place. Not only did I see how differences in cultural rhythm upset us, I could actually feel it there, on the banks of that Laotian river. Analyzing diversity and inclusion using the language of rhythm is a way of strengthening our bonds. That language offers several advantages: it's neutral, it's often energizing and we all speak it.

Rhythm: repetition, variation and synchronization

In her book *Rhythm*, Dutch medical doctor and philosopher Marli Huijer writes that a sound or a movement becomes a rhythm only when it is characterized by at least these three elements: repetition, variation and synchronization. Repetitious patterns create order in our lives. That might sound monotonous or boring, but most people don't experience it that way because there's always something that gets lost or added in the repetition. Today's exchange at the water cooler is a bit different from yesterday's and what we talk about isn't exactly the same either. Rhythm provides stability, but also constant, subtle change. Simple repetition is not a rhythm: that just establishes tempo and doesn't introduce any change. By itself, variation doesn't create rhythm either; without some constant, we have only chaos. In other words, rhythm is the variation in repetition that happens in synchrony with all other rhythms that constantly exist. Rhythm emerges in experience and thus in cooperation, too.

Everything has a rhythm. Your heart, your breathing, the days, the seasons, the phases of life. Every person has their own rhythm. Locations have rhythm, even things have rhythm (see p. 242). We can make good use of these rhythms while jamming. If our rhythm is disrupted too much, we get unhappy and we can't get into a flow or synchronize. And that brings us back to the question of how much diversity we are willing and able to handle. If our environment is very diverse, repetition is challenged, synchronization gets harder and there might be too much variation to even call it a rhythm.

Cultural worlds of rhythm

I call the rhythm created by groups of people cultural worlds of rhythm. A cultural rhythm is the sum total of daily actions and an annual calendar of festivals, holidays, sports events and other events. A cultural rhythm balances moments of calm and action, quiet and noise, festivities and routine tasks. It has a beat, a regular basic rhythm that encompasses the group's variation in behavior. It is the beat to which we move, work and live. And it's unique to every cultural group. Recurring annual rituals, like Christmas, Ramadan or Mardi Gras, create continuity. In the workplace too, we create a cultural rhythm through our work schedule, shifts, HR cycles, quarterly meetings and the office Christmas party or summer barbecue. Every group intersperses its daily routine with extraordinary moments like festivals, team building sessions and holidays. It is by by breaking our routines that we can continue the rhythm.

Our shared rhythm makes us feel safe and connected with each other and our surroundings. Rhythms create a sense of interdependence. Every cultural group creates its own, distinct rhythm.

Cultural World of Rhythm
The beat that groups of people create to work, live, and be together.

Rhythm of speech

People speak at different speeds and their speech also varies in the number of syllables per minute and the length of their pauses. This differs from individual to individual, but also from one language or cultural group to the next. The average Italian speaks faster than someone from Laos; a Dutch person will generally wait their turn while a French person rattles on; then again, Dutch people generally speak much louder than most other Europeans, but they are topped by the average American. Naturally, these are stereotypes: there are many individual differences. When two people with very different mutual rhythms meet and when each of their rhythms differs from what the other expects in a given situation, those two people won't understand each other. Worse yet, their rhythmic differences are bound to generate distrust. This is caused by the different ways in which people express their universal needs in a conversation (see p. 188).

Rhythm of speech

Some people	allow	long silences	to fall.

Otherpeopletalkalotandfastandoftenacrosseachother.

And yet others. Wait exactly. Until someone has finished talking. Maximum four-seconds silence.

IMAGE: BASED ON AN IMAGE BY SUGGESTION & ILLUSION, FROM: WOW! WHAT A DIFFERENCE!

Rhythm of daily schedule

Our daily routines also have a rhythm that differs from culture to culture and from subculture to subculture. For example, Dutch people will grab a quick bite to eat for lunch—often a homemade sandwich from a brown paper bag—while lunch in many other countries is a drawn out, several-course affair. In the Netherlands, we eat a plate of hot food at 6 p.m.; in other countries people sit down for dinner at 10 and in yet other countries, there's always a pan of food on the stove from which people fill a plate whenever they feel like it. We tend to stick to our own rhythm, even when we foray into a different culture. At a campsite in France, I witnessed how every evening at 6:45 p.m. the Dutch campers lined up to do their dishes in the communal sinks, and sit down in front of their caravan or tent with a cup of Dutch coffee afterwards. Just like they would do at home.

Differences in working rhythm can be stark too. When construction workers are done for the day at 4 p.m., some people in the hospitality industry are just starting. Farmers have to be home to milk the cows or harvest the corn; writers can work wherever and whenever they want, bookkeepers experience peak times at the end of the fiscal year; beach bar managers cram a full year's work into one season. Some organizations have more than one fixed working schedule with its own rhythm and etched-in-stone breaks, for example, one for sales

'Stuttering is simply an immeasurable love of one syllable.'
– Robert Sabatier

*A disrupted rhythm
equals stress*

Stress is caused by
a disruption of your
rhythm, according to
Marli Huijer. Being stuck
in traffic, for instance,
is not stressful in and of
itself. After all, how bad
can it be? All you have to
do is just sit, and while you
wait you can listen to the
radio. It won't last forever.
It's stressful only when it
interferes with your other
rhythms, because you have to
pick up your kids from daycare
before closing time, or you have
to make it to a meeting by 9.

Hard work, in and of itself, doesn't
cause stress either. Most people
can handle it fairly well. It gets
harder, though, when someone expects you to keep doing what you're
doing, while also reflecting on what
you're doing, finding your kid's soccer
cleats, or adding this extra hour of an
out-of-sync job. Those things interrupt your working rhythm.

Accepting that things are going differently than planned helps to relieve stress.
It's the same mechanism as what I call
'opening up' in the Jam Circle.

reps and one for the back office, or one for the office and another for the production floor. Or think of how different your rhythm is when you rush through the supermarket after work to get groceries for dinner from that of a bunch of schoolboys on their after-school snack run. The contrast is clearest in the check-out line, when you're behind them with your hastily collected items from your shopping list, waiting for each of them to pay separately for their single items of potato chips and soda.

When shared daily rhythms disappear

When we lose a shared daily rhythm, we lose connection. We no longer sit on the couch watching the same TV show, because anybody can watch whatever, whenever. That's convenient, but it eliminates a shared time, a time to strengthen bonds. The same can be said about church on Sunday: because most of us don't go, we've lost another opportunity to connect. Similarly, kids don't play on the streets so much anymore. And so on. At the same time, we're introduced many new rhythms: Ramadan, step counters, social media posts. The same is true of rhythms in the workplace. We no longer all have nine-to-five jobs, and many of us no longer have our own desk. Lifelong employment in the same company is a relic. At the same time, our smartphones have made us available 24/7 for work-related messages, so we need to find a new work-life balance.

Today we have the individual freedom to live our lives in accordance with our own rhythm. The the drawback of that freedom is that sharing the same rhythm with others doesn't go without saying. There's a lot of variation. Everybody is locked into their own variable pattern and synchronizing our patterns is a big challenge. Part of the social unrest we're experiencing these days is due to these disrupted rhythms. In 2008, Dutch public broadcasting decided to reschedule Sesame Street's airtime by half an hour. All the parents at my kids' school were up in arms. Our collective playtime-dinnertime-bathtime schedules had to be rearranged! Everyone was out of sorts. And no,

I am not arguing for a return to the good old days when everything was supposedly better. It just means there's no conductor deciding what our collective rhythm should be. So if we want to experience connection, we need to jam, we need to sync our rhythms. This is true in the workplace, at home and in society at large. Our life beat has a growing number of variations, so we have to attune ourselves to each other's rhythms.

Locations have a rhythm

Rhythms are not just determined by the clock, but also by the context and the emotions evoked by the environment, the company and the occasion. The rhythm at a railway station is not the same as that of a church, soccer stadium, local pub, or movie theater. Your conversations with your aged mother have a different rhythm than your talks with your new love, the cable guy, the little girl next door or your best friends after a good meal.

Objects have a rhythm

Even objects have their own rhythm. Oysters and champagne have a rhythm, which is not the same as that of a bowl of oatmeal. A hammock has a different rhythm than an office chair. A handwritten letter has a rhythm unlike that of an e-mail. If you look around, you'll see that the world is for the most part made up of largish objects, such as your computer, your coffee mug and your own body. Yet, this is illusory, because each of these objects is made up of a fascinating world of smaller parts that are moving all the time: molecules, atoms, electrons, protons and neutrons. We know from quantum mechanics that the smallest particles are waves of energy. Hence, matter is actually densified energy, which is not stationary, but constantly

Whistle while you work
Kids who sing together while carrying out a joint task perform better than kids who don't. Singing (or yelling) together creates neural synchronization, according to neuropsychologist Erik Scherder. That's knowledge we should apply more often in the workplace.

I have literally jammed with international groups where communication had become a cacophony. I had all participants drum their own rhythm on the table—some banged down their fist, some used their fingers, others just put their hands down—and then had them work on creating a more harmonious rhythm. Afterwards, the conversation would usually go smoother.

Singing together in the workplace does require a good introduction. I was at a conference once where people were suddenly asked to sing along. Many people did, but in the break they expressed their discomfort with this collective experience because it lacked any synchronization with the context. Communal singing is an intimate experience that you need to carefully introduce and that may not be fitting if it is too far removed from the (cultural) context.

vibrates. Energy is never still. Everything surrounding us has its own frequency of vibration.

Clash between biorhythm and cultural rhythm

Your biorhythm can be different from your cultural rhythm. Some studies have shown that teenagers perform better if school starts an hour later. The same is true of adults, by the way! Looking at a smartphone or tablet screen late at night also has a negative impact on our sleeping rhythm, because the blue light prevents our brains from going into sleep mode. It takes many people weeks to adjust after we switch to daylight savings time or back. Canada has carefully studied the statistics and found that on the Mondays after daylight savings time begins, there are 8 percent more car accidents than normal. Similarly, some people cannot handle shift work that includes night shifts. Or the 24 hour shifts hospital staffers have to do. And some people are affected much more by jet lag than others.

Rhythm makes us feel and remember

'Figure out the rhythm of life. And live in harmony with it.'
– Lao Tzu.

Rhythmic sentences with recurring words, usually grouped in threes, are easier to remember and are more readily accepted as true. That's because they sound so good. Not only do we remember the phrasing better, but we're more likely to respond emotionally, too. Using rhythm is a great way to make an emotional connection to large groups of people. Speech writers are well aware of this. Let's look at an example from President Obama's inaugural address (2 × 3):

'Homes have been lost, jobs shed, businesses shuttered. Today I say to you that the challenges we face are real, they are serious, and they are many.'

Another example is Churchill's speech on the eve of England's involvement in World War II:

'We shall fight on the beaches, we shall fight on the landing grounds, we shall fight in the fields and in the streets, we shall fight in the hills, we shall never surrender.'

Rhythms are neither good nor bad. Hitler, too, knew how to use rhythm and repetition to enthrall the masses. And marketeers know how to use this tool too, in slogans like Intel Inside, in product names like Coca-Cola, and even in the names of entire businesses, like Dunkin Donuts (and its arch-nemesis, Weight Watchers).

Rhythm and time perception

Different perceptions of time are a key underlying cultural factor in scheduling and planning. It's a cultural difference that becomes visible in strategic planning and the way in which teams deal with deadlines and promises. Does 'now' mean later, later today, or this minute? Is ten minutes past the deadline late or not? When does your future start? And when does your past end? Do you measure time in days, weeks, months, multiple lives?

To avoid unnecessary irritation, it's important to make explicit agreements about when 'late' becomes 'too late'. In some people's way of thinking, time is money. Based on that idea, time can be measured and days can be divided up into small units that help you plan your days. For others, clocks and calendars play no role in the decision to start on something. Time is relational, and the higher someone's status, the longer an hour can last. Others see time as something that can pass and can run out. Yet others see it as something that's simply there, as a cyclical movement, with the sun rising and setting. In that view, time is not scarce and the past provides the context in which to interpret the present.

According to anthropologist Edward Hall, time is a complex whole of concepts, phenomena, perceptions and systems that for the most part determine our life and working rhythms. Time is the core system around which we shape our image of the world. We're all connected by an endless web of rhythms, without realizing it.

Time is much more than a bunch of numbers on a dial. Time is about status, relationships and respect. Is it more respectful to be right on time, a few minutes early or an hour late? These feelings and ideas are expressed in team planning, in the times set for meetings and in the importance of meeting deadlines. What is it that determines your schedule: the appointments in your calendar or the unpredictability of your day and your relationships with people? Another factor influencing this is your set of assumptions about how much control you have over your future and your environment. I experienced this once when I was arranging a second meeting with a Ugandan. I said, "I'll see you again in two months. Same place, same time." His response was: "Ah! How do you know?"

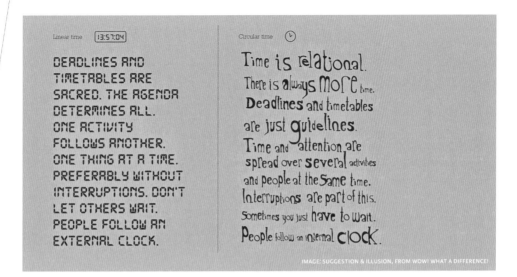

Linear time `13:57:04`	Circular time
DEADLINES AND TIMETABLES ARE SACRED. THE AGENDA DETERMINES ALL. ONE ACTIVITY FOLLOWS ANOTHER. ONE THING AT A TIME. PREFERABLY WITHOUT INTERRUPTIONS. DON'T LET OTHERS WAIT. PEOPLE FOLLOW AN EXTERNAL CLOCK.	Time is relational. There is always more time. Deadlines and timetables are just guidelines. Time and attention are spread over several activities and people at the same time. Interruptions are part of this. Sometimes you just have to wait. People follow an internal clock.

IMAGE: SUGGESTION & ILLUSION, FROM WOW! WHAT A DIFFERENCE!

Rhythm and music

Every cultural group on the planet makes music. It goes without saying that music has rhythm. It also has a very special place in our lives, because it can transcend words and deeds. Parkinson patients can walk better when listening to music. Dementia patients can access old memories better. Singing and dancing together, experiencing rhythm, significantly increases the level of oxytocin—the happiness hormone—in our bodies. If you're interested in how music affects your brain and sense of happiness, I recommend you read *Singing in the Brain,* written by neuropsychologist Erik Scherder.

Music puts us in touch with emotions we can't express in any other way. Everybody knows that hardcore metal evokes a different feeling than a calm classical concerto. Music can soothe or agitate. It can lighten your mood, evoke sadness or help you deal with your anger. It can even help you recover from illness, or make you feel worse. Music brings people together. Religions and sports put this knowledge to good use. If you're backpacking around the world and you think you see a fellow American somewhere, all you need to do is whistle a few bars of 'Born in the USA' and watch their reaction to see if you're right. In the Netherlands, where patriotism is more understated, there's been a revival of interest in the Dutch national anthem. Whether you like it or not—and many Dutch people don't—it's no coincidence. It's being used to boost people's national pride. Elevator music and those soothing tunes piped in to every waiting room aren't random either. There's a reason why marching rhythms accompany military parades. Think of film scores, too. Music is used to evoke and conduct emotions. In politics, in sports, around campfires and in the workplace.

We're always subconsciously looking for the rhythm that fits us best and once we've found it, we're loathe to let go. It's weird for someone to drink a glass of wine at work, at 10 a.m. They're not sticking to the rhythm. But you can also play with that same rhythm: organize a champagne breakfast for your team at work and you'll see that it has special impact. It creates an extraordinary slice of time in which the conversation can take a different turn than usual.

Vibrations and frequencies

Music is made up of frequencies. It affects your pulse, blood pressure, breathing, circulation, metabolism and heart rate. Its tones and textures can influence your body and mind. Listening to music releases hormones and every frequency releases a different one. Hence, combinations of frequencies release specific combinations of hormones which are linked to our emotions. Low tones can make us feel languid, calm or relaxed, while high frequency notes can activate us and stimulate attentiveness.

We can make each other sick if we don't keep our working and life rhythms in sync. And speaking unkindly also affects human health; words do hurt.

Tiv Time Chambers

People don't all live by clock time. In some cultures, people's sense of time is determined by a series of activities that are used as units of time. Take the Tiv, a group of traditional farmers who live in het savannahs of central Nigeria. For the Tiv, activities alone determine the rhythm of a day. Time is a frame into which activities are fitted like the pieces of a jigsaw puzzle. The anthropologist Paul Bohannen explains that each activity—bringing in the harvest, for example—has its own *time chamber*. Once an activity has started, the time chamber is hermetically sealed, separated from other activities and secured from interruption. You do not disturb a Tiv during an activity and multi-tasking is completely out of the question. When the Tiv participate in magical activities, such as ceremonies, magical time does not so much run parallel to the daily clock as it replaces the daily clock.

In the Tiv system, every activity is attached to a period of time and a place. Time, space and action are, thus, in complete harmony with one another. It's an arrangement that many Western employees would envy. In our organizations today, it is rare to find the time and space to undertake an activity completely free from disturbance or distraction. Even the highest boss, even during a *magical session*, is not entirely immune to intrusions from daily reality.

— Excerpt from *The Corporate Tribe: Organizational Lessons from Anthropology*

If we jam well, something magical happens. The session becomes bigger than ourselves. You can see it happening. Just like you see it in a live performance, when you sense that the musicians are discovering something new in the moment. Or in improv theater or stand-up comedy, when a joke appears out of thin air. The audience is part of this. It's a shared, contagious energy. If a team in the workplace jams well, it lifts everyone. It's intangible and it eludes description. In *On Dialogue*, physicist and communications expert David Bohm calls it 'the tacit level'. It's that sense of celebrating the Fourth of July on a wonderful, warm, sunny day or of suddenly playing an extraordinarily good game of basketball with your friends. That same, sudden sense of greatness—flow—can occur in the workplace: in group projects, in a start-up or even in the boardroom. It's more than doing things in a way everyone agrees to; it's lifting each other up in the moment.

If a jam session doesn't achieve this dynamic, it might just run aground. Very diverse teams tend to either overachieve or underachieve. One thing they're not known for is average achievement.

'If you want to find the secrets of the universe, think in terms of energy, frequency and vibration.'
– Nikola Tesla

When dialogue stops, there's no more flow and we descend into fragmentation (see p. 54). Joint dialogues are essential for our society. Shared meanings, but also that elusive, tacit flow, are the mortar that keeps us together. They are the antidotes to fragmentation. Bad mortar means that the whole structure falls apart and sounds hollow.

In a good jam session, everyone tries to find each other's extremes, in opinions, or sounds, without drowning each other out or going on for too long. We share our opinions and thoughts without attacking the other or defending ourselves. We get into a flow.

From Mihaly Csikszentmihalyi's famous book on flow and happiness I learned that flow makes us feel strong and alert while it allows us to do our jobs effortlessly. It gives us the feeling that we know what we're doing, and that we're delivering a peak performance. We lose all sense of time and for a second, we seem to leave our bodies. Flow is described as a state of utter concentration blended with intense joy.

To me, flow means that everything is in motion. Opinions are fluid, new insights are formed, and there is a shared spirit to which individual minds are not subordinate. We build on each other's input and seek a shared meaning without everyone having to agree on everything. That's what I believe inclusion is all about: living your life fully, alongside others. Jamming.

Aligning communication

Rhythms become visible in communication and communication can be aligned. You can communicate about the same thing in various language frameworks at the same time, both verbally and non-verbally. We can learn to communicate like people who play in a jam session, speeding up and slowing down at times, not when a conductor directs us to, but by taking turns being the leader. Sometimes we need to take a break so we can process what's been said. And if the time between beats is too short, we lose our place. If the time to pause for thought is too long, we get bored or impatient.

We can't jam all the time

The aligning process never ends. Yet, we can't jam all the time; we would all keel over from exhaustion. We need time to process new insights, to let them filter into our system and to recharge, so we can continue to develop these new ideas with renewed vigor. We need demarcations that signal our transition from one moment to the next. There are times we want to act on routine, and to retreat for a while into our own group. If variations in rhythm are lost, we lose track of time and we live as if we're in Las

Aligning rhythms

There was a team whose members considered each other incompetent. This created friction and a growing gap between them. Their manager directed them to explore what was going on. They concluded that a lot of their judgments had to do with their different communication styles. Some people were loud and interrupted each other a lot, while others hardly dared speak up. The question the group tried to answer in a brainstorming session was: how can we give each other space and respect each other's communication style? People came up with all sorts of suggestions: use a kitchen timer and give everyone three minutes to make their point; use a talking stick to ensure only one person speaks at a time; use the time-out sign if you want to speak up; put a colored building block on the table if you want to say something; count to three before reacting to someone, etc. In the end, the team opted for the louder individuals to wait three seconds before responding and for the quiet ones to use the time-out sign to indicate they wanted to say something. They also decided that everyone was responsible for ensuring that everyone could speak their mind. It took a few weeks for these habits to take hold, but from then on, there was more room and respect for everyone to participate in team discussions.

Vegas, where you have no idea what time it is, what season it is, or whether it's day or night. By experiencing changes in rhythm, we're better able to be ourselves and we're less bothered by the confines of the dominant group's norms. If we lose the cadence, or demarcations, we get lost.

Three basic beats and endless variations

In *When Cultures Collide*, British linguist Richard Lewis divides the world into three types of culture. Obviously, this is stereotyping. There are all sorts of variations and differences within those three cultural groups. But as I argued in Chapter 1 on difference, stereotypes can be useful for understanding the world. I have taken Lewis's groups of nations and studied them in terms of their traditional music and dancing styles. I then asked Dutch musician Tudor Rutjes to come up with a basic beat for each of these cultural types. I went to his recording studio and came out with three basic beats. Like I said, these are sweeping generalizations with many possible variations, but they do give us an interesting frame to listen to the world. On the Human Dimensions YouTube channel, you will find a video where I demonstrate these rhythms. Below I will sketch in broad strokes the different meanings of these rhythms, which you can perceive as three different worlds of rhythm. Which rhythm do you identify with and when? Which rhythm applies to your family? To your in-laws? To your workplace? To your customers or clients? Do you feel each other's rhythms, or are you out of sync? Do your rhythms bring you closer or cause misunderstandings and raised eyebrows?

1 Linearly active: task-oriented

Task-oriented cultures tend to value the written word. The focus is on factual information, on the content of what is being conveyed. Honesty trumps diplomacy and confrontations are met with logic rather than emotion. Communications are intended to convey information. People wait for others to finish their sentence and then respond, after a short 'beat' of silence. Communication is about substance rather than the way in which the information is expressed. Loss of face is experienced as unpleasant but not insurmountable. You can say and ask anything; if your interlocutor doesn't like it, they will say so. Structure is considered very important in many aspects of life. Actions are planned in a linear fashion, preferably back to back and not simultaneously. Planning and schedules are taken very seriously. Taking a practical approach with very little emotional fuss is the norm. In business, punctuality, high performance and quality are key. Phone calls are short and to the point, and people respond quickly to written communications. Status is earned through work done and leaders tend to operate on an almost equal footing with their inferiors. Time is money and money is important.

2 Multi-active: people-oriented

People-oriented cultures value direct interpersonal dialogue, emotions and relationships. The focus is on intuition, on who conveys information and how it is conveyed. Communication is lively, with many gestures and few pauses. Talking and listening overlap; passion and emotions are important and can be expressed. People do more than one thing at a time and don't strictly adhere to calendars and structures. Scheduling and planning are not an end but a means; deadlines are postponed on a regular basis. Time is not determined by the clock, but by the relative importance of the relationship. Everything starts when it starts. Flexibility and improvisation are considered important competences. In business, contacts and networking are more important than products. In business discussions, people start off by inquiring about each other's well-being and families. Official rules are not considered very important. People respect authority to a limited extent, but accept everyone's place in the pecking order. Leaders are expected to provide strong, directive leadership.

3 Reactive: harmony-oriented

Harmony-oriented cultures value listening and silences. Communications are preferably monologues, with sufficient pauses for reflection and for others to think about how they want to respond. People tend not to interrupt each other. Emotions are not readily shown and non-verbal communication is subtle. The context in which things are said or written, the person who says them, when and how, determine the meaning of the words. Loss of face has to be avoided. The unwritten rule is that interlocutors are responsible for the other's loss of face. This requires very careful, and usually indirect communication, especially when trying to convey opinions. Preferably, confrontations are avoided. Networking and contacts are very important.

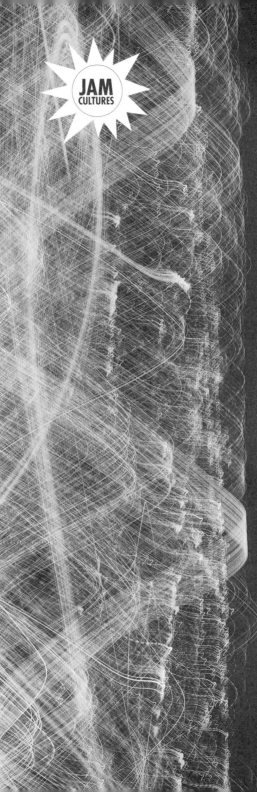

JAM CULTURES

Vary the rhythm

Our trust deepens now we both speak our minds and hearts. The tension of the project drives our passion to achieve our targets. Cooperation takes on new meaning now that we've let each other's rhythm enter the coldness of the neon-lit conference room with its acoustic ceiling tiles and its brown plastic coffee cups.

We work our way through the agenda, dealing with items one by one, as fast as we can. Tsjk, tsjk, tsjk. The depth of our thinking manifests itself effortlessly in the cha-cha-cha of our discussion. And then suddenly. Silence. Shush. We will never say the most important things out loud. We all know it, but we don't say it. The bass resonates in the silence of the drum. A rhythmic agenda.

Sizzling teamwork. Our sounds make love to the rhythm of our thinking. I listen to the vibration in your speech. We are silent, but not still. We dance from bullet point to bullet point. We take the risk of hearing each other out. We tune in to listen to our feelings. We try to make music, not just noise.

Jitske Kramer

No flow without risk

Being gutsy is easier when you feel safe. But when you feel too safe, it's also very comfortable to leave everything the way it is. After all, it's fine the way it is. In Chapter 1 on difference, I described the Jam Circle. When you apply this process to the way you collaborate with people, you can get into a flow together. Flow is an appealing type of energy that lets you really take off, enabling you to surprise yourself at how much you can handle. It's a state of continuous slight stretch, with just the right amount of challenge. You need to use your talents and skills to work together, but not to the extent that it's overwhelming. It's the opposite of routine. Diversity gives you the gift of flow and creativity, provided that you and the people you work with are able to channel the underlying emotional and power dynamics.

Jamming creates flow

It takes courage to time and again hold genuine conversations with each other. We're often called upon to 'bring our whole selves to the workplace' and we've all said that we want to 'put people first'. But we're all real people with all the faults and virtues humans have. Using our full potential often is a messy business of trial and error, of reaching the end of your tether, wanting to go back to the way things were so you don't have to try so hard. And that's exactly when we have to trust that things will turn out okay. That's when we can get into a flow. The structure provided by the Jam Circle can help you achieve this, I believe. The circle moves from certainty to uncertainty to certainty, with built-in moments of reflection that are consistently transposed into action, so that the music we call collaboration can continue. You can use every type of conversation in this book, and every other type you know of, to facilitate this process.

Studies into flow suggest that seventeen percent of people are in a flow most of the time, says Belgian motivational speaker and coach Jan Bommerez in one of his newsletters. The rare individuals who mostly live in a state of flow are the small group of people who continue to learn and grow throughout their lives. They are those who know how to realize the essential needs of safety, fulfillment and attachment in this growth. As Csikszentmihalyi says, "Flow is a state of total involvement in which pleasure and creativity spontaneously emerge." Jamming evokes that state.

Striving for more diversity and inclusion means working together to tap into that magical state of flow. In order to live in a state of flow, we need to learn to distinguish between physical danger and psychological or emotional insecurity. We do this in the opening-up phase, when we look to find safety in ourselves and try to connect by feeling where we're at. Living and working in a state of flow requires courage. Jamming is acknowledging and feeling our fear, but not letting it take over. Taking the leap with your eyes wide open and allowing new insights in. Having the courage to say what's on your mind. Saying what you want, what you feel. Sharing and doing what makes you happy. Connecting with yourself and others. The easier this gets, the more self-confident we feel in this tense moment of insecurity and the more freely we can jam. This may strike you as idealistic. It is. And it's not an easy process at all. But that doesn't mean it's unrealistic. It does happen. And when it does, it's wonderful. And it all starts by thinking in terms of what's possible, rather than what's standing in your way.

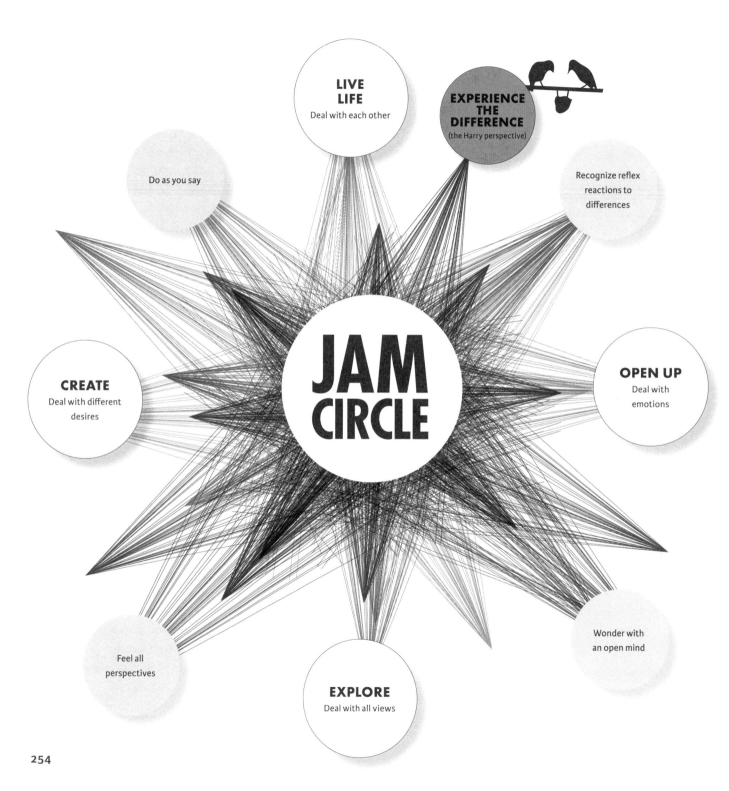

LIVE
LIFE
Deal with each other

EXPERIENCE
THE
DIFFERENCE
(the Harry perspective)

Do as you say

Recognize reflex
reactions to
differences

CREATE
Deal with different
desires

JAM
CIRCLE

OPEN UP
Deal with
emotions

Feel all
perspectives

Wonder with
an open mind

EXPLORE
Deal with all views

254

Passion and intimacy create flow

After one of my masterclasses on inclusion in the workplace, a gentleman named Harry van de Wiel introduced himself to me and asked whether I was aware that what I described touched on the core of his field. I asked him what field that was. He turned out to be a professor of human sexuality. I was startled because I had never looked at it that way. I had been talking about teamwork, making space for talent, taking a different perspective, participation processes, diversity and inclusive decision-making. After our enlightening talk, I read his inaugural address and could only agree with him wholeheartedly. In a business context, we use technical, masculine words that mask a deeper, human layer of emotions. If I leave aside this technical language, we're looking at a deeply human, emotional image of inclusion. It reveals which personal and essential fears are at play in our interactions and our perceptions of difference.

The dynamics of diversity and inclusion touch on power, vulnerability, modesty and shame. Clearly, these dynamics are not exactly the same in the workplace as they are in the bedroom. Yet, in business relations these deep, human emotions are at play, too. In the dynamics of power and difference, intimacy and passion play an important part. This is even true in the office and the boardroom, whether we like it or not. I'd like to clarify this statement by discussing how Van de Wiel defines intimacy and passion.

Intimacy

In his definition, intimacy means revealing ourselves to the other in several ways. Opening up can be scary. What if you fall short of expectations, or you're 'found out'? What if the other doesn't react sensitively to your personal stories? Intimacy occurs when you cross boundaries together. It comes about when we leave the mundane behind and jointly embark on an exciting journey, or manage a complicated project, or even deliver bad news to someone. In order to experience intimacy, we need to take risks and overcome our fear of losing face. The reward is grand: we experience deep feelings of unity, bonding and security. In showing ourselves, our strength and vulnerability, and in entering the unknown together, we achieve that coveted sense of connection. This is scary in any relationship, both in love and in the workplace. Even more so when we feel very different from each other and don't know exactly what the other expects of us, either.

Many organizations want their employees to excel in *customer intimacy. To* be people-oriented. To put people first. These are just marketing and management expressions to ask employees to enhance their mutual intimacy.

Passion

And then there's passion. We experience passion when something or someone sets us ablaze. Many organizations hope for people who throw themselves passionately into their work and feel excited to serve their customers or contribute to their core activities with a passion. So many job ads make use of the word 'passion,' it's now on the verge of becoming a cliché. I talked to someone the other day who was skeptical about his manager's latest rant about passion for the job. 'All this talk about high energy, excitement and passion... You know, I still have to answer fifty emails and fill in my time sheets. And forgive me, but I don't exactly feel passionate about those tasks.' While talking, we came up with the idea that preparing and completing Excel sheets might be similar to changing the sheets on your bed in the hopes of having a passionate night. In other words, it's not the actions themselves that spark the fire in you, but those actions could lead to something big and exciting. And when you give it all you've got, and the other does the same, we can experience that special bond that passionate people can share. At the same time, experiencing a shared passion is daunting, because the more passion we feel for someone, the bigger the fear that they will just up and leave. Passion gives us wings, but it also heightens our fear of rejection. And if we want to hang on to passion, we run the risk of quenching it. Passion requires most of all that we let go, that we lose ourselves in each other and our activities, to keep the inspiring energy flowing.   .

In order to get into that prized state of flow, we will need to work through our fear of rejection. We will have to let others in and show ourselves. Despite being nervous about whether we're good enough or making an ass of ourselves.

The creative energy of inclusion

Inclusion always goes hand in hand with feelings of fear of being together and fear of being alone. Inclusion is about creative energy: jamming with passion and intimacy to create synergy and get into a flow. It's an emotional chaos full of potential that needs to be channeled by taking risks, stretching limits, regulating fears and engaging in a real dialogue about this.

Jamming with passion and intimacy takes courage

Intimacy is the result of self-disclosure and transgressing boundaries
To experience intimacy you need to take risks:
- Self-disclosure means opening yourself up and figuratively, or even literally, baring yourself. Running the risk that you might fall short of expectations. The other might find you weird or ugly and you'll be rejected in all your vulnerability and nakedness.
- By crossing borders together, by embarking on an exciting adventure, you increase intimacy. This adventure can be a special project, making a hard sale together or dancing to a weird tune at the office Christmas party.

Rewards for the risk you take:
• A sense of unity, security and connection with the other.

Passion is the result of complete surrender
To experience passion you need to take risks:
- By giving it all, emotionally, by losing yourself in the moment, in the activity or item on the agenda, or in the other. It means taking the risk that the other won't give it all they've got, and you will have made a fool of yourself with all your passion.
- If you put your all into it and the other does too, this creates a special bond. You're into each other or the project. Still, you run the risk that the other suddenly quits and leaves you behind empty-handed. That idea can be really scary when your bond is special or the projects has high stakes.

Rewards for the risk you take:
- An enormous zest for life, high energy, engagement and many intense climaxes.

Loosely based on Harry van de Wiel's inaugural address *Happiness Isn't Everything*

One key question relating to inclusion is whether we want to embark on this precarious adventure with everyone. Who do we want to associate with and with whom do we want to connect? After all, we're social animals and others judge us partly by the people we surround ourselves with. And what if I want to and take the first step, and the other backs away? Also, real contact can be painful. The person I talk with might turn out to be talking on behalf of others. He or she might pass on our intimate exchanges to others, or hide something, or only want to benefit his or her own group, or have a hidden agenda. And how deeply connected do you really want to be with your co-workers, your manager, your students, your customers, your clients?

Too much safety kills the fire

Flow requires us to feel our fear, but not get overwhelmed by it. Getting passionate about something or someone can be scary, because you're about to surrender completely while taking the risk that the other can simply leave you. Intimacy is scary because you bare your soul, transgress boundaries together and then the other may think you're weird once they really get to know you. Hence, we say we need to feel safe enough to have the guts to take the leap. And that's right. We need a basic sense of safety to know that the other won't eat or club us. But the tension we need is in taking the risk. The only way we will ever find passion, intimacy and flow, is if we dare to take that leap. And if we try to hold on to passion or intimacy, for example, by literally holding the other tight, or holding them back, wanting to safeguard what we have and prevent the other from moving on or leaping, we'll lose the flow.

For a state of flow, we need just the right amount of safety. If we feel too safe, too comfortable we don't feel like taking risks. It's just too much trouble. Plus we'd be putting our cherished safety on the line and we don't want to do that. As a consequence, though, safety may smother us like a blanket. We may end up sitting it out, covered in the blanket of love. Conversely, taking too much risk, too quickly, may result in real insecurity. We may experience a rush of new impulses and great climaxes, but we'll crash because there's no foundation and no connection. It would be utopian to think we can always strike the right balance between safety and risk, but at heart, inclusion is about aiming for more self-expression while also striving for stronger, mutual bonds and relationships. As we saw, there's a similar dynamic in the power-love polarity (see p. 176).

IMAGE: UNSPLASH

The Quest for Flow, for Meaningful Encounters: A Story

Once upon a time, there was a human being. An ordinary human, just like you and me. This person was fed up. He or she, but let's call her a 'he,' worked day after day on things he didn't consider valuable. He worked with people he didn't particularly like. They were okay, but there was no real connection. They didn't click. Everybody just did their thing. There was no sense of community. The days blurred together without any excitement, energy or sense of trying to accomplish something together. He went from nothing to nothing. People in his organization expressed concern about the employees' lack of engagement. HR called for more involvement. Coaches were called in to help people find their passion. Managers talked about energy and excitement. But our man felt he was stuck in a place where there was **nothing to experience**. He felt no passion, no intimacy.

He dreamed of **meaningful encounters**. Encounters where everyone would help each other shine, where he would work in a team full of synergy, looking for a win-win situation. A team in which people looked out for each other, so everyone benefited. A team in which he would feel passionate about collaborating with others on goals and missions. A team with differences, with diversity, with power and love. With passion and intimacy, with drive and trust. A team that would be ready to take on the world. That would push every one of its members and the people beyond, to dig deep. A team where 1 and 1 would add up to at least 3. That type of thing.

Egged on by management's call to show more passion, take more responsibility and think like an entrepreneur, he found his inner strength and jumped at the first opportunity to join a project team. The energy that was unleashed was unreal. Years of built-up tension were set loose. He had never worked on anything with so much passion. He passionately worked on achieving the goals set. His team met and surpassed, their targets with ease. He wore his best suits to work and felt like a boss. His success did not go unnoticed. And he kept going. And going. His relationships with other people became less important than achieving his goals and priorities. He was on a roll. Every deadline gave him a thrill, but the tension was **released** every time he succeeded.

And so it went. On and on. And on. Tiredness was not a reason to take a break. He rushed from dopamine rush to dopamine rush. Addictive adrenalin ran through his veins. Endorphins took care of any pains. His desire for the tension to be temporarily relieved kept growing and growing. Passion for the project and people turned into pursuing a high. He seemed not to have any limits and pushed his co-workers and customers to try ever harder, ever more, ever longer, ever higher, ever faster. Gradually, he lost himself in that sense of being invincible. He was trapped in lusting after more. And then, one day, he drowned in his own intensity. He had lost touch with his body, with himself. He was deprived of any real, human, emotional contact. Brimming with passion. Full of lust, but lonely and isolated. Devoured by the **tyranny of lust**.

Rest, relaxation and routines helped him to regain a sense of normalcy. He improved his diet, went to bed earlier, exercised and created a clear daily structure. He started communicating again, with himself and others. He took note of the signals his body sent him, listened to his wants and needs, and fears. And talked about these with the people in his life. By being honest with himself and baring his soul to others, an energy that he had missed so badly started to flow again. His encounters were connective and soft. They fostered togetherness and intimacy. Others also started telling him more about themselves. That was exciting. By challenging his own limits, he found a sense of community, security and trust. Together with others, he had new experiences. Bonds became stronger. Oppositions and conflicts faded into the background. Targets were important, but so were mutual relationships. Attention was the key. He was given a T-shirt as a present. It read: It's not the *destination, but de journey that counts. He felt a sense of familiarity, togetherness, **belonging**.

The warmth and the sense of unity kept growing. It was great. It was peaceful. Everybody was nice to each other. But slowly, he started having misgivings. There was never any disharmony on the team. In order not to cause any waves, people stopped themselves from saying what they thought. There were clear habits and routines that everyone stuck to and whenever someone didn't, it would cause raised eyebrows. No one ever spoke a cross word. The fear of spoiling the sense of togetherness and being excluded from the group caused him to stifle all his own impulses. Everyone conformed to everyone else in this **tyranny of togetherness**. The cloak of love had become a smothering blanket.

He was desperate. He missed the tension of passion. Too much togetherness bored him to tears and all the intimacy was too much for him. He wanted passionate friendships, the familiar fireworks of working hard, of good old fashioned teamwork... He longed for **meaningful encounters** and collaboration, with fire and passion, but also with the softness of connection. In all honesty, he had to admit that what he wanted was the tension without the risk. Because with the passion came the fear of suddenly losing that feeling. Or losing himself. And every time he bared his soul and bonded with someone, he became afraid that the other would break off this close and special relationship and run away. Slowly, he got used to the idea that truly meaningful relationships could only develop along with the tension of risk-taking. He took a deep breath and started getting comfortable with the fear of tension and insecurity. He learned to **deal with the risk and the fear of commitment**.

He also faced up to the tyranny of 'not acting up.' He saw how authenticity, being yourself and sticking up for your own values are all important, but also very convenient excuses for not budging. Excellent reasons to lose your curiosity. Meaningful conversations were possible only when there was

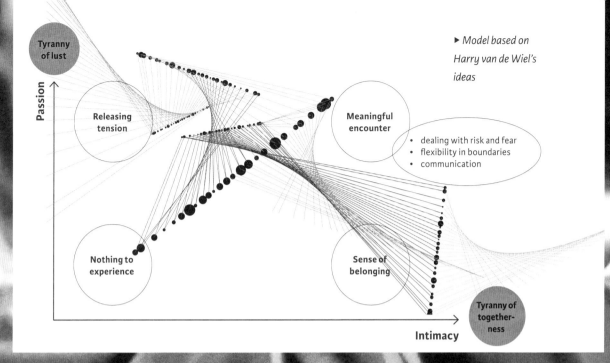

Passion

Tyranny of lust

Releasing tension

Meaningful encounter

▶ *Model based on Harry van de Wiel's ideas*

- dealing with risk and fear
- flexibility in boundaries
- communication

Nothing to experience

Sense of belonging

Tyranny of together-ness

Intimacy

room for doubt, when people were willing to transgress their own limited thinking and to challenge others' ways of thinking. He even questioned how bad it was to cross his own lines. And he bought a T-shirt that read 'Outside of your comfort zone is where the magic happens.' By being less rigid and becoming more **flexible with his own boundaries**, he discovered new people, new emotions and new stories.

And that became his new mindset in his team, workplace and life. Pushing the envelope, facing his fears. Not everyone liked this. And if that was the case, he listened. He discovered that real encounters happened on the edge of not-knowing. He learned to balance together, to test the limits, to take risks without being overcome by fear. He learned to stretch, not panic. He found that meaningful encounters come about when you manage to talk to each other about your wishes, desires and limits. Better **communication** generated moments of quiet time, created space for feeling small and vulnerable. But also moments of greatness, sparkle and fireworks.

He established a rhythm. If it got too boring, he took action. When he noticed he started needing the rush too much, he took a break. It was like breathing in and out. A rhythm for him and the people around him. And he found himself daring to look the other in the eye during difficult talks and peak moments. He no longer lived in the dark, but with the lights on. In a state of flow. Jamming. Searching. Finding.

Rebel mindset and moral courage

There are many, complicated issues that urgently need solutions today. Climate change, wars and poverty, to begin with. We also have crises in healthcare and education. And if there's one thing that sets humans apart as a species, it's our ability to work with large groups of strangers to anticipate and adapt to changes. Bees and ants are also known for their excellent teamwork in large groups, but they are unable to quickly change their complex systems. How can we use our unique abilities to become more inclusive in teams, the workplace and society as a whole?

Just like other mammals, like elephants, chimpanzees, wolves and dolphins, our collaboration is based on social relations. In this context, the number 150 circulates as the maximum number of people with whom we could develop a loving or hostile intimate relationship. We can't deal with more than 150 personal relationships. At the same time, though, we are able to work together with large groups of people. Just look around: we live in cities and countries with large populations and this generally works smoothly, aside from an occasional incident and a few persistent and quite horrible conflicts. How come? Because people are able to collectively come up with stories that we believe in wholesale, that create a bond. These stories give us a made-up and hence imaginary, order that becomes so ingrained and normal, that we start to see it as the absolute truth. This is called culture.

The notion of culture in a nutshell, again

We live in a world where nothing has meaning in and of itself. This means that we're faced with a gigantic, chaotic number of possible meanings. To deal with this, we create cultures. A culture orders the world in which we live and classifies it into categories. It provides direction by giving clues about what is real and true, and what isn't. Culture provides moral signposts, because it teaches us right from wrong, and aesthetic signposts, because it defines what's beautiful and what's ugly. If lots of people say the same thing about any of these categories, this becomes the truth and any other interpretation becomes false. Also, these rules and frameworks not only create order in our lives, they also give meaning to what we do and how we do it. They help us make sense of the world and answer our questions about why we do things. They give us principles to live by. Culture is not so much intended to reproduce uniformity. Every group has subcultures and variations on its rules and stories. Culture organizes diversity in such a way that we can navigate it. The cultural truth we grow up in then shapes our personal truth and outlook on life. It gives our personal thoughts, feelings and actions direction. In short, people shape cultures and culture shapes people in a never-ending interaction.

If I ask you to point to your nose, you can do this without missing a beat and without words. If I ask you to point to the economy, you'll use metaphors and tell me a bunch of stories. Economy, religion, education, society, organizational culture and so on, are all made-up stories. They're fictions with a very tangible impact on our daily lives, our bodies, our relationships and our emotions. By realizing these are fictions we have authored, we become more aware that we can rewrite them, too.

Breaking through the imaginary order

The ability of humans to create and pass on stories cannot be over-estimated. It has given us, Homo sapiens, so much power that we are now ruling planet earth. In *Homo Deus, Israeli historian Yuval Noah Harari explains how all large-scale forms of human collaboration are based on imaginary orders. These are collections of rules that exist in our minds only, but feel as real as gravity, comparable to the mindbugs I discussed in Chapter 3 on truth. This is great for mutual trust, which we direly need, because if everyone believes in the same story, repeats the same story and lives according to the same story, it's easier for us to assess and predict each other's behavior. This creates order in the chaos of possible interpretations and infuses our relations with calmness and trust.*

The problem is just that if we accept or are forced to accept more diversity, we'll need to adapt our existing divisions and stories. This is especially true if our current stories disadvantage some groups. It takes courage on everyone's part to enter the debate on this. There's something weird about our feelings of unfairness, though. If we experience unfairness in a small group, we get all emotional, but if we see it at a larger scale, we are less deeply affected. If, for instance, on a five-person team, one of the team members got paid significantly less money for doing the same work, we'd be all up in arms. However, we also know that the person in India who sews our jeans lives below the poverty line. Even if this strikes us as unfair, few people get upset about this daily. How come? Harari explains that large groups of people act differently than smaller groups of people. The farmers toil in the shadow of the palace. The factory workers are working up a sweat around the corner from the air-conditioned boardroom. Somehow, we think of this as normal. People are not equal, as we saw in Chapter

▶ We live in a made-up, constructed story with collections of rules and patterns that exist in our minds only, yet feel as real as gravity. A bit like in the movie The Matrix.

IMAGE: FLICKR.COM/D_PHAM (CREATIVE COMMONS)

2 on power. It's the order of things. That's the way the cookie crumbles. White collar workers usually earn more than blue collar workers. And products in the supermarket aren't ordered alphabetically, Dutch philosopher Tim Fransen argues in *Letters to Koos*. Our stories create stable, human hierarchies that facilitate massive cooperation, but they're not inescapable laws of nature. They're fabrications. But because they are part of the long history of our species and embedded in our procedures, rules, buildings, laws and privileges, they feel natural.

Do it yourself, don't wait to be saved

It's not easy to change existing realities. Not even at the level of the individual. Like me, you might have a fitness club membership and sincerely mean to go exercise at least once a week, but nine times out of ten fail to find the time. Sometimes it takes a health scare or a partner who starts to complain about the shape you're in for you to change your ways. Sometimes, it takes a bunch of friends who go to the same club and sweep you up in their enthusiasm. And on rare occasions, you might manage to motivate yourself, if only because you hope to get compliments from others.

We can let changes toward more inclusion develop slowly and step-by-step, waiting for things to unfold in an evolution. Or we can break with the current state of affairs more radically and quickly, through revolution. I believe both ways can lead to important, sustainable effects. But what if we want to see a major shift in a short span of time, like ensuring that half the members of Congress are women, or thirty percent of kindergarten teachers are men, or bicultural people are proportionately represented in top-level jobs? To achieve that, we have to take risks and stretch our limits. More diversity and more inclusion means combatting the status quo, which often requires a rebel mindset. More revolution than evolution, in other words.

Real revolutions are few and far between. For one, because they are not beneficial to those in power, and therefore people with power actively prevent others from joining forces to oppose them. I once worked with the middle management of an organization where worker dissatisfaction was high. The meetings people held were always strictly departmental. When I suggested they change that and organize interdepartmental meetings, so that the various managers could share and learn from each other's best practices, my audience became restive. There was no way they were going to do that, because senior management would interpret that as a coup and that would kill their careers. Far too risky.

Particularly if we want more diversity and inclusion, we shouldn't wait for the powers that be to arrange it for us. The odds are extremely slim that they would ever do that. Which is a shame, because it would be the fastest route. As I said before, if those at the center of power want something, they can make it happen in a snap. Well, that's overstating it a bit, but when there's a will, there's a way. Our current leaders, who are in a position to influence the meaning of our collective thought and actions, stand to lose a lot. And so do we. The chaos of change affects everyone, for different reasons. And change is something you create together, with people from both minority and majority positions. Dominance blindness disappears and minority stress is shared.

Moral courage and doubt

People are naturally inclined to stay themselves and cling to their own identity. This is true especially when dealing with diversity. We're prepared to make radical decisions, to move, to change jobs or partners in order to maintain our identity without having to work hard for it. We want to stay within our network. However, we can't control the world; it just keeps turning and changing. So we have to get moving, we have to change and our identities and loyalties change at the same pace. Because we'd prefer to stay inert, taking action requires courage and a rebel mindset on the part of our leaders and those making the change. It requires us to face the truth and act accordingly, so we can create meaningful encounters that everyone can participate in.

Discussing diversity issues often boils down to raising points like unwritten rules and dilemmas and the redistribution of privilege. Those are things that usually don't earn you any brownie points. Change generally involves sacrifice. Inclusion touches on issues of integrity, loyalty, honesty, leadership and discrimination. No one wants to go down in history as a bad boy in any of these respects. That's why it's important to talk about these issues in a non-threatening, high-energy manner. That takes courage, self-confidence and, ironically, a heaping helping of doubt. Doubt creates the necessary curiosity to deal with contrasts, polarities and conflict.

'We draw real strength from the stories we make up.'
– Yuval Noah Harari

It gets messy, our attempts

I can find it pretty difficult to talk about inclusion. Sometimes, it feels like things are not moving along fast enough or that others are too stuck in their own prejudice, which also impedes my own flexibility. Stretching your limits and deferring judgment has to be reciprocal. It helps to remind myself that people, including myself, regularly make stupid choices, even if they should know better. It helps to remember that life tends to get messy and that everyone is simply trying to make the best of it. We may hope that our leaders know best, but they're just people, too. And in their own clumsy human way, they, too, can fall short of perfect. Working together on more diversity and inclusion is not a matter of following an orderly logic and ticking off boxes of a well-structured plan. Prepare for emotion, lots of it, a bit of craziness here and there and absolutely no miracles. If you do that, it might just turn out a tiny bit better than you expected.

'People who are crazy enough to think they can change the world, are the ones who do.'
– Steve Jobs

A movement rather than a manifesto of change

If you want more diversity and inclusion, you need more than a policy document or a vague statement of intent by management. A good first step is to make public promises, by signing a manifesto, for instance. But the real work is what comes next. How do we guarantee that everyone gets to participate, speak their mind and really help make decisions? Inclusion is a complicated tangle of conscious and unconscious emotions, needs and interests. And it also includes the feelings, sto-

How to start a movement

- Some of the lessons I took from Seth Godin, described in his book Tribes.
- • Publish a manifesto.
- • Be available to your community, so they can share your language.
- • Make sure your followers can find each other.
- • Keep in mind that money is not the object of your movement.
- • Track your progress.
- • Practice transparency, since it's the only way we can see where we stand.
- • Let the movement be bigger than yourself.
- • Dare to follow someone else as well, since movements grow and you can't control everything.
- • Hook up with similar movements.
- • Resist opposing movements and the status quo. Exclude outsiders from the start. Be faithful to your goals and beliefs. Plan your own path and don't let others sidetrack you. Draw from your own strength and act on it.
- • Follow your heart. Draw a picture of the future and move in that direction.

– Seth Godin in *Tribes*

ries and behavior of the brave souls who went before us. These are not changes that you can manage or implement using an action plan or through knowledge exchange. It's not a process you can manage and control. It is, however, a movement you can kick-start, contribute to and push forward.

Good intentions are not enough

Greater diversity can make us question our current norms. Striving for more inclusion, and hence for more different voices to chime in, can create confusion. It causes people to think twice about the made-up protocols and codes of conduct that everyone believes in. Many people find this upheaval annoying, because the status quo provides them with a familiar, safe order. In other words, diversity is not for the faint-hearted. You have to be strong, know why you want to do it and find people who are willing to support and help you. At the first signs of opposition, you may be tempted to think: never mind, at least I tried. But that's not good enough. If we don't put our money where our mouth is, we'll never get to jam and dance.

Slash and burn

If you decide to take the hard, confrontational approach, it's simple. All procedures, habits and behaviors that are obstructing inclusion need to go. Just stop doing them. Slash and burn. In practice, this is not easy to do, but the principle is very simple. It starts with raising consciousness. For example, keep track of every example of exclusion you notice in yourself, in others, at work, at home, on the street, in the media. These can be big issues, like the pay gap, or ageism, but also small things like the invitation to your office summer barbecue promising 'plenty of beer and whole sides of pork'. This might reflect the writer's idea of the best barbecue ever, but others might think: 'OMG, how macho can you get?' or 'I guess I'll just pass on the meat, if there's no Halal beef,' or 'I'll just bring my own vegetarian salad, then'. Once you've kept track of these examples, you can think of what you want to do with the insights you now have.

If you decide to discard all excluding behavior and procedures, this is the ultimate power issue in the power-love duality. You take the lead. You stop making any 'jokes' about women, gays, Arabs and so on and start calling out others when they do. Every time. That's not easy, because others might feel caught out or under attack. And you're the party pooper. But this changes in the dialogue that takes hold. And after a while, people start catching on to the fact that exclusion is undesirable behavior. Together, you start to come up with new ways of behaving, new and more inclusive ways of dealing with each other. A new culture is shaped by stacks of micro-decisions. As a man, say no to panel discussions that consist of men only. As a young entrepreneur, explicitly invite seniors to apply to jobs in your start-up. Hire a visually challenged, new co-worker and find out what adaptations you need to make in the workplace. Shake those foundations, yank those chains, do something. Take action and change the power dynamics in your space. Know when a compromise is unacceptable and have the courage to take the unbeaten path. Inclusion requires everyone to adapt, including minorities. Be yourself, yet adapt – it's a two-way street!

Holding space

While we're going through the upheaval of change, we need to make room for the stress caused. We need the love side of the equation, we need to create a safe foundation for discussion and resolution of problems, as we saw in Chapter 4 on trust. This can sometimes require the patience of a saint. Part of this is accepting that people don't all change at the same pace. So we need to listen really well, do our best to relate to what people tell us and help those who stumble to get back up. In the case of profound changes, this may take months or even years.

This patience is inclusive leadership too. Stop explaining why change is important and stop making recommendations on how inclusion could be done better. Instead, listen to each other's personal stories, talk about difference and similarities. Increase intimacy and discover shared passions.

You mean women actually have to be paid more?

I was once asked to do several sessions about inclusion, specifically gender inclusion, for the senior management of a large accountancy firm. When they invited me, they had fifty partners, only one of whom was a woman. Our conversations were wonderful, full of aha-experiences and very open. It wasn't the first time the firm had put the issue on the agenda and various questionnaires had shown that the company's policy not to allow part-time jobs had led many women in their thirties to leave. There was also a great deal of dissatisfaction about the pay gap: men earned a higher salary than women who did the same work.

I asked the participants how important they considered greater diversity. Very important, they said. *I asked how bad it was for them and for the business, that so few women were rising to the top. Terribly bad, they said. I asked how high on the agenda the issue was. It was their No. 1 challenge, they said. So I asked them how they usually went about urgent, high-priority business issues.* We establish a temporary taskforce with a full mandate to tackle the issue, they replied. Alright, I said. That seems like the right approach for this issue. Okay, they replied, but what should that group actually do? Um, I said, create part-time jobs and close the pay gap? A stunned silence ensued. Do you mean that all women should get paid more? Yes, I said. Or pay the men less, of course. They said they'd think about it.

Several weeks later I received a call. No, no taskforce had been established, but would I please come back for a repeat performance? They'd like to organize another inspiring session for their women's network. I said I'd gladly do it, but only if they'd first set up a taskforce and take the first real action.

That was the last time I ever heard from this firm.

Maybe I should have been more patient. Maybe I was too focused on creating space and not enough on holding space. Perhaps I wanted too much revolution and would have gotten further with a quiet evolution. But I didn't have the patience and I got the impression I was simply an item on a checklist. Good intentions look good on policy documents. Real change requires taking action.

Widening relationship circles

We like to have it good with the people around us. We tend to put a lot of energy into those relationships. When our own well-being or that of our group is threatened, a powerful force is unleashed to protect us. It's fairly simple to use this force to create more diversity and inclusion. If everything has to be pleasant in the circle we've drawn around ourselves, than the only rebellious action we need to take is to all widen our relationship circles. Not so wide as to span the globe, but wide enough to include your neighbors, or your co-worker from a different department. Imagine what would happen if you decided that your group did not just equal your team, but also included the whole department. This means you have to make different practical decisions. In this way, the energy you put into creating favorable circumstances for 'your group' will extend to more people. Thus, our natural penchant for tribalism and 'putting our own group first' can be used to the benefit of more people.

The principle is the same in our battle against the plastic soup in the ocean and general environmental pollution. It goes without saying that you pick up a soda can and an empty candy wrapper in your front yard. If everyone would practice 'Leave No Trace' and pick up all their own garbage when hiking or after a day on the beach, but would also pick up just three items of trash that other people had left behind, it would go a long way. The effort required from each individual is small, but the impact is great. Similarly, if everyone were to expand their group just a tiny bit, we'd become much more diverse and inclusive.

Warriors without swords

It is hard to stand up to polarization without becoming a pusher. The call for radical nuance, to listen to the shades of grey, sounds dull. Mobilizing the silent midfielders doesn't have a very sexy ring to it. Black and white statements and expletives sound more powerful than talk about togetherness. Not to mention how hard it is to come up with tough-talking soundbites about inclusion. I've personally experienced how hesitant TV producers are to invite me as a guest on their talk shows, because 'you look at everything from all sides, and that's a risk for a medium like TV'. Language is important. Words are, in fact, actions.

In the end, inclusion is about love, compassion, understanding and humanity. Soft talk that tells us to push hard to get change started. Sadly, diversity and inclusion often have to be fought for with all our might. There is a lot of resistance. Organizational consultant Margaret Wheatley talks about inclusion warriors who go on the warpath with soft weapons that can hit people hard in their hearts. Inclusion is not a rational issue. It's not about comprehension, but about feelings and willingness. By creating new connections you disrupt the status quo and hence the whole gamut of ranking, power differences, privilege, norms and values.

Do it together

All too often, diversity managers in organizations work hard with inadequate funds, a weak mandate and a lack of connections in strategic positions. I've seen it time and again. It's not necessary though. Let's work together or let's act as leaders, to ensure that the various project teams that work on inclusion can join forces and don't have to vie for budget and time on the management team. Don't sideline diversity, but give it the attention it deserves. Rank it up! More diversity among your customers, production chains and networks can only be matched with more diversity in your team and organization.

As a group with a mission, you need to reach out to other groups. There's a fascinating yet damaging dynamic at work in many groups that strive for similar innovations: they tend to backbite and compete over which method or approach is best, most radical or most effective. Like vegans and vegetarians can squabble about whose eating habits are better and healthier. Neither group eats meat, so that could be their common characteristic. But as we know by now, when several people or groups of people want the same thing and perceive scarcity, this becomes a source of conflict...

And even though groups share characteristics, obviously there are different ways of fighting social injustice, lack of diversity, discrimination and exclusion. There are both ground-breaking, activist groups and conservative groups that go about change step-by-step. Each is valuable in its own way. I think it's important to join forces. Just as in the wake of the #MeToo debate, the next step seems to be that women all over the globe are rising up against the abuse of (sexual) power. Let men support them in this.

Step-by-step: calculate the risks

A rebel mindset doesn't always have to involve chaining yourself to a gate and being dragged away by the police. Not everyone can be Pussy Riot. There are many roads that lead to Rome. Revolutions can also be fought one step at a time. One person, one action, one word can start a mass movement. Many of us probably wonder how we can speak up and call people out on their unacceptable behavior without being a do-gooder or hurting our own careers. It helps to know exactly why you want something and what you're prepared to put on the line for it. Calculate the risks. You'll always risk something, but make sure that the risk you take is in proportion, that it still feels okay to you.

If you think this approach is too cautious and doesn't get you results fast enough, you'd probably like to take more radical action. Put your foot down. Set limits. Remember that any activist action will unleash a backlash, as we saw in Chapter 4, where I discussed polarization dynamics. That's the drawback.

I believe that all these efforts together create change and more diversity and inclusion. Personally, I try to find ways to prevent further polarization, yet still have the courage to start deeper conversations with people. I try to foster inclusion by raising difficult, uncomfortable issues and by helping others do the same, while validating and supporting everyone involved. I try to do this by speaking my mind and by listening to others with radical nuance. By empathizing with the different perspectives. This is not easy, particularly when people's perspectives are worlds apart.

IMAGE: © ANP FOTO / ANDREJ ISAKOVIC

Tips from Pussy Riot

Pussy Riot is a Russian political punk rock band that consists of women who wear colorful balaclavas. They protest Putin's dictatorial behavior with eye-catching, but strictly non-violent demonstrations. Co-founder Nadya Tolokonnikova was imprisoned for two years for a protest that consisted of song and dance. In her 2016 book *How to Start a Revolution*, she gives tips for starting a revolution:

- Every gesture you make has meaning, even when you're unaware of it. Every gesture you make prompts rules. There is not a single decision you make just for yourself.
- Redefine your criteria for success. Start now.
- You're not likely to win by force and violence. If you win, that'll be because of your resourcefulness and being a little crazy in the head.
- Speak up, keep speaking publicly and writing until the very last, because we have only one way of winning this unequal struggle—with our thoughts, our feelings and our sincerity.
- Smile when you protest.
- Don't forget to thank your enemies for the services they've provided for you.
- Take what you need. Play proactively. Take the upper hand.
- Penetrate like skin cream. Get into the pores.
- Make sure that you know that which you criticize inside out. Take back the initiative.
- Lose yourself and then find yourself again.

It just takes a small group of committed individuals

The good news is that all it takes is a small group of committed individuals to change the bigger story. This small group needs to have a clear mission, which they all believe in, to spread this story in every possible way. These individuals also need to show behavior that's consistent with their beliefs. And this behavior needs to be easy to copy. They need to tell stories that are so attractive that other people will be eager to pass them on. If these other people happen to have a large network, the ball will really start rolling. New behavior can spread like a virus. That's how cultural change works, in a nutshell.

A powerful, inspiring story

You can't create an inclusive jam culture on your own. It's a team effort. To this end, we need a language that gives us energy and a story that connects us and melds our differences together. That is not to say that we should all want and do the same. As long as we're able to arrive at temporary, workable agreements that leave room for our differences and that help us to move toward a more inclusive culture. So we keep taking action.

But, but …

Many businesses find reasons not to hire a more diverse workforce. With reference to hiring people with special needs, for instance, many cite the following reasons for not doing so: the job is too specialized; the environment is too hectic; the pace is too high; we've already hired a couple of people with special needs; and, it's not convenient because we're in the middle of a restructuring operation. I see quite a few assumptions that need to be debunked. In 2015, the Dutch government passed the Participation Act, hoping that the business community would clean up their act a little. The law is aimed at encouraging individuals to participate in the labor market to the extent they're able to, and at encouraging businesses to hire people with special needs. The ultimate goal is to make people less dependent on social security. Unfortunately, the law has not been very effective (SCP report November 2019), so more and different action is needed.

'Never doubt that a small group of thoughtful, committed citizens can change the world; indeed, it's the only thing that ever has.'
– Margaret Mead

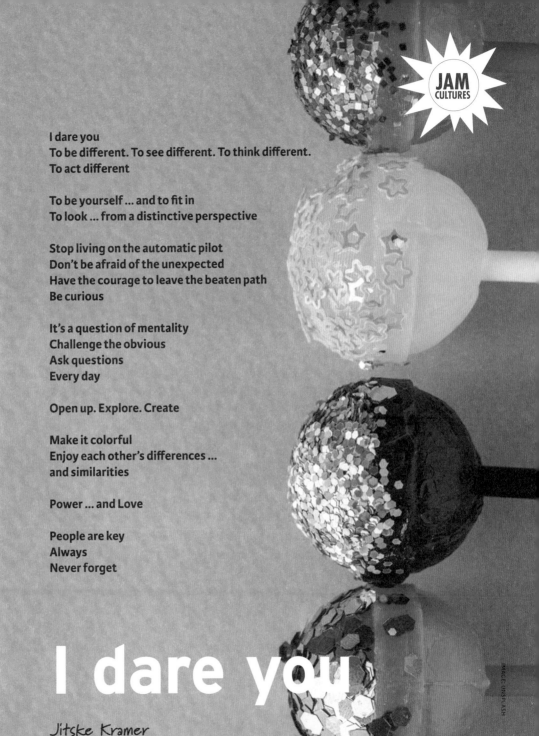

I dare you
To be different. To see different. To think different.
To act different

To be yourself ... and to fit in
To look ... from a distinctive perspective

Stop living on the automatic pilot
Don't be afraid of the unexpected
Have the courage to leave the beaten path
Be curious

It's a question of mentality
Challenge the obvious
Ask questions
Every day

Open up. Explore. Create

Make it colorful
Enjoy each other's differences ...
and similarities

Power ... and Love

People are key
Always
Never forget

I dare you

Jitske Kramer

Bij deze tekst heb ik ook een film gemaakt. Geeft een mooie start voor vergaderingen, trainingen en events:

https://www.
youtube.com/
watch?v=R_
GXM7s7NkI

An energizing web of compatible stories

We'd like to see ourselves as rational, smart people who act consciously. Maybe not when we're on vacation, but most definitely in the workplace. There, we act with purpose, according to objective logic. That's a story we'd like to believe, but the reality I've observed suggests something else. We're much more driven by social logic. Our emotions are often the decisive factor in firing an employee, selecting people for a project team or launching a new product.

Stories condense and pull people together. At the same time, a good story can make room for difference, especially when it uses metaphors that are ambiguous and leave room for multiple interpretations. One example of such a strong metaphor and story is Kate Raworth's *Doughnut Economics*. This helps all the different actors to tell a shared story. Narratives are an inestimable part of the solution of complex issues. Narratives provide a language and a framework for us to act in, so we don't have to helplessly wait around for 'politics' or 'management' to do something. That's why the story and the way it's told are so important. It's not about shouting popular slogans or firing blanks. The story has to be right, it has to be genuine and it must be told in a way that leaves room for others. A story provides identity. The !Kung people in Botswana put it like this; 'you're an adult only when you can tell your own story'. We could extrapolate this to: 'you're a mature group only when you can tell your own story,' and then only if your story leaves room for different perceptions. In other words, a story that is compatible rather than communal.

Diversity and inclusion: asset or liability?

Every year, the Netherlands Institute for Social Research (*Sociaal en Cultureel Planbureau*; SCP) polls the population about how well they and the country are doing. According to the SCP, we're doing great! The Dutch had rated their lives at 7.8 out of 10 for three years in a row, according to the SCP 2018 report. Our optimism is on the rise. In 2008, 20% of the respondents reported they were optimistic, while 60% said they were pessimistic about the future. In 2018, there was a big shift. In that year, 50% of the respondents said they felt optimistic about the future and only 40% reported they felt pessimistic. The number of people with a higher education keeps growing. Crime keeps falling. Fewer people are victims of a crime and fewer people feel unsafe. However, there is one problem that is a constant: living together. Almost all the respondents call living together their greatest concern, greater than their concerns about the economy, immigration and healthcare.

In other words, we're happy with our own lives, but we find it hard to be happy together with others. The reasons people give for this are: lack of respect, intolerance, antisocial behavior and egotism. It goes without saying that only other people are guilty of this, never the respondents themselves! The solution the respondents suggest are: become more tolerant, more social, less egotistical and show some more respect. That will make everybody even more happy. It looks to me like we've set ourselves a clear task by way of the SCP poll. To achieve this, we need to look at diversity in a more positive and perhaps more realistic, light.

Whether you regard diversity as positive or negative, depends on your outlook on life. As I stated in the Introduction, in terms of diversity, people believe in one of two extremes. Living together, living with diversity is either possible or impossible:

Story No. 1: Living with diversity is impossible
People seek out others who are like them. That's always been the case and that's not going to change. That's the stuff we're made of. We protect our own people first, set clear boundaries and build walls to protect ourselves. Diversity is complicated. It's a hassle and not a good idea.

Story No. 2: Living with diversity is possible
No two people are the same. That's always been the case and that's not going to change. That's the stuff we're made of. People have always sought out others, for trading purposes and to exchange knowledge and beliefs. Diversity is fun, productive and something to be enjoyed.

Both stories are true. Diversity causes less social integration and makes organizations more susceptible to conflict. However, diversity also makes organizations smarter, more innovative and more flexible. We can't choose between these two stories and we don't have to. We can stop debating this. It is a polarity. It's not an either-or issue. It's like breathing, in and out. Sometimes you set limits, sometimes you open up. If you set too many boundaries, you get lonely, because no one can come and visit anymore. If you open up too much, you get lonely because you lose touch with yourself.

Still, your actions are informed by your point of departure. If you believe in Story No. 1, you spend your time building walls and determining where you'll put the windows and the drawbridges. If you believe in Story No. 2, you live with on a piece of land without a fence, and you decide where you need to build a wall or a moat to make the place feel safe and authentic.

The debate shouldn't be about who is right, but on how we can open up some of the time and set boundaries at other times. The debate should be on how we can benefit from our differences. How we can use the tension this creates to fuel the energy we need to jam. How we can utilize our differences instead of pitting them against each other.

Too often, the inclusion story is reactive

Inclusion warriors use soft weapons, like I said before. The message of love, connection, compassion, dialogue and listening to each is often a lot less resounding than the battle cries of power, force, 'our nation first', drive and debate. This makes it look like the inclusion story is a response to other people's stories. For example, people respond to some alt-right statement or something an angry neighbor says, and every time we do that, we inadvertently help promote the other's story and get sucked into further polarization. Which is exactly the opposite of what we want. Which prompts us to shout that you shouldn't discriminate, that it's wrong to exclude, that the other should 'act normal' and show some respect. Thus, inclusion becomes the antithesis of exclusion, while we should work together on determining how and where we want to set which limits. Freedom is achieved by taking a flexible attitude towards boundaries. Freedom is the result of arranging meaningful encounters in the liminal zone.

Don't get me wrong. You have to take a stand against wrongdoing and defend yourself against opinions that harm others or yourself. But before you know it, you could end up fueling a polarization you're trying to end. It's key to turn the story into something we all have in common.

*'People don't believe what you tell them.
They rarely believe what you show them.
They often believe what their friends tell them.
They always believe what they tell themselves.
What leaders do: they give people stories they can tell themselves. Stories about the future and about the change.'*
– Seth Godin

Moral high ground

The problem with sustained action for more inclusion is that the people who are aware of and point out the unconscious dynamics of exclusion and mindbugs are often seen as highly irritating. They get branded as 'a bunch of know-it-alls that just tell us what we're doing wrong the whole time' or as 'sad do-gooders who think they're better than us'. Or people put them down for spoiling things: 'It used to be fun, before they showed up. They've ruined it.' Or people suggest that 'all that talk makes it out to be more serious and worse than it really is'. The people who raise the issue of inequality are under a microscope: if the actions of people with strong ideals are not 100% in accordance with their message—say they eat meat or take a plane while they're advocating sustainability—they are viciously attacked for it. Their message tends to get lost in personal attacks and jabs. Particularly on social media.

This moral jousting is difficult to tackle and blocks many conversations. The way Gloria Wekker writes about 'waking up from white innocence' seems to imply that 'all white people' have been asleep for years, while 'everyone else' has been 'woke' since the beginning of time. I know she is writing about whole groups at the level of society as a whole, but it makes me, as a white individual, feel stupid and makes me want to defend myself and my peer group. Uncovering institutional racism is painful in so many ways for everyone involved. Those afflicted by dominance blindness can suddenly feel hopelessly naive and caught out, locked in a matrix whose existence they were unaware of. Personally, I dressed up as Black Pete for my children for years and had great fun doing so, while as a teenager I had already been aware of inequality and had written a critical poem about the phenomenon—'The December feast of ginger bread is like society itself/one white guy is the leader/the black man is his serf.' These two realities existed side by side in me, though if I can now no longer imagine how this was possible. The more aware people become of inequality, privilege and power imbalances, the more cultural shocks, identity issues and sensemaking questions they're confronted with. That's part of the process. Dominance blindness dissipates, stress is shared and the possibility for a new order emerges. That is the zone of discomfort where everyone has to face their own pain, fear and shame. That's where we have to keep each other on our toes and where we have to hold on to each other.

Again, fighting for more inclusion takes courage. Some people will make you out to be a nag and a drag, while others will put you down for being too soft. Yet others may call on you to instigate more dialogue. You can never please everybody. No one said it was going to be easy.

The Ideal Story

The question we need to answer is this: how do we plant a powerful, high-energy story in people's minds that does justice to all the different viewpoints, fears, hope and inclusion and exclusion mechanisms? A story with the right balance between reason, facts and fiction. Fiction, you say? Indeed, fiction. Because it has to be an emotionally appealing narrative that gives us an ideal, a collective fantasy that we can believe in. It has to be a story with—new—rules that open our eyes of ways of working and living together that are more equal and more satisfactory, that are challenging but doable. A story that tells the inconvenient truth, but doesn't rub it in too hard. A story that you'd like to participate in, no matter what your ideas on diversity are. Because you're human. A story that provokes and piques your curiosity. A story that's grand and mythical, and yet small and practical enough to start applying right away. A story that's easy to put into practice. A story that invites you to write the next chapter. A story that provides ethical guidance. A story with a constant alertness to change and renewal. And nuance. And doubt, because doubt expands your world.

Like that.

...

So now what?

...

Well...

...

Uhm

...

?!

...

The good news, I think, is that this story doesn't have to be a grand, complete narrative with a clear plot and fully worked-out script from the get-go. It's about all of us together creating a visible web of stories and experiences. Big and small. With examples, thoughts, actions, poems, songs, new laws, procedures and measures. With language that touches people's hearts and helps us gain a firmer foothold. Everyone does what they're good at, what they feel comfortable with. Without direction from a central coordinator or conductor. Are you good at devising procedures and adapting laws? Go right ahead. Do you excel in writing policy documents? Incorporate inclusion! Do you have a large network? Connect people with each other! Linking diverse actions in diverse contexts helps you create powerful stories. Talk about what you do. Share your actions, thoughts, fears and dreams with others.

The best I can hope for is that this book contributes to that joint effort. The appendices include a Jam Cultures Questionnaire and a Jam Cultures Canvas that can help you start the conversation about inclusion in your workplace. These tools can also help you take the actual, concrete steps to improve the situation, so that your organization doesn't just talk the talk, but also walks the walk.

How to find the courage to jam

More diversity isn't served on a silver platter. More inclusion isn't just conjured up out of thin air. These issues require us to stretch our boundaries, take risks, find our rhythm and sync it with others, deal with tension and oppositions. And each of us individually, but also the group, the team, the department, the organization and society as a whole, has to take part in this. That's a hefty challenge. We can't wait around. We need to get to work right now and start solving the complicated situations and problems of today, tomorrow and the day after. We must do this step-by-step, but we need to bring a rebel, revolutionary mindset to the task.

Questions to reflect on and discuss with others

Plenty of food for thought, I think. Here's a list of questions you can explore, either by yourself or with others. Share your insights on social media, so we can all benefit: #jamcultures.

- Do you have enough faith in inclusive cultures? How can you increase your faith?
- For what cause would you walk through the fire? I was at Robben Island and the jail where Nelson Mandela was held prisoner for decades. A daunting place. The guide asked me the question I now put to you: 'For what belief would you be willing to risk a thirty-year prison sentence?'
- What examples can you recall of people showing compassion for you as a person or for the situation you were in? Can you describe this experience? Can you recall that feeling? What strength can you derive from this?
- How do you make sure you are aligned with the people you live and work with?
- Do you make people adapt, or do you adapt your way of working with them?
- What is a source of stress for you: other people or activities? Can you identify rhythm problems in these?
- What negativity do you regularly exude? How can you change this?
- What does participation mean to you? What do you do to include others and to make sure they can participate too?
- How would you answer these questions from a workplace perspective? And from the perspective of your professional role?

Do something

Reflecting and talking are important, but so is taking action. Below I've provided a few ideas that are ready to be put into action. Clearly, this is not intended to be exhaustive. Add your own ideas and make the list longer. Share your insights on social media, so we can all benefit: #jamcultures.

- Stop intimidating and silencing the people that challenge you. And stop saying you don't do that.
- Create unusual, non-obvious connections in unorthodox places. Arrange strange encounters and encounter strangers. Your teachers are right in front of you. Learn from passers-by. Invite that third grade teacher to come talk to the CEO of Unilever. And if you happen to be the managing director of a large wholesaler, shadow a registered nurse for a day. Mix stories and experiences. Shake things up and regularly refresh your mind by creating new input.
- Hunt down clichés and debunk them. On your own, or with your team, or your family. Why do people do the things they do, and in the way they do them? Why don't they behave differently? Raise these issues, read about them, get out there to find the stories.
- Don't give the diversity portfolio with minority issues to the minorities (people of color talking about people of color, women about women, LGBTQ+ about LGBTQ+, special needs about special needs...). Don't! Let high-ranked individuals from the mainstream deal with minority issues and people from minority groups with mainstream issues. Everywhere: in the workplace, in politics and in the media. Obviously, not on islands, but in connection with each other.
- Don't turn diversity into a separate issue, a fun, optional add-on. Make diversity and inclusion part of the main issues on the agenda in your workplace. Make it part of your core business.
- Have the courage to prioritize diversity and inclusion not only on paper, but in your actions and decisions, too. If those at the center of power decide it's important, they can take the necessary action in no time at all. Take that as your leaping-off point. Assume a can-do attitude.
- Don't think things will go right by themselves, that time is the great equalizer. Recognize the urgency. Make it part of your recruitment policy, traineeships, mentoring. Define inclusion targets. Be bold and be brave.
- Call on senior management to actively support the cause and show behavior that sends the right message.

Inclusion Principle: Vary your rhythm

- Attune your rhythm to others, to the goals at hand and the context.
- Slow down, so you can hear others and yourself.
- Change the procedure, not the people.

Inclusion Principle: Do it together

- Fight for togetherness.
- Break with procedures and habits that hamper inclusion.
- Openly support good initiatives.
- Make room for informal, human contact.
- Create an energizing, compatible story about inclusion.

- Make yourself and others responsible for inclusive behavior. Talk about it: share stories, make it a topic of conversation. Discuss what concrete steps can be taken: who is selected for what position; who is involved in the decision-making; who do you talk to about this, and when?

- Include inclusive behavior as a requirement in job descriptions and job evaluations. Demand that any third-party training institution you hire includes inclusion as a core issue in all its programs, regardless of whether these are about leadership, strategy, sales, personal development or communication. And if you offer such training programs, make sure to include these issues in all your programs, even when your clients don't explicitly ask you to.

- *Walk the talk.* Do as you say and say what you're going to do. Display behavior that sets a good example.

- *Talk the walk.* Tell others what you do about inclusion and diversity on your team, in your workplace. Spread the word. Share your best practices, talk about the difficulties you encounter. Make it an upbeat, contagious story to inspire others to copy your inclusive behavior.

- To determine what your point of departure is, you can use the Jam Cultures Questionnaire and the Jam Cultures Canvas (see Appendices). These help you to identify areas for improvement and decide how much diversity you think you can handle. You can repeat these tests at a later time to check how much progress you've made.

- Surprise someone by talking to them. It only needs to take a minute, while waiting in line in the checkout lane at the supermarket, or at the bus stop. Or it could take two hours, when you decide to rekindle that friendship with a long-lost friend. Turn this into a habit.

- Find a small thing you'd like to change. For example, get up fifteen minutes earlier, or walk around the block every day, drink two liters of water every day, call your mother every other day. Do this at least seven times in a row. During and after take the time to feel how this made you feel and to note how your environment responded to it.

- Make a banner and take to the streets if you think that a particular viewpoint needs more public attention. Also, be aware that this might fuel a tension you'd rather see diminished. Find your own way. All voices deserve to be heard.

Our Story: Human Dimensions

This is the story about inclusion that is the basis for Human Dimensions. This is how we jam and how we use the Jam Circle. This is what works for us. I'd like to share this to inspire others. I'm curious to hear about your best practices and your ways of creating an inclusive culture in the workplace. Let me know. Preferably on social media, so we can all benefit. Please use #jamcultures, so we can find each other. You can find us on LinkedIn, Facebook, Twitter (@HumanDimensionJ) and on Instagram (@humandimensionsjk).

For Human Dimensions, inclusion is key in all sorts of different ways. It's important to us as individuals, but also as an essential part of all our core activities. Our core value is the 'independently together' polarity. This is the principle underlying our collaboration and all the work we do for clients. Once a year—and every time a new member joins our tribe—we have a heart-felt dialogue about what these words mean to us. To this end, we use the Jam Cultures Canvas and various conversation models from the Lewis Deep Democracy method and other techniques from *Building Tribes.*

We use these dialogues to distill our best practices, which we then translate into Temporary Work Agreements. But we also collect our *tough questions*. These are the things that we run up against, things that suck. It's not always easy to have these dialogues, but it is very important. And it helps us to formulate workable agreements, our temporary work agreements (see p. 209), which we refer to all year long, so we can adapt and change what turns out not to work so well. For example, we'd like to create more space for peer supervision and we're all struggling with our time commitments. Because this is a known issue, we're looking for ways to improve on this. Another area of improvement is our own diversity. We're happy with our own and our clientele's demographic diversity (30-65 years of age); gender diversity (though slightly more women than men); religious diversity; educational diversity; industry diversity (slightly more public than private, though); diversity of skills; and cultural diversity (though we'd prefer more). Areas of improvement include our wish to reach a more diverse audience and how to increase the diversity of color and cultural background in our own—growing—team and collaborations.

Another principle underlying our way of working is based on what I learned during a trip to Iran. The principle is based on the Iranian concept of *taarof*, a complex form of etiquette and implicit rules of conduct. It's a subtle form of communication that revolves around politeness and deference. *Building Tribes* describes this subtle art of etiquette in more detail. At the time, I made my own translation of what I understood taarof to mean. We use these questions to identify the value of our product and our collaboration. They inform our pricing and our choice of the type of work we accept or reject. When dealing with complex issues, we often literally refer to these questions:

- God or the universe: does it make the world a better place?
- Suppliers: are the suppliers, manufacturers and the designers remunerated appropriately for the energy they've put into the product or service?
- Customers: is this the best deal for the customer, in terms of money and value?
- Ourselves: as a human being, do you get a good feeling from the deal? And as an entrepreneur?
- Fellow entrepreneurs: is there a good balance between give and take on the market?

Our dialogues based on the Jam Cultures Canvas have led to very practical set of rules, that we use as a basis for any collaboration. Currently—but open to change—our rules are:
- Always and at regular intervals ask whether anyone has a different view and whether we've heard everyone's viewpoint.
- You speak up about your own preferences and ideas, you defend them, but you also gladly attack them. Looking at an issue from every possible angle enables us to make the best decision at the time.
- Always start a meeting with a check-in. Include in this the questions you're scared of, that bother you, that you hope will not be asked. And always ask: what gossip do we need to share?
- Everyone can stand on their own two feet. You're invited and challenged to have and develop your own style of working and thinking. Procedures and scripts are nothing but guidelines; own them and share your new discoveries. We don't need to be in complete agreement on everything. Though the differences must be compatible enough to co-exist. If we can't reach a workable agreement, earlier best practices are leading. If even those don't help us to reach an agreement, Jitske—as the founder of Human Dimensions—decides.
- We assume that we can always learn more and that curiosity, wonder and doubt are our best guides.
- We want to become the best. That means that everybody can tag along and watch over each other's shoulder.

- We believe that stretch is the best way to learn and add value for ourselves, each other and our clients. We challenge each other, seek out comfort for the essential work-life balance and avoid panicking. Should panic strike anyway, then we raise the issue right away. And we keep an eye out for each other in this respect.
- We work with heart and soul. That means we hit highs and lows and that we find great enjoyment in our work, but that it also takes blood, sweat and tears. No one needs to feel bad about sharing their successes, blunders, nightmares and dreams. Everyone has their own rhythm, and their own degree of enthusiasm or restraint. We appreciate that.
- We're only human. Interaction is a messy process in which we assume everyone has the best of intentions.

We're on the road a lot and see each other in between our forays in different configurations and convene in full force about six times a year. We make sure we stay in touch through *Slack* (a sort of expanded messenger app). We have a #randomfun channel and a #randomshit channel to share different emotions about the same situation. Plus a #allthingsorganizational channel to solve practical issues. And we call each other on the phone and grab a coffee together. Or a glass of beer, or wine, or a soda. Our contract is just half a page long. We work together for as long as we like working together.

This is the contract that regulates our collaboration in Human Dimensions. It's based on trust, on equal footing, with room for difference, and a minimum number of binding agreements:

HUMAN DIMENSIONS

Independently Together

We agree to collaborate for as long as it feels good to both of us and we feel the values we exchange are equitable. We agree to work based on mutual trust and in total openness. This enables us to build each other up and to grow and help each other grow. We have a clear pricing arrangement and agree to carry out certified levels of Deep Democracy only under the Human Dimensions label. We commit to convening a few times a year at our Human Moments, where we share what we've learned. We also commit to learn together, from, about and to the benefit of, each other. We try to achieve for ourselves what we promise our clients. That's our goal and that's what we seek each other out for.

'Human Dimensions wants to activate organizations to be irresistible places of employment for all employees, but also for their customers, suppliers and society at large. Strong tribes. Safe for diversity. Ready for change. Strong tribes connect wherever possible, fight whenever necessary, repair where possible and part ways as a last resort.'

Utrecht, DATE

Jitske Kramer   Human.....................................
HumanDimensions

Bronnen

Braun, Danielle & Kramer, Jitske (2018). *The Corporate Tribe: Organizational Lessons from Anthropology*. London: Routledge.

Csikszentmihalyi, Mihaly (1990). *Flow: The Psychology of Optimal Experience*. New York: Harper and Row.

Fransen, Tim (2018). *Brieven aan Koos. Avonturen van een zolderkamerfilosoof. [Letter to Koos: The Adventures of an Arm-Chair Philosopher]*. Amsterdam: Das Mag Uitgevers.

Godin, Seth (2008). *Tribes: We Need You to Lead Us*. London: Piatkus Books.

Hall, Edward (1984). *The Dance of Life: The Other Dimensions of Time*. New York: Bantam Doubleday Dell Publishing Group.

Harari, Yuval Noah (2016). *Homo Deus: A History of Tomorrow*. London: Harvill Secker.

Huijer, Marli (2011). *Ritme. Op zoek naar een terugkerende tijd. [Rhythm: In Search of Recurring Time]*. Amsterdam: Uitgeverij Boom.

Kramer, Jitske & Braun, Danielle (2018). *Building tribes. Reisgids voor organisaties. [Building Tribes: Travel Guide for Organizations]* Deventer: Management Impact.

Modood, Tariq (2018). *Multicultural Nationalism*. Blog post-dated August 13, 2018: Open Democracy, https://www.opendemocracy.net/en/can-europe-make-it/multicultural-nationalism/

Scherder, Erik (2017). *Singing in the Brain. Over de unieke samenwerking tussen muziek en de hersenen. [Singing in the Brain: About the Unique Interaction Between Music and the Brain]*. Amsterdam: Athenaeum.

Tolokonnikova, Nadya (2016). *Pussy Riot: How to Start a Revolution*. London: Penguin.

Wheatley, Margaret, J. (2012). *So Far From Home: Lost and Found in Our Brave New World*. Oakland, CA: Berrett-Koehler Publishers.

Wiel, Harry van de (1999). *Geluk is ook niet alles. Naar een gedifferentieerde seksuologie. [Happiness Isn't Everything: Toward a Differentiated Sexology]. Inaugural address, dated January 19, 1999, University of Groningen*.

Jan Bommerez writes about flow and letting go. His website (in Dutch): www.lerenloslaten.com

APPENDICES

I Jam Cultures Questionnaire: Inclusion in Attitude and Behavior

This is an overview of the attitudes and behaviors which are key to achieving an inclusive corporate culture in Jam Cultures. This questionnaire has been divided into sections that reflect the chapters in this book. In each section, rate every statement on a scale of 1 to 10, where 1 is 'absolutely not applicable' and 10 is 'totally acceptable and frequently observable'.

The first questionnaire asks about you as an individual. You can fill it out yourself, or ask a co-worker to consider your behavior and attitudes and fill it out for you (and you can do the same for them). The second questionnaire asks about your group, team, department or organization as whole. Every respondent scores their own perception of the prevailing culture at the collective level. The results can be used to start a dialogue and to come to new agreements that will improve the situation. Full disclosure: I have been asked more than once whether this questionnaire has been validated. The answer is no. I compiled it based on my own study of many inclusion tests and my personal experiences in working on this issue.

How inclusive are you? Answer these questions for yourself, or ask someone else to answer them about you.

1 Difference - Don't clone *About our tendency to clone, and the pros and cons of stereotyping*	Rating (1 - 10)
1. I appreciate visible differences (clothes, age, gender, skin color, hairdos) among my co-workers or my customers. I like these differences and support them.	
2. I appreciate invisible differences (opinions, viewpoints, religions, characters, level of education) among my co-workers and my customers. I like these differences and support them.	
3. I understand how my appearance and preferences influence my decisions and ways of seeing.	
4. I deliberately work with people who are different from me.	
5. I judge ideas, not people.	
6. I consciously and actively question my prejudice and mindbugs.	
7. I keep learning about other cultures and religions by reading about them, visiting museums, talking to people and traveling.	
8. I base my actions on the idea that 'everyone is welcome, but not every type of behavior is acceptable'. I am aware that this boundary is different for every individual and every culture, which is why I am open to talking about this boundary.	

2 Power - See the power of power *About the pecking order and who has the power*	Rating (1 - 10)
1. I am fully aware of the issue of who sets the norm.	
2. I use my privileged position and place in the pecking order to the benefit of the larger community.	
3. I actively try to share my privileges with others (e.g. inviting others to give presentations or speak at conferences; open my networks; contribute financially; generate publicity; offer a vacation home for the weekend).	
4. I respect co-workers who rank higher on the ladder than me, but continue to see them as normal human beings; I neither demonize nor glorify them.	
5. I respect co-workers who rank lower on the ladder than me and continue to see them as normal human beings; I do not patronize them.	
6. I can see that ranking is multifaceted, that my co-workers can rank higher on some items than on others, and that the same can be said of me.	
7. I speak up when I notice that people are being excluded, patronized, ridiculed or bullied.	
8. I know how to address these issues respectfully, without being afraid of rejection or compromising my own position.	
9. I recognize resistance in myself and others.	
10. As soon as I notice myself or others displaying resistant behavior, I raise the issue, even if this is hard to do.	

APPENDICES

3 Truth - Challenge the truth and go for 'both' *About how to deal with multiple truths*	Rating (1 - 10)
1. I fully accept that there are multiple truths.	
2. I'm not scared to question my own opinion or group standards.	
3. I initiate honest talks about similarities and differences.	
4. I continue to actively look for the flaws in my own thinking.	
5. I don't see different opinions as obstacles and I do accept diversity as a given.	
6. I always look for the 'no', the dissenting opinion. I make sure to ask whether anyone sees things differently than the rest of the group and, if so, what they need to go along with the majority decision.	
7. I may act from an 'either-or' perspective at times, but I strive to act from a more inclusive perspective whenever possible.	
8. I involve the people who are affected by my decisions in the decision-making process.	
9. Leaders and other people invite me to join the decision-making process about issues that have an impact on my work or my day-to-day life.	
10. I often find myself having more questions than answers and I'm not afraid to question my judgments and choices.	

4 Trust - Enjoy the unknown *How discomfort releases energy*	Rating (1 - 10)
1. I regularly break with fixed patterns and routines and try new things. I love doing that.	
2. I create safety for myself by taking an open, inquisitive attitude.	
3. I recognize and acknowledge tension and uncertainty in myself and others. When necessary, I talk about it.	
4. I actively create a safe space for myself and my team to make room for differences and uncertainties.	
5. I am good at continuing to act when faced with uncertainties.	
6. I don't shy away from a challenging debate or conflict. That's part of life.	
7. I have good interview techniques and skills to work through conflicts with others, and I use these, both one-on-one and in teams.	
8. I know when I am playing the part of pusher, joiner, bridge-builder or silent midfielder when dealing with a polarized issue. I know how to stop adding fuel to the fire	

5 Courage - Jamming in a flow and with extremes *About jamming with rhythm and flow*	Rating (1 - 10)
1. I am committed to connection and I openly support inclusive initiatives.	
2. I create room for informal, human contact.	
3. I have enough moral courage to oppose the mainstream.	
4. I understand the Jam Circle's flow and I take the time to learn to jam with my co-workers and to compare notes on what we need from one another to make that happen.	
5. I can, and do, phrase my communication and collaboration needs.	
6. I ask others what they need to work with me and truly take their answers on board.	
7. I attune my communication and behavior to others, to the goals at hand and the situation. I change the procedure, not the people.	
8. I take the risk of baring my soul.	
9. When I feel passionate about something at work, I dare to fully and openly show this and act on it.	
10. I try to have meaningful encounters with others and am willing to take risks to create these.	

How inclusive are we? Answer for your team / department / organization.

1 Difference - Don't clone *About our tendency to clone and the pros and cons of stereotyping*	**Rating** **(1 - 10)**
1. We appreciate visible differences (clothes, age, gender, skin color, hairdos) among our co-workers or customers. We like these differences and support them.	
2. We appreciate invisible differences (opinions, viewpoints, religions, characters, level of education) among our co-workers and customers. We like these differences and support them.	
3. We understand how everyone's appearance and preferences influence their decisions and ways of seeing.	
4. We deliberately work with people who are different from us.	
5. We judge ideas, not people.	
6. We consciously and actively question our prejudices and mindbugs.	
7. We keep learning about other cultures and religions by reading about them, visiting museums, talking to people and traveling.	
8. We base our actions on the idea that 'everyone is welcome, but not every type of behavior is acceptable'. We're aware that this boundary is different for every individual and every culture, which is why we're open to talking about this boundary.	

2 Power - See the power of power *About the pecking order and who has the power*	**Rating** **(1 - 10)**
1. We are fully aware of the issue of who sets the norm.	
2. We use our privileged position and place in the pecking order to the benefit of the larger community.	
3. We actively try to share our privileges with others (e.g. inviting others to give presentations or speak at conferences; open our networks; contribute financially; generate publicity; offer a vacation home for the weekend).	
4. We respect co-workers who rank higher on the ladder than us, but continue to see them as normal human beings; we neither demonize nor glorify them.	
5. We respect co-workers who rank lower on the ladder than us and continue to see them as normal human beings; we do not patronize them.	
6. We can see that ranking is multifaceted and that each of us can rank higher on some items than on others.	
7. We speak up when we notice that people are being excluded, patronized, ridiculed or bullied.	
8. We know how to address these issues respectfully, without being afraid of rejection or compromising our own positions.	
9. We recognize resistance in ourselves and others.	
10. As soon as we notice anyone on the team displaying resistant behavior, we raise the issue, even if this is hard to do.	

3 Truth - Challenge the truth and go for 'both' *About how to deal with multiple truths*	Rating (1 - 10)
1. We fully accept that there are multiple truths.	
2. We're not afraid to question our own opinions or group standards.	
3. We initiate honest talks about similarities and differences.	
4. We continue to actively look for flaws in our thinking.	
5. We don't see different opinions as obstacles and we do accept diversity as a given.	
6. We always look for the 'no', the dissenting opinion. We make sure to ask whether anyone sees things differently than the rest of the group and, if so, what they need to go along with the majority decision.	
7. We may act from an 'either-or' perspective at times, but we strive to act from a more inclusive perspective whenever possible.	
8. We involve the people who are affected by our decisions in the decision-making process.	
9. Leaders and other people invite us to join the decision-making process about issues that have an impact on our work or day-to-day life.	
10. We often find that we have more questions than answers and are not afraid to question our own judgments and choices.	

4 Trust - Enjoy the unknown *About the energy created by discomfort*	Rating (1 - 10)
1. We regularly break with fixed patterns and routines and try new things. We love doing that.	
2. We create safety by taking an open, inquisitive attitude.	
3. We recognize and acknowledge tension and uncertainty in ourselves and others. When necessary, we talk about it.	
4. We actively create a safe space for individual team members and the team as a whole to make room for differences and uncertainties.	
5. We're good at continuing to act when faced with uncertainties.	
6. We don't shy away from a challenging debate or conflict. That's part of life.	
7. We possess good interview techniques and skills to work through conflicts with others, and we use these, both one-on-one and in teams.	
8. We know when we are playing the part of pusher, joiner, bridge-builder or silent midfielder when dealing with a polarized issue. We know how to stop adding fuel to the fire.	

5 Courage - Jamming in a flow and with extremes *About jamming with rhythm and in a flow*	Rating (1 - 10)
1. We are committed to connection and openly support inclusive initiatives.	
2. We create room for informal, human contact.	
3. We have enough moral courage to oppose the mainstream.	
4. We understand the Jam Circle's flow and we take the time to learn to jam with our co-workers and to compare notes on what we need from one another to make that happen.	
5. Our team members can, and do, phrase their communication and collaboration needs and the team is able to take those on board.	
6. We ask others what they need to work with us and truly take their answers on board.	
7. We attune our communication and behavior to others, to the goals at hand and the situation. We change the procedure, not the people.	
8. We take the risk of baring our soul.	
9. When someone feels passionate about something at work, we dare to let them act on it.	
10. We try to have meaningful encounters with others and are willing to take risks to create these.	

II Jam Cultures Canvas: Talking Points, Strategy and Action Planner

On the next two pages you'll find the Jam Cultures Canvas with an overview of questions that can help you create a powerful inclusion story, strategy and concrete actions. Copy or print the canvas. Use post-its, flip charts, and any other facilitation tricks you know to get the conversation going and keep it going.

Jam Cultures Canvas

Diversity Mix

Difference
- How much, and what type of diversity do we have in our workplace? And our customers?
- Are there any mindbugs at play?
- Do we take ownership of diversity?

Leaders
- How diverse are our leaders?
- Jam Cultures mindset?
- Jam Cultures behavior?
- Education or training needed?

Employees
- How diverse is the workforce?
- Jam Cultures mindset?
- Jam Cultures behavior?
- Education or training needed?

Conclusions & Actions
- What do we do well?
- What do we not do well?
- What action do we want to take?
- Who could help us?
- What can we do ourselves?

Inclusive Culture

Power
- Privilege: is power distributed fairly?
- Our 'Us vs. Them' dynamics: asset or liability?
- Which procedures are blocking inclusion?
- Any resistance at play?
- Do we have humaneness and equality in every layer of the organization?

Jam Cultures Story. What does diversity and inclusion mean to you?
- What role does diversity and inclusion play in your personal life?
- What do you consider good examples of inclusion in your workplace, your own job, your life?
- Do you have a role model, someone who is really applying inclusion, either inside or outside the workplace?
- What behavior goes with inclusion? Be very detailed and clear.
- What behavior do you, as a human being, need to change in order to foster inclusion? And in your corporate role? How are you going to do this? How are you going to call out others on this behavior?
- Which procedures and structures enhance inclusion? Which ones block inclusion? What actions do you need to take?

Trust
- Is there enough safe space? Are we holding space?
- Do we welcome dissenting opinions?
- Are we stretching? Are we panicking?
- Are we aware of our knee-jerk reactions and can we talk about them?

Conclusions & Actions
- What do we do well?
- What do we not do well?
- What action do we need to take? Make them KPIs?
- Who could help us?
- What can we do ourselves?

JAM CULTURES

	Revenue

 Truth
- Is there room for multiple perspectives?
- Can self-evident truths be questioned?
- Are liminal zones put to good use?

 Products & services
- Mindbug-free?
- Match with customers?
- Added value: customers, the world, ourselves, our ideals, sales?

Results
- Is it fun? Is it challenging, does it teach us something?
- Does it have impact? Numbers, quality, story.
- Do we earn money? Are our fees fair to us, our customers, in relation to the competition and suppliers?

 Courage
- Do you have a powerful, inspiring inclusion story?
- Do we walk the talk?
- And do we talk the walk?
- Moral courage: slash and burn if need be?
- Flow and rhythm: are we taking risks?

 Internal collaboration
- Mindbug-free?
- Privilege and power fairly distributed?
- Open communication? Conflicts?
- Jamming, flow, intimacy, passion?

Conclusions & Actions
- What do we do well?
- What do we not do well?
- What action do we need to take?
- Who could help us?
- What can we do ourselves?

DIFFERENCE

Don't Clone

- Understand how your preferences influence your decisions.
- Widen your preferences.
- Consciously work with people who are different from you.
- Judge ideas, not people.

POWER

See the Power of Power

- Stay aware of the importance of who decides the rules of the game.
- Discuss rules and behavior that exclude people.
- Use your privileged position and ranking for the greater good.

TRUTH

Challenge the truth
- Dare to put your own opinion and the group's norm up for debate.
- Have candid conversations about differences and similarities.
- Actively try to uncover where you're wrong.
- Accept that there are multiple truths.

Actively look for alternatives
- Don't shun dissenting viewpoints.
- Respectfully say what needs to be said, without fear of being rejected or losing your position.
- Personally involve people with a stake in the matter in your decisions.
- Listen sincerely to their opinion.

Not either/or, but both
- Don't regard a different opinion as an obstacle.
- Have an 'it's both' mindset and keep your eye on the common goal.
- Work from your own preference and add the qualities of others to the mix.

TRUST

Enjoy the unknown
- Break fixed patterns and try new things.
- Create safety by taking a learning attitude.
- Recognize and acknowledge tension and uncertainty.

COURAGE

Vary your rhythm
- Attune your rhythm to others, to the goals at hand and the context.
- Slow down, so you can hear others and yourself.
- Change the procedure, not the people.

Do it Together
- Fight for togetherness.
- Break with procedures and habits that hamper inclusion.
- Openly support good initiatives.
- Make room for informal, human contact.
- Create an energizing, compatible story about inclusion.

ABOUT JITSKE KRAMER

Jitske Kramer travels all over the world to learn from traditional healers, leaders, surprising innovators and random strangers. She views the world and individual organizations through the eyes of an anthropologist. Her discipline, cultural anthropology, questions what it means to be a human being amidst other humans in organizational settings and beyond. In 2012, she introduced Deep Democracy in the Netherlands, where she and her Human Dimensions team provide training. Kramer is always looking for new ways to build strong tribes and reinforce mutual ties. She shares her knowledge with people in the world of organizational consultancy, collaboration and leadership by means of top-notch lectures and master classes. Her goal is to improve individual and group effectiveness and results (while also making the world a vastly more pleasant place to be). She trains people, so that we will never again have to hold meetings, but have lively and honest conversations instead. She captivates you with stories that create space for new ways of seeing and behaving. As her stories progress, what seemed normal to you becomes strange, and what was strange becomes familiar.

Jitske Kramer (1973). Corporate anthropologist. Public speaker. Entrepreneur. Facilitator. Founder of Human Dimensions. Trainer of the year 2013. Author of *Managing Cultural Dynamics, Deep Democracy – The wisdom of the minority, Wow! What a Difference!, Voodoo – A Journey to Find Yourself Through Ancient Rituals* and co-author of *The Corporate Tribe* (Management Book of the Year 2016, published in English, German, Russian, Dutch and Vietnamese) and *Building Tribes*. Kramer works in Dutch and English. For more information, see www.jitskekramer.com, www.humandimensions.nl, www.deepdemocracy.nl and www. jamcultures.nl